LIM_

HOTEL

ROMEO

By
Karen McGarr

JANUARY

1st ~ Miriam & Hank's, Orlando Florida

It was the kind of kiss you get lost in and lose all sense of your surroundings, which was surprising, given that we were smack-bang in the middle of the dance floor, of the overcrowded club.

With Gabriel's hand loosely resting on my hip, we tried keeping time to the music but after one too many overzealous fake guitarists crashed into us, Gabriel motioned to outside. Snaking our way through the denim clad crowd, we pumped our fists in the air, singing, "I'm hot sticky sweet, from my head to my feet." Aside from being a huge crowd pleaser, it's been my ear worm all day.

Sweeping past the bar, we waved to Colin, who looked pleased as punch, talking to a girl whose hair equalled half her height. From her calf length cowboy boot, a tattooed serpent wound its way around her leg, disappearing under her fuchsia rah-rah skirt.

Out on the street, the cacophony from the aptly named *noise makers* was deafening and with cheers of, *Happy New Year*, filling the air, it was the perfect setting to continue ushering in 1989.

I hadn't planned on going to the airport last night, but when Colin said he was going to pick up pizza, his sister Carina gestured for me to go with them. Once we were in the car, they let me in on the surprise, and at the gate at Orlando airport, Carina was first to spot her older brother.

Wrapped in a bear hug, Colin and Gabriel joked that it'd, "been a while," when in fact they saw each other last week. I felt a little awkward just standing there but when Carina introduced me to Gabriel, his smile reached all the way to his crinkly blue eyes that reminded me of a certain someone, and for that reason alone, I was more than happy to sit in the back seat with him.

"Hi guys," their dad Kevin said, waving his hand behind him, which Colin smacked on his way past. When Liza came into the living room, asking where the pizza was, Gabriel stepped through the front door. Liza lunged at her son and in floods of tears, she went from squeezing him, to looking at him, and back to hugging him.

Hogmanay has long been my favourite night of the year, and last night was the first time in years I didn't spend it with Ben. I don't know how New Year's Eve is celebrated in Italy, or what Ben planned on doing, but that's what comes of having an ex. I'm still not used to thinking of him in those terms, but maybe this year will change that.

After minimal shut eye, Liza announced brunch was ready, and wearily, we trickled into the kitchen, filling our faces with the first meal of the year.

On the couch, groaning in satisfaction, with MTV humming in the background, Carina and I rolled our eyes after the guys began speculating when Martha Quinn might return. Carina agrees that "downtown" Julie Brown is much more entertaining.

At the pool with Carina, her brothers and a handful of their friends, I kept my baggy top on, thankful the weather was cool enough not to have to worry about wearing less. There was much chat about college (Gabriel) high school (Carina) and the working world (Colin).

After Gabriel and Carina dropped me off at Miriam's, I was glad to find Donna home alone. "You and Gabriel were makin' out *big time* in the club last night," she smirked. "You like him, huh?"

"He's alright," I joked, feeling my cheeks flush. I was dying to get the scoop on Gabriel, but I knew Donna would only tease me, so I left it at that.

I spent more time with Donna today than I have since arriving last month, and tonight is the first time she hasn't gone out with her boyfriend, Robbie. Because Donna's mum and mine have been best friends since they met during their teens, in Glasgow, it's a given we're friends, but we're very different.

I didn't expect to be awake for *The Tracey Ullman Show*, but after a good natter with Pamsy, I perked right up. As usual, she wanted, "all the dish," but conscious of the cost of the international call, I rattled off the short version. When I told her I'd kissed Gabriel, she cooed, "Blimey! What a start to the new year."

2nd ~ Miriam & Hank's, Orlando Florida

At the crack of dawn, I stumbled into the kitchen to find Carol hunched over the breakfast bar, tucking into one of the pre-made meals that show up in a box marked, nutri/system, whose tv ads urge us to call 1 800 321 THIN. Today! I was craving fluffy pancakes, doused in the goopy syrup that comes in a plastic bottle (tastes nothing like the Tate & Lyle stuff I'm used to) but I didn't think it'd be fair to gorge in front of Carol, so I filled a bowl with Special K, hoping to be transformed into the girl in the ad in that *oh so perfect* white swimsuit. After polishing off her paltry portion, Carol asked if I wanted to go to the alligator farm. There's such a place? I thought, but all I said was I wasn't in the mood.

With my vitamin D levels topped up (I was the only one at the pool) I made my way back to the condo and sat outside. I was about to sink my teeth into, *The Mysteries of Pittsburgh*, when Robbie showed up in the biggest truck I've ever seen. Flashing what I've heard him call, "a shit eatin' grin," he climbed down from the cab, shielding his face from the sun, whilst wearing his baseball cap, backwards!

"She here?" he asked, presumably about Donna.

"Nope," I clucked. From behind the dark lenses of my new Ray Bans, I feigned interest in the book but kept a beady eye on him. With his thumbs loosely tucked in the belt loops of his stiff Wranglers, Robbie circled his new toy, pausing every few seconds to rub the gleaming body with the hankie that hangs from his back pocket. After a few revolutions, he made a big show of climbing into the cab and when he left, the engine roared so loud, I instinctively covered my ears, cursing him after I lost my page.

Colin rang and asked if I wanted to go and see, *Rain Man*, but he's heading back to California tomorrow so I figured his parents would want him home. After I wished him *Bon Voyage*, he said he'd enjoyed meeting me. I echoed his sentiment, but it's his brother I'm interested in.

3rd ~ Gabriel's, Orlando, Florida

I'm in Gabriel's bed…alone! It's five eleven am, and we just called it a night, after talking (and kissing) out on the sun porch. I feel totally knackered (read as; slightly tipsy) but I'm getting ahead of myself (how unusual!) so I'll start at the beginning.

The area surrounding Miriam & Hank's is flat, which makes cycling a breeze. I went to the bank to exchange more sterling for dollars, then popped into Winn Dixie's, hoping to nab a handful of the chocolate chip cookies they bake on the premises. I scoffed one on the ride back and stashed the other two in my bum bag. I can't exactly stuff my face around Carol, when she's trying so hard to lose weight (unlike moi!).

Carol's school bus is full of spotty teens, wearing sweatshirts emblazoned with names of colleges and sports teams but it seems most of her friends will be driving to school, as soon as they get their driving licence. I don't recall any of my friends ever driving to Stantonbury Campus and when I told Carol I rode my bike throughout secondary, she looked positively gobsmacked.

On the way over here in the car with Miriam and Carol, I thought it might be awkward seeing Gabriel again but across the dinner table, we stole the odd smile, and underneath, his foot found mine. When the conversation turned to Scotland, Miriam and Liza said the thing they miss the most is family, but that overall, they consider America home. When Liza asked if I miss living in Scotland, I shared how devastated I was, after mum and dad broke the news that we were moving to England. Surrounded by accents very different to mine, I felt like a fish out of water but after I made friends with Sarah, and Lucy, things began to look up.

While we were in the kitchen washing up, Gabriel asked if I wanted to go out, laughing when I responded with an enthusiastic, "Yes, please!" We quickly finished the task at hand and made a hasty exit, after his dad agreed to let him borrow the car.

Walking into the bar reminded me of the movie scenes, where the saloon doors swing open, and the music stops dead. Gabriel said he, "Gets a kick outta dive bars," and wasted no time ordering a beer. When I asked the burly bartender for a Bartles & Jaymes, I caught him snickering.

In the loo, the colourful plastic mushroom shaped air fresheners lining the cracked sink held my attention, as I made a poor attempt at washing my hands under a rusty tap that only doled out drips.

When I found Gabriel seated next to the pool table, he slid a drink across the coaster encrusted high top. Clinking the sticky glass against Gabriel's bottle of Budweiser (the neon sign in the window may have prompted his choice) I chirped, "Cheers!" before taking a huge gulp, only to discover the liquid I'd mistaken for cranberry juice was laden with vodka.

"Phew!" I exclaimed, shaking my head. "What is this?"

"It's called a Cape Codder, do you like it?"

"I do," I nodded, enthusiastically.

"It usually comes with a lime slice," Gabriel said, gesturing to the bartender, "but I didn't wanna get thrown out on my ass!"

The pool table was in high demand and when a guy with big hair asked for our names, to add to the list, I drawled, "Bonnie and Bobby." Once he was out of earshot, Gabriel leaned across the high-top. "Hey *Bonnie*, you know the expression, the higher the hair the closer to God?"

"I do now," I laughed.

Twisting on the bar stool in time to ZZ Top's, "Sharp Dressed Man,", a guy Gabriel later described as, "A tall glass of water," passed me the cue. After discovering I'm the worst pool player ever, we gave up and grabbed two seats in the lounge. Crammed together on a tiny, makeshift stage in the corner, the band played mostly Johnny Cash songs. Gabriel was well impressed that I knew most of them, all thanks to dad. We stayed 'til closing time and Gabriel asked if I needed to get back to Miriam's but I doubted she'd appreciate me stumbling through the door in the early hours.

Parched from a delicious amount of kissing out on the sun porch, I dropped heavy hints about how much I'd love a cup of tea. Smirking, Gabriel returned, swinging a bottle of tequila.

"That is *not* tea," I whispered.

Grinning in a way that made me want to kiss him again, he said, "This is waayyyyy better."

4th ~ Gabriel's, Orlando, Florida

Perched on the edge of the bed, Liza talked ten to the dozen, as mum is apt to do. Liza reminds me a lot of mum, not only because they're both blonde but in their mannerisms and obvious zest for life.

After I was showered and dressed (in clothes borrowed from Carina but wearing the extra pair of knickers mum has always suggested I keep in my toiletry bag!) I found Gabriel in the kitchen.

"How's your head?"

"Pounding," I groaned.

Gabriel gave me something called Advil that along with milky tea, worked wonders, and over pancakes drenched in syrup (finally!) we made plans to go to Daytona.

I enjoyed taking in the sights and in between listening to the radio, our conversation covered the gamut, from favourite music to the difference in cars between here and the UK, prompting Gabriel to ask what I drive.

"I don't have a car. I only got my licence a few months before I came here, so I use public transport, mostly the train."

"That's crazy," he said, shaking his head.

"I love being on the train, it gives me time to write."

"That's cool. My girlfriend likes to-"

My head spun so fast I cricked my neck. "You have a girlfriend?"

"Maybe not." He sounded sheepish with an expression to match. "We got into a fight the night before I left."

"I didn't know you had a *girlfriend*!" I snipped, pressing my fingers against the back of my stiff neck.

"You sound pissed."

"I can't be, we stopped drinking hours ago."

"Pissed, like, angry," he explained, sliding into the fast lane.

"In that case, I'm *very* pissed. You should have told me."

"I'm sorry," he muttered, glancing in my direction as I adjusted my posture.

"Well? Tell me now."

He inhaled deeply and exhaled slowly. "I had a girlfriend, but we...*I*...said some shit before I left. It was bad."

I kept my eyes fixed on the road.

"Do you want me to take you home? We're just about there but I can turn back." After a long pause, he added, "If you want."

With my thoughts whirling, I knew whatever I said would come out sounding jumbled, so I kept quiet.

After finding a parking spot, Gabriel shut off the engine and turned to me. "I'm sorry," he said, reaching out his hand, a gesture I ignored. "I should have told you about Maria. But right now, there's no Maria. And you know what? It feels good...being away..spending time with my family again. Hanging out with you."

"Oh, so it's all her fault, is it?"

"He shook his head. "No. I can be a real asshole sometimes."

"You can say that again!"

He started to laugh but stopped. "Before I opened my big mouth and screwed up, I figured we'd get some bikes and go exploring but if you wanna go home, I understand."

"Let me get this straight," I said, facing him. "Do you or do you not have a girlfriend?"

"Do not," he said with a heavy shrug. "Like I said, the night before I left, we got into it, and I said some dumb shit-"

"Gee, quelle surprise!" I blurted, not meaning to.

"She said she wanted a break."

"You didn't mention the part, about the break. What did you say?"

"Ok."

"Just like that?"

"Uh-huh, just like that." Leaning forward he craned his neck to the sky, in an exaggerated way. "It looks real nice out there. Be good to get out and see what's happenin'. Whaddaya say?"

8

"Since we're already here," I sighed, unbuckling the seatbelt. "We good to go?"

I nodded and he scurried out of the car and darted to my side, but I already had the door open.

"You have a temper," he grinned.

"And you," I said, with a prod to his shoulder. "Have a terrible memory."

5th ~ Gabriel's, Orlando, Florida

Gabriel had tickets for a comedy show, but we skipped it to meet his family and Miriam, Hank and Carol at Phineas Fogg's. After we'd devoured a towering dessert, Gabriel made me laugh when he said, "You ready to blow this popsicle stand?"

I don't remember the name of the bar, but the DJ was super slick and when Gabriel suggested we request a song, my mind went blank, so he chose.

Well into the evening, after I'd asked about Maria, Gabriel said he was interested in hearing more about Ben, and how we met. I was about to tell him, when slicky announced, "This one's for the beautiful Brit, from the amazed American."

Gabriel held out his hand and onto the dance floor we went, to the intro of, "She's Like the Wind."

"Amazed? Is that all you can come up with?"

Without missing a beat, he said, "Yup, that's all I got. I'm still in college."

"This song is terrible."

I know," he said, pulling me tight to him. "But this is an awesome way to dance."

6th ~ Miriam & Hank's, Orlando, Florida

I was at the sink, getting some water, when Gabriel crept up behind me. Encompassing me in a hug, he said, "Did you have fun yesterday?"

"I did," I said, quickly abandoning the task at hand, opening my neck to his kisses. When I turned to face him, his lips moved to my mouth and desire (nature!) began to take its course. With our hands searching one another's bodies, I could feel myself opening to the possibility of a lot more than kissing but (fortunately?) the sound of the front door interrupted the moment. Liza, back from her morning walk.

"Morning honey," she beamed, handing a newspaper to Gabriel, who (for obvious reasons!) had quickly taken a seat at the table.

"Hey, mom."

"How are you, Karen?" Liza said, squeezing my shoulder.

"Fine, thanks. Ehm, I hope it's ok that I'm still here, we were out late again last night and-"

"Miriam knows you're here, it's fine. Besides, you're always welcome."

Gabriel looked up and smiled. Returning his smile, I said, "I should probably be getting back to Miriam's soon."

"I was thinking about going for a wee drive, seeing as it's such a nice day."

"Mom, it's Florida, it's always a nice day!"

"Aye, I know that Gabriel, but today is *especially* nice. Do you fancy going out?"

"Sure," he said, spreading the newspaper across the table.

"Come with us, Karen?"

I looked at Gabriel's for his reaction, but he was engrossed in the sports section.

"We'll stop somewhere nice for lunch," Liza said, confirming the invite.

Eyeing the surfboards at Ron Jon's (cool shop) I thought about Pamsy's arrival, next week. I bought her a t-shirt and few bits, but it's somewhere I want her to see. Besides, I'd love to stop at the tawdry motels we passed, some of which looked straight out of *Psycho*.

Over yummy seafood, Liza suggested I go to Miami with Gabriel, when he visits his grandparents. Seems it's a few hours from here, so I imagine it'll be an overnight trip, which could be interesting.

Liza talked for most of the ride back, thereby reminding me more of mum. Carina was home from school and when she said she was happy to see me, I joked, "You're obviously looking for help with your English homework." I did end up helping, but the algebra stumped me, so we gave it a miss and watched MTV. When the "Wishing Well" video came on, we stood in front of the tv, mimicking the hand movements of the backing singers/dancers but when Terence Trent D'Arby did the splits, we just stared in awe.

At Miriam's, while Gabriel and I were out on the balcony watching the sunset, I wanted to bring up Miami, but he seemed a little pensive, so I refrained from mentioning it. From the other side of the French doors, Miriam and Liza chatted animatedly and when I caught Miriam's eye, she raised her wine glass and flashed a mischievous smile.

7th ~ Gabriel's, Orlando, Florida

It's been an interesting night and I'm so tired I just want to curl up in bed, but going with the expression, no time like the present, I'm glad Miriam wasn't up to witness the old banger truck that rumbled up after ten, with Gabriel and his two friends.

Chad and Cliff seemed a little impersonal, but in Wings at the Marriott Hotel they soon came alive, chatting up one girl after another at the bar, before quickly deciding to leave. In the parking lot of Bottle Bar, they snorted cocaine with ease and in the backseat, I shot Gabriel a look he clearly understood.

"Catch up with us inside, guys," Gabriel said, as I bolted out of the truck.

"You ok?" Gabriel asked, halfway across the parking lot, where it suddenly dawned on me why Cliff had parked so far away from the entrance.

"Yeah, that's just not my-"

"Not my thing either," Gabriel said, reaching for my hand. "Boneheads! You sure you're good?"

"Yeah, I'm fine."

"Hey," he said, stopping mid-step. "You're coming to Miami, right?"

"Ehm…"

"Awesome!" he yelled, breaking into a sprint.

The atmosphere in Bottle Bar was exhilarating and when, "Wild Wild West," came on, Gabriel and I strained our vocal cords, "She's so mean but I don't care, I love her eyes and her wild, wild hair."

"I think these guys are Brits," Gabriel yelled.

"They sound American."

"Everybody sounds American when they sing," he laughed.

"Brits! Americans!" we screeched, back and forth, dancing like maniacs.

8th ~ Miami, Florida

I like that Gabriel asks lots of questions and appears genuinely interested in the things we talk about (pretty much everything!) and I think being here temporarily makes it easier to talk openly about stuff I'd usually keep close to my chest. Having said that, Gabriel is easy to talk to and always seems keen to delve deeper into whatever we're discussing.

When I asked if he's missing Maria, he shrugged and asked if I miss Ben.

"He's always floating about in my head somewhere, but the intensity varies."

"But you guys are totally broken up, right?"

"We finally called it a day before I left to come here. I cried all the way across the Atlantic."

"You got it bad, girl," he said, shaking his head.

After a while I asked Gabriel if he minded shutting off the AC because it was giving me a headache. The fresh air felt so much better, but it was difficult to hear over the noise from the motorway (Gabriel calls it a highway but apparently in California it's a freeway).

Gabriel knew all the lyrics to, "Every Rose Has Its Thorn," and sang it in such a heartfelt way that I felt a little teary but not sure why as it's not the sort of music I usually listen to. When I joined him in the chorus, he looked chuffed. I meant to ask him who sings it, but totally forgot. The tables turned with, "Need You Tonight," and I sang while Gabriel moved his head in time to the beat, playing his imaginary harmonica in all the right places. I told him when I went to the INXS concert in London (with Ben) a smattering of girls tossed their knickers on the stage. That little snippet sparked an interesting chat that dominated the remainder of the drive.

When we arrived at Gabriel's grandparents in the early afternoon, they came out to greet us, and quickly ushered us inside. Within minutes I was chilled to the bone (AC was blasting) and when grammy (as she introduced herself) showed me to the guest room, I wanted nothing more than to wrap myself in the pink and green palm treed bedcover.

"They've been this way forever," Gabriel said in response to the bickering voices coming from the kitchen. "You wanna go out?"

"Do you fancy going for a walk? That was quite a long drive."

"We don't walk here!" G & G stated in unison as they came into the living room, all smiles!

"Come on," Gabriel said with a wink. "I'll show you the sights."

The hotels dotted along South Beach were a combination of dingy and deluxe but either way I was mesmerised by the shimmering sea and art deco architecture. We walked on the beach and *wow*, not a lot of fabric to be found, even the men were in G-strings! I can't imagine ever having the confidence to bare my body in public, in nothing more than a pair of shoelaces.

Music pumped out from a multitude of bars facing the expansive beach.

"So?" Gabriel said after we'd downed our first Mojito. "What do you think?"

"I love the vibe," I said, as another group of supermodels swanned past. "And the view isn't too shabby, either," I said, trying to keep a straight face. "But I know you brought me here for the architecture." No sooner were my words out, when a girl in a sheer top and a pair of bikini bottoms that'd fit my pinky (maybe!) cycled past.

"To the architecture," Gabriel grinned, clinking his empty glass to mine.

After being out in the sun G&G's house felt like an igloo. When Gabriel handed me a sweatshirt, emblazoned with *Miami Dolphins*, I uttered, "I didn't know there was a Sea World here." For a split second he thought I was serious, until I broke into laughter, prompting him to roll his eyes in such a way that made me laugh even more.

When grammy said we were going to a friend's house for dinner, I assumed it'd be close by, but the drive was lengthy enough to watch the landscape go from congested to almost barren, with the odd billboard advertising churches and others providing a telephone number, should anyone be interested in repenting their sins.

Earl and Ali's huge brick house sat at the end of a winding driveway, and they seemed pleasant, until they started insisting I, "Talk in your British accent!" I was tempted to go on a diatribe about *Her Majesty, scones, tea, the tube, mind the gap, Bob's your uncle* and all that, but instead I flashed my best Princess of Wales smile.

I've never seen so much meat (or condiments) and after what felt like an interview for an ambassadorship, Earl suggested we, "Eat up good before we go ridin'." I assumed he meant horses, but it was quad bikes. I was hesitant to ride solo, so Earl suggested Gabriel, "Sling her on back a yours!"

"Before or after he drags me by the hair, back to the cave?" I was tempted to say.

Halfway across the field, Gabriel shut off the engine. When he turned to face me, his mustard tongue found my ketchup lips and we made the most of a few quiet moments before Earl and his cohorts caught up to us.

When Gabriel offered to drive home, grampa boomed, "Nobody drives my Caddy!"

In the plush back seat, we nodded in acknowledgement as G&G continued to squabble all the way home, by which time I felt like I was suffering from hypothermia.

9th ~ Gabriel's, Orlando, Florida

A few minutes after I shut off the light, Gabriel tiptoed into the room, whispering, "Are you awake?" I waited until I felt his breath, before I flashed open my eyes and shot my hands up towards him. Following a string of expletives that I doubt his grandparents would approve of, he climbed into bed beside me, and in hushed tones, peppered with the odd kiss, we talked until the sun came up.

A few hours later I drowsily (lack of tea and sleep, and excessive AC) stumbled out of bed and followed the sound of music to the kitchen, where in between sashaying in time to the salsa rhythm, grammy cracked eggs in a bowl.

"Morning cutie," she shouted. "Go grab some oranges."

Prompted by my blank expression, she motioned to the back slider. Of course. Florida. Orange trees.

With the sun glinting through the trees, I took my sweet time picking an armful of oranges, before stepping back into the freezer. Belting out a song in Spanish, grammy juiced the lot, filled a tall glass to the brim, and danced her way in my direction, all without spilling a drop. No doubt roused by the noise, Gabriel appeared and joined us as we circled the breakfast bar.

Grammy, looking at Gabriel, "This gal can dance."

Grammy, to me, "Shake it honey!"

Grammy to Gabriel, mid spin, "You want coffee?"

Hoping Gabriel's telepathic skills were up and running, I flashed him a pleading expression.

Gabriel, to Grammy, "You got tea?"

Grammy to Gabriel, "You get that tea thing from your mother! Go grab the teapot from the china cabinet."

The result? Loose leaf tea, in a warmed pot, complete with tea strainer and tea cosy. China cups and saucers, sterling silver teaspoons, plump blueberry muffins, and a side order of chattering teeth.

In Palm Beach, a bevy of svelte beachgoers (average age 80) flashed expensive smiles, as they cavorted in the sea, bringing to mind an expression mum is fond of; *The sun's a tonic.*

On our way back to the car, Gabriel and I stopped for frozen yogurt (is that the sexy seniors' secret?). There was enough in my dish for four, but I still managed to polish it off.

G & G argued their way through dinner, mostly about whose turn it was to wipe off the sticky clumps of ketchup on the lid (a universal issue!) but when it came time to leave, they were all smiles and hand in hand, they waved us off.

Liza looked delighted to have her son home and had a barrage of questions, most of which I answered while Gabriel was in the shower. At the kitchen table, surrounded by piles of homework, poor Carina looked miserable, so I helped a little with history but everything else looked like gobbledygook.

A whiff of minty Cool Water by Davidoff (thanks to duty free, us hosties know our fragrances) prompted Carina to screw up her nose and gesture, *way too much*. When the kitchen phone rang, Carina made a move to answer it, but Gabriel reached in and grabbed it. He turned his back, and I tried not to listen but a few words in, the piercing sound of the caller's discontent mingled in the air with his cologne.

"Maria," Carina mouthed.

When I whispered, "Very healthy vocal cords," Carina chuckled and nodded in agreement.

After Gabriel hung up, he disappeared but when he came into the kitchen a little while later, he asked if I wanted to go out. When I said I felt a bit knackered and would rather stay in, he looked more than relieved. Watching *Risky Business*, my only child status became more appealing, when Gabriel relentlessly teased Carina about her crush on Tom Cruise.

Liza suggested I spend the night, so I rang Miriam to let her know I won't be back/home. Again!

10th ~ Miriam & Hank's, Orlando, Florida

On our way to Miriam's, Gabriel and I popped into the pharmacy so I could pick up the Christmas pictures I just had developed. Usually, there's a handful of good ones from a twenty-four exposure but most of this bunch are keepers.

Much to my delight there were plenty of chocolate chip cookies in Winn Dixie's, so I bought half a dozen. Munching our way through them in the car, Gabriel agreed they're the best cookies ever.

"You sure you don't wanna come over for dinner?"

"It's your last night," I said. "I've been there so much, it's probably best I don't."

At the edge of Miriam's driveway, Gabriel's sigh matched mine. "I guess this is it."

"How long is your flight, tomorrow?"

"I don't know, I gotta change in Cincinnati, home of the Bengals. They're playing in the *Superbowl*, in Miami. We shoulda waited!"

"No idea where Cincinnati is, and is that football?"

"Yeah, the Superbowl is football," he laughed, shaking his head. "And Cincinnati's in Ohio." Still smiling his lovely smile, he opened his arms. "Gimme a hug, you."

I slid my arms around his sweatshirt and returned the squeeze. "It's been awesome hangin' out with you."

"Thank you for everything," I mumbled into his chest.

"Goodbye's suck," he said, holding me at arm's length.

"Then let's say see you later."

"Not yet," he grinned. "I wanna kiss you."

"We're in public!"

"Yeah, and the first time we kissed we were in a crowd of how many people?"

"Point tak-" I started to say but his lips were already on mine.

"Good luck with British air," Gabriel said, getting behind the wheel. "And I hope Ben gets a clue and stops being a jerk."

"Good luck with Maria," I said, closing the door. I almost suggested he pick up some ear plugs before seeing her. When he rolled down the window, I leaned in and gave him one last kiss.

"Peace out," he said, making the sign.

"Peace," I smiled, doing the same.

We each held the gesture while he drove off and at the end of the street, he beeped the horn, and turned the corner.

11th ~ Miriam & Hank's, Orlando, Florida

When Gabriel rang from the airport, I got the impression he was sad to be leaving. I know how wrenching it can be, saying goodbye to family, so I let him do the talking.

"Hey, I was thinking that we might meet again?"

"Maybe. If I make it through training with Bri-"

"When!"

"Ah, you confident Americans," I teased. "*When* I start flying with BA, I imagine at some point, I'll get to California."

"Or I might go to Scotland again to visit mom's family."

"I live in England."

"I know. I guess what I'm saying is that we might meet again, somewhere."

I kept an eye on the clock and when it came time for Gabriel's flight to depart, I made a wish that he'll be happy, in whatever life brings him.

12th ~ Mary-Kate's, Orlando, Florida

Trying to get comfy in this cramped spot on the pullout, but Donna just threw her leg over mine, so now I'm trapped. Misty is in Mary-Kate's room, hopefully asleep, which is what I ought to be doing but fuelled by ample white wine spritzers, I'm not ready to call it a night just yet.

Donna and Robbie are, *Taking a time out,* so I joined her and her friends at the Cheek-to-Cheek lounge. Misty disappeared for ages and when she came back, she moved like she was made of rubber. Gesturing, *What's up with her?* to Donna, she shrugged and asked if I wanted to dance. The singer was murdering Huey Lewis's "Power of Love," so I stayed with Misty. When I asked if she was ok, she tossed her head back so far, she almost whacked it against the illuminated planters (plastic foliage is never a good aesthetic).

"You seem a little out of it," I shouted.

"You wanna go out?"

"No," I said, inching closer to her. "You seem out of it. Are you ok?"

"Bay beeeee, I'm more than o kay," she slurred in her deep Southern accent. "You want some?"

"Some what?"

"You know," she said, slipping her way down the velour couch. "You wanna spliff?"

18

I thought she was saying something about being spiffy, so I said, "Yes! Your outfit is very…ehm, snazzy." Snazzy isn't the word I'd usually use to describe corduroy dungarees, but I was trying to relate. Swaying her Aqua net tresses, she said, "A blunt hun eeee pie. You wanna blunt?" I was utterly stumped. Was she accusing me of being blunt?

"A doobie?"

I held up my hands and shook my head in confusion.

"Fatty?"

Slightly taken aback from being called fat, I glared at her, finally clicking when she gestured smoking.

"Ah, a joint! You're asking if I want a joint?"

"You got it sugar bear," she breathed, pointing to her bag, as she slid all the way down the couch.

13th ~ Comfort Inn Hotel, Orlando, Florida

Travelling on a staff travel standby ticket can be dicey, but fortunately Pamsy made it. At the airport, Hank took care of the rental car for us, and even drove it to the hotel, which was a great help because Pamsy had just flown across the pond, and there's no way I'm driving here.

With the price of the hotel room, I thought it might be a little dodgy, but with two double beds and a decent bathroom, it's perfectly adequate. We wasted no time unpacking, then popped out to pick up a pizza. The box was so huge we had to tilt it to get it through the door!

With pepperoni and mushroom filled bellies (and gooey cheese, yum) we fell into our beds.

"I want to hear *everything*, from the second you met Gabriel, all the way to the last word."

"I already told you most of it."

"I haven't heard about the last few days."

"True."

"Ahhh," Pamsy sighed, readjusting the pillows. "Your first American."

"What?"

"Gabriel. He's the first American you kissed."

"You're right, he is."

"However," she said tartly. "I highly doubt he's the last."

14th ~ Comfort Inn Hotel, Orlando, Florida

We planned on spending the afternoon, lounging by the pool but we soon got bored and ended up at the Florida Mall, where we took turns trying on tops and jackets, all with shoulder pads straight out of a David Byrne video.

After dinner at Rosie O' Grady's (thank you, Miriam, always so generous) we made our way to the Cheyenne Salon, where a pair of gormless guys sidled up to us at the bar. Somehow managing to keep a straight face, after they asked our names, I drawled, "I'm Charlene Buchanan and this here is ma friend, Tiffany Wells."

"Y'all look like models."

"We're hosties!" Pamsy chirped.

"Like at a rest a ront?"

"No, not a hostess," Pamsy said. "Hosties!"

"You two are a caution!" the hairier guy guffawed. "What's a hostie?"

"We circle the globe in a tin can."

"Stews? You guys are *stews*?" The hairier of the two had just discovered his booming voice. "What airline d'y'all fly?"

"Piedmont," I lied, as the kick to my ankle told me it was time to go.

15th ~ Comfort Inn Hotel, Orlando, Florida

Leisurely breakfast at Wags after which the plan was to drive to Ron Jon's surf shop in Cocoa Beach, so off we went, with me claiming I'd remember how to get there, until Pamsy pointed out I'd gone from Gabriel's.

"Don't worry," she said, as I clicked through countless country radio stations. "I'm sure we'll find it."

Church after church dotted the flat, barren landscape, all with oversized parking lots, filled to capacity.

"Where do all these people live?" Pamsy asked, echoing my thoughts. Shutting off the crackly country crooners, I pointed to a petrol station way in the distance, hoping they'd have snacks.

Inside the stark wooden structure, two men with matching pot bellies, sat side by side.

"We'd like some petrol, I mean, gas, please," Pamsy said in a sunny tone.

Stretching as though he was being roused from time in a tomb, the younger man (son?) slithered behind the counter, all the while wiping his meaty mitts on a t-shirt that might have started out white. Pamsy handed over two $20 bills, and if only to avoid seeing what dirty t was chewing (definitely not hubba bubba) I caught the eye of the older man.

"Boy howdy," he said, presumably in greeting.

"How do you do," I responded, as chewy slid the bills into a wooden drawer, before flopping into an armchair that'd seen better days.

From the other side of the car, while Pamsy fiddled with the petrol cap, I said, "I think we just went down the rabbit hole."

"Spot on, Alice," Pamsy said through gritted teeth. "Can you see them?"

"They're staring at us."

"Flash 'em your biggest smile," she said as the gurgling halted. "Must be full, and it was only four dollars, so you know what that means."

I came out to find Pamsy in the passenger seat. "This is the perfect road for you to drive."

"No way! I haven't driven since I passed my test."

"All the more reason to give it a go," she said, patting the seat. "And don't worry, I'm right here."

Bolstered by Pamsy's encouraging words, I got behind the wheel, and when I turned the key, the seatbelts activated and attempted to strangle us.

"Ugh," I groaned. "This whole seat belt, lap belt thing is such a rigmarole."

"Total palava," Pamsy tutted as I adjusted the mirrors. "It's automatic, so you'll be fine," she said, encouragingly. "It's just like being on the dodgems."

"Which I *hate*."

"Start by keeping your foot on the brake and move the...*oh shit*, give it some welly!" she yelled. "Here comes Tweedledum!"

I slammed the gas pedal and kept my foot on it until the rear window was clouded in dust.

"Well done you," Pamsy chuckled as I took a deep breath.

"What a scary pair!"

"Us or them?" joked Pamsy.

16th ~ Comfort Inn, Orlando, Florida

The woman from Texas we spoke to in the ticket queue for EPCOT wasn't kidding when she said it should be renamed, *Every Person Comes Out Tired*. Pamsy is further proof of that because she's already out for the count, no doubt dreaming about the fantastic day we had.

Parking was a cinch and we walked mile after mile through the World Showcase, enjoying a taste of what each country had to offer. I especially loved Japan and bought a hand painted fan I used most of the day. In England, we popped into the Rose and Crown, if only to see how authentic it was. Filled with, to quote Pamsy, "Skinny blokes staring into pints," we got chatting to a few of them. One of them suggested meeting up later and scribbled his phone number on the back of a beer mat.

Over fettucine at L'Originale Alfredo di Roma, my thoughts turned to Ben. Savouring the warm sensual feeling he ignites in me, I imagined him flying down the slopes of the Italian Alps, in more than a hurry to get back to the chalet. *To me.*

"Have you heard from him?" Pamsy said, spookily interrupting my lurid thoughts.

"Eh, yeah, I had a Christmas card. And a letter."

"What did he have to say for himself?"

"Oh, you know, the usual," I said, feigning nonchalance when in fact my stomach was churning, but not from the food.

"I know you miss him, but you have so much to look forward to when you get home. I mean with BA. Isn't it exciting?"

"I hope I hear from them soon. I'm a bit concerned that I don't have a start date yet."

What I didn't tell Pamsy is that the second I wake up, I mentally add six hours to the time, then spend way too much time pondering what Ben might be doing. Throughout the day, I do the same and again at night, especially after I shut off the light.

17th ~ Comfort Inn, Orlando, Florida

I have a date! I have a date! I have a date! Woke up with Miriam on the phone. "I know it's early honey, but I'm just off the phone with your mammy. She was up to high-doh. A letter arrived from British Airways, requesting you give them a call."

A minute later, with Pamsy on her bed, facing me, I dialled the UK prefix, followed by the London number.

"Why are you crossing your fingers?"

"I'm superstitious. And really nervous."

After a slightly posh voice reeled off her name and job title. I blabbed something about the letter I received (couldn't very well say I was over four thousand miles away!) and nodded in response to the request to hold. Pamsy grinned through a thumbs up.

"Yes, I'm still here and no, I'm not sure why there's a time delay on the line."

Pamsy covered her mouth, but the shake of her shoulders gave her away.

"Yes, I understand, but the thing is, I was rather hoping for a later date."

Pamsy's mouth fell open in question.

"Yes, I can wait, thank you."

"What're you doing?" Pamsy said, edging closer to the end of the bed.

"I can't start next week," I whispered, my hand covering the receiver. "You just got here."

"But what if that's the only date available?"

"Then we'll start pack-"

The voice from London was back on the phone.

"That would be wonderful," I gushed into the phone. "And yes, that date is much more agreeable."

"Only you," Pamsy mouthed.

"Thank you, and yes, I'll expect the confirmation letter in tomorrow's post. Thank you very much."

At a hole in the wall breakfast joint, we celebrated with runny eggs, undercooked sausages and tepid tea that tasted like dishwater, but none of that matters, because thirteen days from now,

I'M JOINING BRITISH AIRWAYS!!!

18th ~ Comfort Inn, Orlando, Florida

After a brilliant day at Disney World, we fell into bed early. Pamsy's still adjusting to the time change, so she usually zonks out first, after which I read until the book thumps me on the face, a sure sign I'm nodding off.

Because I was unsure when I'd be going home, I flew here on a one-way ticket, so this morning, we went to Orlando airport (MCO, formerly known as McCoy Air Force Base and named for Colonel Michael Wright McCoy). The most economical flight I could find, at almost $500, connects in Newark (EWR) which I only know is in New Jersey because it's close to where mum lived, during her time in New York.

Pamsy added her name to the standby list and hopefully she'll get on the same flights, but if our track record is anything to go by, I shan't hold my breath. We had a good giggle recalling our disastrous attempts at getting out of CDG and ACE.

Once again, we set off in the direction of Cocoa Beach but while we were on the highway, I spotted a Winn Dixie. It didn't take much to convince Pamsy she didn't dare leave Orlando without experiencing you know what. Laden with cookies, snacks and drinks, we gleefully got back in the car and ended up taking a wrong turn, which put us on another highway. As if that wasn't bad enough, the traffic was horrendous so when I spotted the sign for Liza's, Pamsy suggested we pop in for a visit.

Carina and a friend of hers were home from a half day at school and Liza welcomed us with open arms. After devouring most of the cookies with tea, Liza insisted we ring Gabriel.

"Hello stranger!"

"Hey you, howz it goin'?"

"Great, I just bought my ticket home-"

"You got your date with British Air?"

"British *Airways*," I laughed. "And yes, I start January the thirtieth."

"Oh man, that's awesome, congrats." His tone was so sincere it made me smile.

"I must admit I'm chuffed, and relieved. How are you getting on?"

"Good, yeah, school's good."

"Why aren't you in a lecture?"

"I'm done with class for the day," he explained. "Wednesdays are the bomb."

"How's Maria?"

Without missing a beat, he yelled, "Loud!"

When I finally stopped laughing, I said, "You're very naughty," to which he replied, "Girls love a bad boy, right?"

Pamsy was chomping at the bit for me to pass the phone and once we were back in the car, she said she'd enjoyed talking to Gabriel and that he sounded as lovely as I'd made him out to be.

"I had so much fun with him."

"Not to mention the hanky panky," she teased, smacking her lips.

"Yeah, there woz a bit of the 'ole slap and tickle," I said in a cockney accent I knew would make her laugh.

"Sorry to change the subject, but how stunning was Carina's mate?"

"Totally drop dead! I found it hard not to keep staring at her flawless skin. Her features were so perfect, she almost didn't look human!"

"That sounds funny, but you're spot on."

"I can't imagine all the attention being that gorgeous would bring."

"*You're* gorgeous," Pamsy said.

"Am not! I'm fat!"

"You are not fat!" she snarled. "I don't know why you always say that."

"I made you turn around so I could buy cookies!"

"That I ate *with you*. And I don't think I'm fat. What do you weigh, like eight stone?"

"Closer to nine," I sighed.

"Well, you're tall."

"And fat!"

"Stop it! You're not fat, say it!"

I looked at her. "Say what?"

"I am not fat!"

"I refuse to say that, but I *will* say something else."

"What's that?" she said.

"Let's stop at Dairy Queen."

19th ~ Miriam & Hank's, Orlando, Florida

Pamsy woke up to find me sitting on the floor, the contents of my suitcase strewn across the swirly seventies carpet.

"What're you doing?" She asked, stepping over my stuff.

"Looking for the purse I keep my sterling in. I need to change more money, I'm almost out of dollars."

"It's all those shoulder pads you've been buying," she shouted from the loo.

After explaining our dilemma to Luis at the front desk, he said, "I'll alert the authorities," reminding me of any number of American tv shows, many of which Pamsy does a great job mimicking. One of the many pluses of a best friend who went to drama school.

26

Sitting across from Pamsy with my back to the door, I watched her eyes widen. "Cor, get a load of that, I hope they're here to see us."

I turned to see two Chippendale's, masquerading as police officers.

"Look busy," Pamsy mouthed, picking up a well-thumbed Cosmopolitan magazine.

After establishing we were the ones who, "Called to report an incident," we learned the officers names were Rodriguez and Sammartino. Between the pair of them, there was a lot to take in, but it was the guns that caught my eye. Officer Rodriguez said I'd need to complete a report and that they'd need to see, "Where the *alleged* crime occurred."

In the lift, making small talk, Pamsy asked Sammartino where he was from.

"Kentucky," he stated, proudly.

"The bluegrass state," she chirped.

"You've been?"

"No, but I watch the Kentucky Derby every year. My dad's a big fan."

With two additional pairs of shoulders, the room felt cramped. At the little table, Rodriguez opened his folder and took down some information, before he asked what was missing.

"A purse, containing sterling."

"Silver?" asked Sammartino.

"UK currency."

Rodriguez nodded in acknowledgement and while he wrote, my eyes rested on beefy biceps that looked like they were about to tear through the short-sleeved shirt.

"How much?" he asked, catching me in the act.

"Fifty pounds, roughly ninety dollars."

"Anything else?"

"The purse itself."

"A pocketbook?"

"I don't know what that is," I said, looking at Pamsy, but all she did was shrug like she does when she says, "Je ne sais pas."

With a quick glance at Pamsy's streaked locks, Sammartino explained a pocketbook is something you'd use, "To carry stuff, like a hairbrush."

"Oh, you mean a handbag," I said. "But no, it's not my handbag that's missing, it's my purse, where I keep my money."

After writing *wallet*, Rodriguez asked what else was missing.

"Donald duck," Pamsy blurted. Rodriguez looked at me.

Pay attention! Pay attention!

"It was for Suzi, she's almost-"

"Just the facts please." His face gave nothing away. Could there possibly be two drama school graduates in the same room?

"Sorry, ehm, Donald Duck, comma, soft toy."

I watched him write Donald Duck followed by the letter c that he promptly crossed out. With the tiny hint of a smile, he asked if there was anything else.

"Yes, a jumper," I said as Sammartino and Rodriguez exchanged a questioning look.

"A lovely white cotton one at that," Pamsy added. "Wasn't that for your mum?"

"It was meant to be," I said demurely. "Until we got robbed blind!"

Who's the actress now!

"When do you think the incident o curd?" asked Sammartino.

Imagining what I'd wear in the courtroom I said, "I believe the incident occurred sometime on Tuesday, January the seventeenth. Nineteen eighty-nine."

"Whilst we were at Disney," Pamsy added.

"How are you spelling that?" Rodriguez asked, stroking a tiny trace of stubble on his chin, the act of which I found more than distracting.

"Would you like me to write it down?" Pamsy was obviously starring in the same courtroom drama. Shoulder pads galore!

"Sure," Rodriguez said, moving from his spot at the table to allow Pamsy to take his place.

With her eyes downcast, Pamsy began scribbling. "You said a jumper, Karen?"

"Correct."

"And what is the approximate value of said jumper?" she asked, completely unabashed. Oh, those thespians!

"I paid twenty-eight dollars and I believe I may still be in possession of the receipt."

This scene alone was clearly going to require a hefty wardrobe budget.

With Pamsy scribbling away, Sammartino and Rodriguez had a bit of a conflab about what a jumper is, mistaking it for some sort of dress.

"Sweater," Pamsy muttered under her breath, as she finished the last of the statement, before handing it to Rodriguez. He had me sign and date the statement (half of which was in Pamsy's handwriting) then asked for a number where I could be reached, so I gave him Miriam's.

"If we find the perpetrator, we'll be in touch," Rodriguez said, shaking my hand. "Is there anything else?"

"Actually, there is," I said. "Can you give us directions to Cocoa Beach?"

20th ~ Miriam & Hank's, Orlando, Florida

After the police left yesterday, we thought it'd be best to check out of the hotel, so we chucked everything in the boot and, with directions in hand, we headed for Cocoa Beach, but somewhere along the way we took a wrong turn and ended up at Sea World! After hours traipsing in and out of shows and exhibits, we decided to come here and when we told Miriam and Hank what had happened, they insisted we stay, where they know we're safe.

Today was our last chance to find Cocoa Beach but due to our excessive talking (shock!) we missed a turn and ended up in St. Augustine. With café's galore, Spanish colonial architecture and an abundance of art galleries, it's on the list for next time. Our attempt at finding a florist failed, so we were forced to buy the supermarket variety, but after we wove them together, they didn't look so bad. I also bought three packets of Chips Ahoy! that are already packed.

And on our last night, America has a new President! George H. W. Bush was sworn in as the 41st President, with Dan Quayle as the Vice President. Pamsy joked that with that taken care of, we can now head home.

21st ~ Flight from Orlando - Newark – Gatwick

UK bound and so excited to be going home.

22nd ~ Home sweet home

Seeing mum and dad on the platform brought home how much I've missed them. As the train slowed to a stop, I watched them scanning the carriages, and when mum spotted me, she clutched dad's arm, pointed and began waving furiously.

The second I was off the train, mum grabbed me, and dad jumped on to grab my luggage.

"We were hoping ye'd be on this yin," mum gushed.

"Sorry I never rang, but I didn't want to miss the train."

"We're glad yer safely home," dad said, tousling my hair. "Yer the picture of health, sure she is, Liz?"

"Oh aye, hopefully ye brought the sun wi ye," mum smiled, linking her arm through mine as we made our way up the stairs to the concourse.

Through the frosted glass front door, I watched Tini's silhouette scampering up and down the hallway. His vocal welcome left me feeling a bit teary-eyed, and he barely left my side all day, but that might have had something to do with the Mickey Mouse treats I drip fed him.

After lunch, we exchanged pressies and dad laughed when I asked him to play Christmas music.

"If I'd known ye still wanted Christmas," mum said, "I'd have kept the tree up."

Two letters from Ben. There's so much more to write about him, but I'm fading fast.

23rd ~ At home

Thanks to the time change and mum's not so quiet movements in the kitchen (directly beneath my bedroom) I was awake early. All smiles, mum wasted no time making t & t (tea and toast) and had plenty of questions about my time away, but when her tone turned serious, I knew what was coming.

"When is Ben due back fae Italy?"

"According to his letter, it'll probably be within the next few weeks."

"Well, don't forget yer gonny be busy during training, so if he shows up when-"

"I know, I know," I said, wanting nothing more than to change the subject. "Don't worry, I won't get distracted."

It's strange coming home after such a lengthy absence because it almost feels like I never left. In between blasting my favourite music, I spent a lot of time on the phone with Pamsy, nana and Stephen.

Now in bed, thinking about Ben (how unusual) and wondering, as I'm wont to do, what he's doing at this precise moment. I know he had airport duty today so there was no way he could ring, but that didn't stop me from wishing the day away thinking he might, if only for a few minutes.

24th ~ At home

Finally got my hair chopped at Braids and when I say chopped, I'm not exaggerating. Tracey got a bit carried away, or maybe it's just that we were talking so much, but I'm fine with it. It's not like it won't grow back and it feels so much better. Oh, where oh where would we be without our hair stylists?

Lengthy chat with Sarah, who I've always pegged as quite traditional so I'm more than surprised to hear she and Simon are moving in together. I expected her to announce their engagement but for the time being they'll be, to quote nana, "Living in sin!" Throughout secondary, Sarah and Jim were tied at the hip and when they broke up, she was beyond heartbroken, so much so that I half expected her to remain single for a very long time. Love is incredibly confusing.

And on that note…in a deep and ridiculously sexy voice due to the fact he'd just woken up, Ben rang! I can't begin to describe how good it felt to hear him say the words I've missed and longed to hear since we kissed goodbye all those months ago. He said he still loves me, hasn't stopped thinking about me and can't wait to come home. I knew from his letters that was how he was feeling but to hear him say it makes me miss him more than ever.

25th ~ Angie's, Surrey

When I lived here during Air Europe days, it was rare for all of us to have dinner together but whenever we did, we'd linger at the table long after the food (mostly cooked by Nadia) was gone, and the empty wine bottles lined the sink.

Tonight, was one of those nights where I laughed myself silly and remembered why I loved being a tenant in this special home, where the landlady has a heart of gold.

26th ~ Pamsy's, Sussex

On the *blink and you'll miss it* platform at Cooden Beach station, Pamsy waved as though we'd been separated for years. Talking ten to the dozen, we legged it to her car but still got drenched. At the beach huts (always our first stop) the slate grey sky looked ominous, which I love, especially when it's blowing a hoolie.

Kitty already moved most of her stuff out of the flat, but fortunately she left the bed. She told Pamsy that she and her three decades older than us boyfriend will be getting married, as soon as his divorce is final. Pamsy and I talked about the possibility of me moving in, but it's too far from LHR (and a certain someone!) so now she's left with no choice but to sell.

With the dining set gone, we ate in front of the tv. Balancing the plate precariously on my lap, I commented on the yummy meal.

"It's just sweet and sour chicken, easy to whip up."

"Maybe for you. You know what I'm like in the kitchen."

"You like baking."

"As much as I'd love to, I can't survive on cakes alone."

Looking pensive, Pamsy asked, "Who said let them eat cake?"

"Marie Antionette and what she actually said was, 'Qu'ils mangent de la brioche.'"

"Which means?"

"Let them eat brioche!"

"Silly cow," Pamsy tutted.

Continuing with the French theme, we caught the last few minutes of a confusing film that confirmed our language skills still require subtitles. While the credits scrolled, Pamsy asked what I expect will happen when Ben returns.

"I don't know, what do you think?"

"Do you want my honest opinion?" She said, taking my empty plate.

Following her into the galley kitchen, I said I did but the only thing I really wanted to hear was gushy stuff about how perfectly suited she believes Ben and I are. Filling the wash basin with a heap of hot water and a generous amount of Fairy Liquid she said, "I think you'll shag him and fall madly in love with him. Again." She swished the bubbles in a circle. "And I think that will put you in great peril of having your heart broken." She plunged her hands deep into the soapy suds. "Again."

"Ouch!"

"I know it sounds harsh, but I can't bear to watch you going through all that again. I loved seeing how happy you were in Florida and how much you enjoyed meeting Gabriel."

"You can't compare Gabriel to Ben," I huffed, defensively.

"The point I'm trying to make," she said, drying her hands, "is that you were happy. Without him." She tossed the dishtowel on the draining board.

"I still thought about him," I confessed.

"But you survived... for months."

Tilting my head all the way back, I released a lengthy guttural sound.

"Only you Scots can make that sound," she laughed, lightening the mood. "Listen, I'm sorry I upset you. I just want you to be happy."

"I know."

"Shall we leave it at that?"

I nodded in agreement.

"Ok now close your eyes, I have a surprise for you."

"What is it?"

"Just close your eyes. And no peeking!"

I listened as the panty door creaked open.

"Ok you can open them."

"Oohhh," I cooed, at the sight of a packet of Chips Ahoy!

27th ~ At home

I'd planned on taking the train to Brighton to spend Friday night with Stephen, but those plans got squashed after he got called out on standby (didn't think to ask where he was going, not that it matters when all he'd be doing was a quick turn-around).

Pamsy was off to Geneva, so she dropped me off at Gatwick. On two trains, and two tubes (sounds like a blockbuster!) it took over three hours to get home, by which time I was in a foul mood, mostly because I had to schlep my suitcase (Pamsy took my third suitcase home with her) up and down one too many broken escalators.

No sooner was I in the door when dad asked how I plan on getting to class on Monday. After I made the mistake of saying I hadn't given it much thought, he started banging on about how much easier things are when you're organised. Gingerly, I reminded him it's only Friday but what I wanted to say was the last thing I felt like doing after hours on public transport was getting more info on public transport.

28th ~ At home

Looking ahead to the warmer climes I'll be frequenting, I spent way too much in Miss Selfridge. Often, when I go shopping, nothing catches my eye but today, I wanted everything. In John Lewis, I found a scientific calculator for dad ("I've had my eye on one of these for a wee while, thanks hen, it'll really help with my job") and several thank you gifts to send to Miriam and Hank.

After getting soaked at the bus stop, I decided it's time to find a car. While I was peeling off the last of my soggy clothes, mum called upstairs.

"Karen! Phone!"

I chucked on my Benetton rugby shirt (so soft from so many washes) and when I went downstairs, mum was still on the phone.

"Oh aye, I hope so," she chuckled. "Right then, here she is. Cheerio."

"Who is it," I mouthed as mum pressed the receiver into my hand, without a word.

"Hello?"

"McGarr!" boomed the only person who calls me by my surname.

"Oh, it's you," I said, chiding myself for wishing it was Ben.

"Yeah, it's me, funny that."

"Sorry, I wasn't expecting it to be you," I said, immediately feeling foolish.

"Hello McGarr, remember me? Ex-boyfriend, we went on holiday a few times, is this ringing any bells?"

"Not a sausage," I teased. "I'm going to need more than that."

"Funny as always," he chortled. "Welcome back! How was Mickey?"

"Appealing, in a quiet mousy sort of way."

"Oh, McGarr, nooo."

"I know, sorry, couldn't resist."

Two hours later (and I thought I could talk!) I was still wedged in the phone chair when Sarah rang. She invited me to their (she and Simon are now *them*, so strange) to watch videos (yawn) and play cards (bigger yawn). When I asked who'd be there, it was so and so and so and so and so and so, basically, all couples.

"Sorry, I just remembered I have a bunch of paperwork to fill out before I show up at BA, on Monday."

"Boo, not fair." Even on the phone, I sensed her sulking.

"What a shame," I fibbed.

"Not to worry," she chirped. "We'll be doing it all again next weekend."

29th ~ At home

I was still on my first cup of tea when mum got home from church, which meant I'd missed breakfast. Typically, I'd make up for it by wolfing down a huge lunch but knowing there's a new uniform to fit into (the thought of which sends me into a tizzy) I stabbed at limp lettuce leaves that mirrored exactly how I felt. The last remaining packet of Chips Ahoy! screamed to be released from the cupboard, but I stood my ground and ignored them (I did, however open the cupboard and gaze longingly at them, before slamming the door shut!).

Mum was full of beans and suggested we clean out my wardrobe to make space for my new uniform. Knowing how she gets when her mind is set on something, I went along with the task at hand, but I soon lost interest. Peeking out from between the hangers, mum asked if I'm nervous about tomorrow.

"Not really," I said, not quite sure I'm not. "I just fancy going out on my bike, I'll help you when I get back, ok?"

"Aye, ok hen," she said, slipping deeper into the wardrobe.

After a steady stream of cursing, I finally yanked my bike out from behind the garden furniture in the shed, and with a strong desire to feel connected to Ben, I rode to his house. Obviously, he's still away but it was so comforting being there, catching up with Susan, while Stan watched the footie.

When I got home after eight (Susan offered to drive me home but, in my absence, dad installed lights on my bike) dad seemed more than agitated.

"Ye shouldnae be oot gallivanting when ye've got such a big day the morra. Did ye get the train times?"

"Er, not yet."

"Did ye book a taxi?"

"I haven't yet but-"

"Did ye fill in the paperwork?"

If only to get him off my back, I almost nodded instead of shaking my head, but I can't lie to my dad.

"Don't forget yer passport and P forty-five, oh, and I'll be up in the morning but set your alarm, just in case."

"Ok, thanks, dad," I said, taking the stairs two at a time.

30th ~ On the train

Sleepy start in the dark and so begins my six-week commute.
Taxi to Milton Keynes Central - 10 mins.
Train to Euston - 55 mins.
Tube from Euston to Hatton Cross – Delay today so not sure, maybe 25 mins, or so.
Walk to Cranebank - 20 mins.
Cranebank is where British Airways cabin crew and pilot's train. It's a squat building with zero appeal but inside it's bustling, and with mostly everyone wearing the BA uniform, it has the feel of a school for grown-ups.

Half of us have previous flying experience, with charter airlines such as Monarch, Britannia and Dan Air, and most of us are in our early twenties. Maura is the oldest and must be in the air before her 30th birthday. Such pressure!

31st ~ At home

I need to be up in five hours so I should probably give this a miss, but never again will it be Day Two of British Airways Long Haul Cabin Crew Training.

The highlight of the day was boarding the TriStar, aka the Lockheed L-1011. With every clanging footstep on the metal stairway, the wings in my stomach fluttered, and when I finally stepped onboard, it struck me how much I've missed flying. When I turned to Lolly, her wide smile matched mine and when instructor Jeremy asked us to take a seat, Carl quipped there weren't enough, which made everyone laugh. I sat next to Kimberly (Manchester) and Sam (London?) and from across the aisle, Lorna (Paisley) rolled her eyes whenever Jeremy mentioned British Airways.

The lower-level galley was a surprise and not a working position I'd ever want to get landed with. Seems it's popular with, "seasoned crew," which makes sense given there's no passenger interaction. All I could think about was getting stuck down there, alone, during an emergency. No thanks!

FEBRUARY

1st ~ At home

I was dead on my feet last night, so I went to bed early, which meant doing homework on the train. What I didn't consider was how long it takes me to wake up, so with the combination of feeling groggy, and the swaying motion of the train, my writing was all over the place. This is where I should vow never to leave it until the last minute, but I know myself better than that.

Today's focus was Economy Cabin Practical's, with the emphasis on service, which I know from being in the States, is key. I imagine I'll be working down the back quite a bit at first, because those are the most junior positions.

Had lunch in the canteen and I think the ice is beginning to crack within the group. Had I known we were going to uniform stores straight after lunch, I'd probably have opted for a salad, instead of shepherd's pie.

The moment I'd been dreading came when the woman in uniform stores took my measurements. I still haven't dared to look at my skirt size but I'm pretty sure it's double digits. We have grey skirts for winter and a red, white and blue striped blouse. Didn't anyone tell the designer Roland Klein that stripes are not my friend? The summer skirt is also striped, and as if that's not bad enough (it is!) there's a belt. A hideous belt that, in addition to the stripes, confirms I joined the airline with the worst uniform.

As well as the basic uniform, there's a full-length wool coat, raincoat, handbag and hat, all of which I lugged home. Everything was wrapped in long, plastic covers and on our walk to the tube, Lolly and I had to keep stopping because we kept tripping over the plastic. I swear she went home with half my stuff.

I got home at half seven, and a few minutes later, Ben rang. I love the sound of his voice so much that I skipped dinner, which I need to keep doing, because four days from now, I'll be kissing him again.

2nd ~ At home

Thanks to a taxi driver with a death wish, I got to the station in record time. To take my mind off the gnawing chill, I conjured up silly stories about the zombie commuters, one of whom came close enough that I stepped back to allow him to pass.

"Karen," he said, catching me off guard.

"Morning," I stuttered, desperately trying to place him.

"Lee," he said coming to my rescue. My first thought was how much older he looked and my second was surprise, that it's been four years since we left secondary. We spilled a quick summary of life since then, but it was all in hushed tones because nobody talks at that hour.

Classes were hectic today and I have piles of homework, mostly pertaining to safety equipment. Walked to Hatton Cross station with Sam and caught the first tube with him.

"Darling," he tutted, his head bobbing in time to the rhythmic carriage. "Your commute is *ridiculous*. Why didn't you move closer for training?"

"My boyfr....a guy I'm eh, rather fond of, is coming home from working in Italy and I'm hoping to see him in the evenings."

Looking like he'd bit into something sour, Sam tutted, "Do you have any idea what we're training for in that stodgy old building?"

I opened my mouth to speak, but Sam beat me to it. "We're training to be international trolley dolly's, which means our entire universe is about to *explode* with possibilities. And you know what that means?"

"What?" I asked, barely able to contain a smile.

"Old boyfriends are cheap as chips and need to be left in the past. Where they belong."

3rd ~ At home

Friday night, and I'm home alone. Mum and dad went to Janice and Terry's for a surprise party, and I only know that because of the note mum left, alongside a bar of galaxy, and a flake.

Most of our group rounded off week one, at the pub. Lolly couldn't make it as she was off to see Eric Clapton at the Royal Albert Hall, Lorna flew home to Scotland for the weekend and fortunately Louise, who never stops waffling on about the strangest things, had some family do to attend.

The pub was packed with locals and trainees from the Boeing 747 course running a few weeks ahead of us. Carl was first to strike up a conversation with some of the girls (all gorgeous, all thin!) so we ended up sitting with them. They've already operated their supernumerary flights and shared some amusing stories about being onboard.

By the time I got on the train, I felt slightly woozy from one too many glasses of wine. My eyes kept shutting, but I knew if I fell asleep, I'd miss my stop, so I stayed alert by thinking about Ben and how I feel about seeing him again…ecstatic comes to mind.

The kitchen light was off, so I knew mum and dad were out. While I was rooting around in my bag for the key, the phone started ringing. Thinking it might be Ben, I got inside as fast as I could and made a mad dash for the phone.

"Hell-o," I purred seductively.

"McGarr! What are you doing home on a Friday night? I was just about to hang up."

"I literally just walked in the door, hold on a sec while I shut it."

Jon seemed interested in what transpired this week, then asked if I'm free tomorrow night.

"Technically, yes, but I have to be up early on Sunday morning to go to Gatwick airport."

"I thought you were going to be based at Heathrow?"

"I will be, but, eh, Ben is coming home from Italy."

I caught the pause before Jon spoke. "I thought that was all done and dusted."

"I thought so too, but we've been in touch quite a bit since I got back from the States and-"

"I just had a few beers with Ralph and Rickie. They said they'd love to see you at our gig tomorrow night. I was ringing to see if you wanted me to come and pick you up and suggest you stay at mine afterwards, in the spare room of course, but now that-"

"That sounds great!"

"What?" He sounded more than surprised.

"I said that sounds great. What time can you pick me up? Oh shit, wait, I can't stay, I have to be here early on Sunday morning."

"I know. You said that. I'll take you home after the gig."

"You live almost two hours away."

"I'm aware of that," he laughed. "One night on the wagon won't kill me. Why don't I pick you up at four, and we can grab some nosh down the pub before I go onstage with the band."

"Do I have to pretend I'm a groupie?"

"If I'm deprived of beer, then yes, definitely."

"Fair enough," I said. "Are you sure you don't mind all the driving?"

"I don't mind at all McGarr. I'm looking forward to seeing you."

4th ~ At home

I was still in bed, daydreaming about my reunion with Ben, when the phone rang. Earlier, mum had popped her head in to let me know she and dad were going shopping, so I shot out of bed and dashed downstairs.

"Uh-oh, somebody had a late night," Pamsy chuckled.

"Actually," I yawned. "It wasn't, but tonight will be. Quelle heure est-il?"

"It's almost noon, mademoiselle."

"What are you up to?"

"Sweet Fanny Adams."

"Good for you. Us hosties need a little r and r sometimes."

"It'll be short lived, I have a night Palma, but check in isn't until six."

"Ugh, is there anything worse than a Saturday night flight? The passengers will be pissed on the outbound, and overdue for detox on the inbound."

"Don't remind me. What are your plans today?"

"Jon is coming over later to pick me up, and then-"

"Wait, Jon, your ex-boyfriend?"

"Uh-huh."

"I didn't know you were still in touch with him."

"Yeah, we're still friends."

"I thought Ben was coming home tomorrow?"

"He is, I have to be at Gatwick early. I can't wait! Anyway, how was-"

"Oh no, don't even think about changing the subject. Start by telling me why Jon is picking you up, and why you're seeing Ben as soon as he touches down in Blighty."

Two hours later, I hung up just as mum and dad got home. My legs were still draped over the armrest of the phone chair.

"Are ye no dressed yet?" mum asked, going into the kitchen.

"Ye must've needed the sleep," dad said, hanging up his jacket on one of the brass hooks under the stairs.

"I've been up for a while. I was on the phone with Pamsy."

"How's she getting on?" dad asked, as mum called out from the kitchen. "I'm making tea, and we bought cakes, so don't disappear Karen."

"Pamsy's fine, dad."

The shrill of the phone startled me and dad laughed.

"This is probably her again," I said, picking up the receiver.

"Is this my gorgeous babe?" Ben breathed.

I felt my insides somersault, and waited until dad was safely in the kitchen, before I croaked my answer.

"Your phone's been engaged for hours."

"Sorry, I was talking to Pamsy."

"I can't stay on for long."

"That's ok, we can talk all day tomorrow, I'm so-"

"Actually," he said, interrupting me. "That's why I'm ringing. I won't be home tomorrow."

"No. Nooooo." I felt the lump in my throat and swallowed hard. "Why not?"

"They need me here for another week."

"But you said you were done. Can't you just leave?" I whined.

Poking her head out the kitchen door, mum asked who I was talking to. With my hand over the mouthpiece, I said, "It's Ben."

"Yer tea's ready," she said, in a not so quiet voice.

"I can't stay on the phone, babe, I have to get back to work."

Through the glass wall that looks into the kitchen, I watched mum's head and hands moving at warp speed, while dad remained still.

"Can you ring back later?" I pleaded, quietly.

"I can't, I have airport duty."

I watched dad shrug his shoulders.

"I'm sooo upset. Are you upset? You don't sound upset," I blurted.

"I'm at a payphone, surrounded by people. I have to go. I'm sorry."

"Ring me as soon as you can. Ok?"

"Karen!" mum yelled. "Yer tea's getting cold."

"I'll call when I can-"

"I love you. I really miss you and can't wait to see you. Ring me as soon as-"

The line went dead. Choking back the tears, I went into the kitchen.

"Whit time is Jon coming fur ye?" mum asked, from the other side of the table.

"I need to phone him."

"Whit fur?" dad asked.

"To tell him I can't make it."

"Uff, noo that's just silly," mum huffed.

"Aye, go wi Jon," dad added. "Ye shouldnae be stuck in on a Saturday night."

I wolfed down a strawberry tart without tasting it. Then I had a cream cake.

"I don't feel very well," I said. "I'm going to phone Jon, then I'm going back to bed."

5th ~ At home

Number one this week is, "Something's Gotten Hold of my Heart," by Soft Cell and Gene Pitney, and while I was poring over every letter I've ever received from Ben, I couldn't get the song out of my head. From reading last year's stuff, it's obvious we experienced a great deal of trying times, but it's a New Year, and time for a fresh start.

On the phone, Miriam made mum laugh so hard, mum made a dash for the loo. Is that what Pamsy and I have to look forward to in our later years? I love that even with thousands of miles between them, mum and her oldest friend remain close.

Once mum was off the phone, I tried getting through to Ben, but no luck. After a few tries, each time with mum making her presence known, she said, "Go and get ready, and we'll go oot."

"I don't feel like going out."

"I'm sure there's something on at the pictures ye'd like to see."

I was interested in seeing, *For Queen and Country*, with Denzel Washington and mum wanted to see, *Roger Rabbit*, but they were both sold out, so it was, *Elvira, Mistress of the Dark*. No need to explain why there were still tickets available.

No sooner were mum and dad out the door tonight, when I tried Ben again, hanging up in defeat after letting it ring forty times, which is probably excessive. Speaking of excessive, I made a glutton of myself with the chicken curry Harry sent home with mum and dad. What an amazing cook he is, there's nothing he whips up that I don't love. As full as I was, I still managed to find room for tea and Club biscuits, which I can't eat without singing the jingle, "If you like a lot of chocolate on your biscuit, join our Club!"

Need to get my uniform ready for tomorrow. At this rate I'll need the next size up.

6th ~ At home

Back to the pre-dawn taxi, train and tube routine, with standing room only on the train to Euston. The trenchies (my name for the commuters in trench coats) had already staked claim to the area around the luggage racks, so I had to stand in the aisle. Unlike the tube, the train has no overhead railing so to keep from toppling over, I dug my nails into the seat closest to me. The scowl on the seat occupants face was not enough to deter me.

I was one of the last to arrive in class today, and it was lovely walking into a sea of uniforms. Everyone looked professional, and so different to last week when we were still in civvies. The morning was taken up with Bar Service, with the focus on the vast selection of wines available in Club World.

It was bucketing down at home time, so I was grateful when Carl offered to drop Sam and I at Hatton Cross. I think Carl could be a bit of a lad, but harmless with it. This is his first experience as cabin crew, and I have more than a sneaking suspicion the lifestyle will suit him to a T.

Before Sam and I had even reached the platform, we got stopped by a handful of people asking for directions, not only to the airport but also to the public toilets.

"Right that way, madam," Sam clipped, pointing to the opposite end of the station.

"Thank you," the woman said, scurrying off.

"My pleasure, madam."

As we made our way down the stairs I said, "I had no idea there was a loo there."

"There's not," Sam grinned wickedly.

7th ~ At home

Standing room only on the train again, fortunately I finished the homework last night. Total brass monkeys walking to Cranebank, which left me chilled to the bone the entire day.

When I rang Jon on Saturday to cancel (felt horrible doing so, especially when he let it slip it was his birthday weekend) he asked if I'd like help finding a car. I only have a thousand quid to spend, so I can't expect too much, but anything will be better than lugging a suitcase on the tube after a night flight.

Managed 98% on today's exam, guess I've been paying attention after all! Louise, who seems to talk nonstop, was asked to, "Go and have a little chat with Sandi." Of the three instructors, I'd say Sandi is the one I'd least want to have a little chat with.

Today felt like a turning point, and I can imagine all of us working together onboard, not that we ever will, but hopefully our paths will occasionally cross on the odd trip.

I was hoping Ben would ring, but not a peep from him. Not even a letter.

8th ~ At home

It's almost midnight and I haven't looked at today's notes, let alone the homework Sandi doled out one minute before we closed our manuals for the day.

Somehow, pizza turned into drinks, and drinks turned into more drinks, and consequently I only rolled in an hour ago. Much to my dismay, I missed Ben on the phone.

My arm is sore, and slightly bruised, from the various injections we received. After the first few, I lost track of what we were being immunized against. Sam said he felt light-headed after the first one and had to sit the rest out, but that just means he has them all to look forward to.

Lolly and I forewent lunch, for a trip to uniform stores, but neither of us could remember where the building is located (we are definitely on the same wavelength!) so we'll try again tomorrow.

I'm so glad I joined this course, and not the one I was set to a week earlier. I can't imagine that group being anything as good as the one I'm with.

9th ~ At home

Met Lee on the platform again, and we even managed to nab two seats together on the train. When I told him I'm tired of standing, he suggested I get a briefcase like the one he and the other trenchies carry.

"A briefcase isn't considered part of BA's uniform standards, so even if I wanted one, which I don't, it's against the rules."

"Are they that strict?"

"Don't you know we're the nations flag carrier?" I said in a mock serious tone, but it was lost on him.

"What other restrictions are there?"

"No chewing gum. No eating. No drinking. No running. Just to name a few."

"I still think you need a briefcase."

"I don't have much to carry."

"Mine is empty, except for a notepad and pens."

"Then why do you have it?"

"It's a weapon," he said, teeny, tiny hint of a smile. "Something that helps get a seat on the train."

On the platform at Euston, Lee made an abrupt stop.

"Are you alright?" I asked, stepping back towards him, ignoring a swell of disapproving grunts.

"Fine, thanks. Listen, I hope you don't think I'm being forward, but would you like to go out for a drink sometime?"

"Sorry, I'm seeing someone."

"Oh. I wasn't aware of that."

We continued walking, and I should have left it at that, but I'm not good with awkward silences. "Actually, you might remember him from school. He's been in Italy for a few months, but he's coming home this weekend."

"I do remember him," Lee said, after my brief explanation. "He was into drama."

"Still is," I muttered under my breath.

"Sorry, what?"

"Just grumbling about how exhausting commuting is."

"That's only because you don't have a weapon."

Day one of Aviation Medicine (AvMed) and the instructor, Bertha, is a battle axe. Her expression remained dour, except for when she informed us, "The face of resusci Annie is based on the death mask of a young woman who drowned in the River Seine in the 1880s."

"That perked her up," Lorna mouthed.

It was still light out when we finished a little earlier than usual. Sam was off to meet friends in Knightsbridge and asked if I wanted to go. I'd have liked to, but I didn't want to miss possibly hearing from Ben.

10th ~ At home

I'd been dreading this afternoon and when I asked Lorna (ex-nurse) to keep an eye on me, she thought I was joking, until I explained I'd fainted during the section on childbirth, at Air Europe. Kicking into nurse mode, she told me not to worry because she'd be monitoring me for any signs of distress.

I've been privy to the horror story of my birth one too many times, so when we turned the page in our manuals to the section in question, I felt reassured when Lorna edged her chair closer to mine. For the first few pages I was ok, until Bertha began stressing birthing terms, and I felt myself wince.

"Just breathe," Lorna whispered.

The final straw came when Bertha strung *fallopian tubes*, *uterus* and *womb* together, in the same sentence. My skin felt clammy, and from the change in my breathing, I sensed I was close to keeling over.

"Later, when we discuss the *placenta*, I'll-"

Lorna's hand shot in the air. "Excuse me, Bertha."

Giving Lorna a probing look, Bertha tutted, "You have a question?"

"It feels a trifle stuffy in here. Can we take a wee break?"

"*Now?*"

Fanning her face, Lorna nodded. "Is anybody else warm or is it just me?"

"I am," I mumbled, pretending to reach for my bag, knowing full well that putting my head between my legs might save me. Much to my surprise (and relief) Bertha agreed to a five-minute break.

In the bathroom, I splashed cold water on my face and thanked Lorna profusely.

"Another wee minute doll," she chuckled, "and you'd have been on the floor, next to resusci Annie."

11th ~ At home

First thing this morning, still in bed, the phone rang. I knew mum and dad were out, so I ignored it and rolled over, but it rang again. And again.

At the bottom on the stairs, I tripped over the scatter rug mum just bought (how many rugs does one house need?) and on my way to meet the floor, I whacked the side of my face against the sturdy phone table leg. I swore. Loudly. Just as I was getting up, the phone stopped. I was so furious I picked up the receiver, and screamed, "arrrrrggghhhghhh," into it, then I slammed it down and plopped in the phone   chair.
When it rang again, I was still in a foul mood and was tempted to ignore it, but curiosity got the better of me.

"Hello?"

"Finally," Ben huffed.

"Did you just ring?" I asked.

"Yeah, I've been phoning you for ages. Just making sure you're still coming to meet me tomorrow?"

"Try and stop me! Your mum and dad are picking me up at eight and your dad said it'll take about two hours to get to Gatwi-" I tried stifling the yawn, but it came out in full force.

"Did you have a late night?"

"I did, actually." Another yawn, inappropriate but oh so satisfying.

"Are you there?" Ben asked, sounding impatient.

"Yeah, sorry about that. A few of us went out for drinks, then dinner in Chinatown." I refrained from adding, *and more drinks*.

"What for?" he asked.

"It was Meryl's twenty-first."

"Who went?"

"I just told you, a few people from my group."

"A mixed group?"

"Uh-huh."

"What are the guys like?"

"Really nice. Carl and Daniel walked me to the tube because it was late, and I had to leg it to catch the last train home."

"You weren't kidding when you said it was a late night." His tone was disapproving, so I figured it was time to change the subject. "What are you up to tonight?" I asked.

"Not much. I need to finish packing. That's about it."

"No big going away bash?"

"Nah, early night for me."

I hate to say it, but I don't believe him.

12th ~ Ben's, MK

Is there anything more exciting than waiting at the airport, for the one you love, the one you've longed to see, since the moment you kissed goodbye.

Waiting. Waiting. Waiting.

The one I flew over four thousand miles to get over, but even with distance and time, I couldn't escape the image of his face, forever imprinted in my head. And heart.

Pacing. Pacing. Pacing.

Through the throng of weary faced travellers, arriving from across the globe, I spotted him. My frenzied pulse and somersaulting stomach left me feeling giddy, and with his eyes fixed on mine like a laser, we moved towards one another.

Kissing. Kissing. Kissing.

I'm deliriously happy to have Ben home. With me. And since our first kiss, twelve hours ago, we've barely let go of one another.

13th ~ At home

It was still dark when Ben came to wake me (about an hour after I'd crept from his bed to the one in the guest room.) I hated saying goodbye after he walked me home, but I had to race to get ready so as not to miss the train.

Everyone in class (except yours truly) appeared lethargic, and Carl teased me about how, "Full of it," I was. Sam reminded Carl that, "Lover boy just got home from Italia," and from that point on there's nothing I'm willing to repeat, but it was all very amusing. And accurate!

I counted down the hours and minutes, until the train finally pulled in, and the sight of Ben on the platform made my insides feel like galloping horses.

Grinning like my life depended on it, we quickly made our way out of the station, to the car, where we snogged for ages, before coming here.

"There's plenty of chicken left, if yeez are hungry," mum said, when I poked my head in the living room, where she and dad were watching the news, with Tini between them, on the couch.

Pinned against the fridge, Ben nuzzled my neck, and whispered sweet nothings that tugged at my desire for him, but with mum and dad right next door, I reluctantly pushed him away.

Ben carried the tray with tea and biscuits into the living room, and dad shut off the tv. True to form, he asked if I had homework and beamed when I said I already did it on the train. On our way out, dad reminded me not to be, "too late."

While we were hanging up our coats at Ben's, his mum said, "There's plenty of chicken leftover, if you two are hungry." Stifling laughter, we made our way to the kitchen, and while the kettle boiled, I tilted Ben's head back and slowly fed him bite sized pieces.

"Stop that you minx," he whispered, looking like the cat that got the cream.

On the couch, with my legs slung across Ben's lap, we watched tv, and just after eleven we left his. After many kissing breaks, I got home just after midnight.

14th ~ At home

Another nightmare commute, with standing room only on the train. As bad as that is, the worst part of the journey remains the walk from Hatton Cross tube station to Cranebank. The weather has been so dismal, I'm surprised I haven't caught pneumonia.

Firefighting drills in the smoke-filled mock cabin really brought home how terrifying a fire onboard would be. I'm not claustrophobic but crawling on the floor trying to locate the exits raised my heart rate. When it was over, we breathed a collective sigh of relief.

The rest of the day flew by (aced the exam) and once again, Ben was waiting on the platform. We came straight to his (empty house!) and in his bedroom, we exchanged all manner of Valentine greetings.

Ben surprised me with a bottle of Obsession and the George Michael *Faith* video, that, unfortunately was playing when his mum and dad got home. It was at the part in the "I Want Your Sex," video where the scantily clad girl walks away from the camera with half her bum cheeks peeking out of her skimpy knickers!

With one look at the screen, Stan, stuttered, "What the-"

"Calm down, dad. It's just a video."

Coming into the living room after hanging up her coat, Susan said, "What on earth are you two watching?" It was at the part where water splashes over the writhing bodies.

"It's George Michael," Ben said to no one in particular.

"Ooh, I like him," Susan said, sitting on the other couch.

"Right, that's enough of that," Stan barked. "Turn it off, Ben."

"Why?"

"Because it's *obscene*."

"Oh Stan," Susan sighed, comically. "Don't be such a prude."

Onscreen, George Michael was writing *Explore,* in lipstick, on a fleshy thigh.

"Oh, I say," Susan chirped. "That's a bit saucy, innit?" Looking up at Stan, she said, "Pop upstairs love and grab me lipstick."

"Mum!" Ben exclaimed.

"Susan!" Stan said, trying desperately to keep a straight face.

"It's a day for celebrating love," Susan said, swatting Stan's arm. "I think you sometimes forget what we were like when we were young. Now, stop acting like an ole fuddy-duddy, and come and give us a kiss."

15th ~ Ben's, MK

Slide drills today, and in order to protect the slides, we donned unflattering jumpsuits. Kimberly could've passed for a model in an aviation mag, while the rest of us looked like we were off to the Michelin man's family reunion.

We received our contracts and they're due back this Friday so I'm going to ask dad to look it over with me. Everyone seems eager to have training over with so I can't imagine anyone refusing to sign.

Finished much earlier than usual so I rang Ben from the payphone in Cranebank.

"I can't pick you up that early, my mum will still be at work."

"That's ok, I'll get a taxi home first, then-"

"Can you come straight to mine?"

"I'd rather go home first, I got soaked again this morning and haven't warmed up all day."

"You can wear something of mine. Just come here first. There's something I need to tell you."

"What is it?" I asked.

"I don't want to tell you over the phone. Just come straight to mine and we can talk then."

All the way home I racked my brain trying to figure out what was so important that Ben felt the need to tell me face-to-face. My thoughts ran the gamut from Ben being diagnosed with some terrible illness to some random girl he'd met, showing up, pregnant.

When the train pulled into the station, I scanned the platform, still hoping to see Ben's beautiful face, but that didn't happen until I was outside his house, paying the taxi driver.

"Hey babe," he said, at the door, with a forced sense of cheer.

"I missed you," I said, throwing my arms around his warm neck.

Inside, Ben took my coat and tried to kiss me, but all I wanted was to find out what was going on. When Ben said he's going back to Italy, I felt my shoulders relax.

"I know that, but summer's ages away. That's it?" I said, relief flooding my system. "That's all you wanted to tell me?" I lunged at him and was about to plant a kiss on his lips, when he stopped me.

"I have to go sooner than expected."

His tone was flat enough to make my stomach lurch.

"When?" I croaked, already close to tears.

"This Sunday."

16th ~ At home

After a sleepless night at Ben's, he drove me home and waited while I got ready. Mum knocked on the bathroom door and asked if I was alright (after Ben's bad news, I rang home and fortunately mum didn't put up much of a fuss when I said I'd be spending the night). My eyes told the story of a tear-filled night, so from the other side of the door, I mumbled something about being fine and that I'd see her tonight.

Wrought from all the crying, I got in the car and when Ben reached the end of the street, I told him to turn left.

"But the train stat-"

"I know where it is," I yelled. "I'm not going!"

He slammed so hard on the brakes that we were thrust forward.

"Karen, you have to go."

"I can't. I feel sick. Look at my eyes!"

"You're just tired, babe. You'll be ok after you get on the train."

"I can't do it. Not today. Let's go back to yours."

Ben tried talking me into going but he soon realised I was holding my ground. At nine on the dot, I rang Cranebank, and spent ages on hold because nobody seemed to know who I should talk to. Shortly after, mum rang. Furious doesn't begin to cover it. Apparently, Sandi rang to find out why I'd called in sick.

"You better get home right this minute!" mum yelled. "If dad finds out aboot-"

"I can't, not yet. I need to stay close to the loo." I hated lying but the last thing I needed, was mum's wrath.

Fell asleep on the couch and when I woke up, Ben was on the phone. He'd moved it into the kitchen, so his words sounded mumbled, but there was no mistaking the name he uttered.

My thoughts turned to a day in London last summer, when we bumped into a girl Ben had worked with, in Spain. A girl who gazed at him with tears in her eyes and body language that screamed of a story with a not so happy ending. For her. *Helena.*

After that chance encounter, Ben claimed their relationship had been short lived and that they'd agreed to go their separate ways when they returned to England, but not long after that, Helena wrote to him. I'm ashamed to admit it, but I read the letter and it was obvious she was still in love with him. Our relationship took a nosedive, but he still had a huge hold over me, and I knew the only way to break it would be with distance (at least that's what I thought at the time) so I left. And went to Florida.

I heard Ben return the phone to its regular spot on the shelf, before coming over to me. Tenderly stroking my cheek, he asked how I was feeling. I knew the second my eyes were open I'd have to act normal, so I kept them shut. When he leaned in and kissed me, I didn't want him to stop until all my anger had melted away.

No sooner was I in the door, when dad started in with a lecture about how irresponsible I'd been. Mid rant, the phone rang (thank you!) and I grabbed it.

"Hiya doll, it's Lorna, just checking up on you."

Dad was within earshot, so I said, "I'm ok, thanks. I'll fill you in tomorrow."

"You'll be back tomorrow?"

"Definitely."

"Listen, doll, I hate to be the bearer of bad news, but I just wanted to warn you that I overheard some rumblings about you being asked to leave the course."

Shit.

17th ~ Ben's, MK

Taxi showed up late, almost making me miss the train. Stood all the way to Euston and got soaked (again) on the walk to Cranebank, so it was with sodden hair that I followed Jeremy down the corridor, towards Sandi's office.

From behind the oak desk dominating the cramped space, Sandi shuffled papers just long enough to make my heart feel like it was beating outside my chest.

"What caused your absence yesterday?" she said in a languid voice, followed by a gesture to *sit*.

Inside, I was quavering, but I held her eye contact as I fibbed my way through an explanation of my absence. After Sandi stressed the importance of attendance in class, she concluded the meeting by informing me a decision will be made on whether I'll be allowed to remain on the present course, or if I'll have to, "Start from scratch. With another group. For which there is currently no foreseeable date."

As if the day couldn't get any worse, I went straight from there to swimming drills. I'd give anything to be waif like and able to wear a swimsuit with confidence, but I had to push all of that aside because I can't afford to put a foot wrong, so even if Jaws had showed up in the pool today, I'd have taken *her* on.

Rang Ben from Euston, briefly filled him in on my diabolical day and said I'd go over after a quick stop at mine but there he was, the love of my life, waiting on the platform.

"I can't bear to have to start all over again on another course," I cried into his jacket. "Or worse still, what if they ask me to leave?"

"I doubt they'll have you do that," he said, smoothing my hair.

"You don't think so?" I sniffed.

"I think they're just making a point, babe. Let's go to yours so you can change, then we'll go somewhere nice for dinner."

"Tonight is so much better than today," I said, finally feeling my shoulders relax.

"And after that," he grinned, "I'll give you what I know you really want."

"What's that?" I said, expectantly.

"Cake."

18th ~ Ben's, MK

Presently on the couch watching, *The Lost Boys*, trying desperately to distract myself from the fact that in less than ten hours, my gorgeous boyfriend will kiss me goodbye, wave from a taxi, catch a train, travel on the tube, then board a plane, bound for Italy. This time tomorrow night there'll be over eight hundred miles between us, which is why I need to keep writing, otherwise I'll cry.

Comments made so far whilst watching this mental, but somewhat amusing movie:

Susan – "It's hard to tell whose legs are whose, with the way you two get all tangled up together."

Ben - (Deep, throaty voice) "We're tangled up in lurv, deep, true, everlasting lurv."

Susan – "You're mad you are. I don't know how you put up with him, my love."

Jill (Ben's sister) "Cor, that Corey Feldman's a bit of alright."

Barry (Jill's boyfriend) "Oi! I'm sitting right 'ere." (I'll never understand what Jill sees in this cretin).

Ben - (In his *I'm Your Big Brother and I Know More Than You* voice) "You've got Jason Patric and Corey Haim in the same film and you're ogling Corey Feldman?"

Me – "The vampire with the blonde, spiky hair is Donald Sutherland's son."

Ben – "Do you remember him in *Stand by Me*? Brilliant film. I remember you drooling over River *too good looking for his own good*, Phoenix."

Me – "Love that film. You should watch it, Jill. Corey Feldman's in it."

Barry – "Oi, don't encourage her!" (Imbecile).

Stan – "This is the stupidest film ever. This bloke's hobby is *taxidermy*? Unbelievable!"

Barry – "It's a bit strange all that stuffing the animals and all that innit?" (Nincompoop).

Me – "I love Dianne Wiest. I think she's a great actress."

Susan – "I agree, she's very talented. I liked her in *Hannah and Her Sisters.*"

Stan – "Michael Caine was in that one."

At the exact same moment, Jill and her dad chirp, "Hello, my name is Michael Caine."

Ben - (In his *I Am Superior to Everyone* voice) "Dianne Wiest was in *Footloose*, but I bet none of you morons knew that."

Barry - Starts singing, "Footloose, footloose, kick off your Sunday shoes. Please Louise, pull me off of my-" Stops abruptly after Ben shoots him a look.

Susan – "Go on Barry, I like that, Kenny Rogers, wasn't it?"

Ben - (In his *I'm The King of This Kingdom* voice.) "No, Mother! Not Kenny Rogers, Kenny Loggins. Honestly, you people."

Susan – "No need to bite me head off!"

Stan – "Have you packed yet, Ben?"

Ben – (In his *I am sooo in love with you forever and ever* voice I'm rather partial to, with an expression to match as he grabs my hand.) "Come upstairs with me, babe."

19th ~ At home

In the early hours of this morning, I woke up with Ben crawling into bed beside me. With our bodies wound together, like vines, we whispered our desires and kissed, until the alarm pierced our little love bubble.

While Ben was in the shower, I got dressed, then crept downstairs. I filled the tea kettle and popped two slices of bread in the toaster. Before the water had a chance to boil, I was already sobbing.

Coming into the kitchen, Ben opened his arms to me. I burrowed my head into his striped shirt and breathed in the scent of his Drakkar Noir. When the toast popped, Ben kept one arm around me while be buttered the toast (not easy!) and I did the same while I made tea.

"The taxi will be here in a few minutes. Are you ready to go home or do you want to stay here?"

"I want to go home," I sniffed.

"Ok, I'll get the taxi driver to drop you off."

"No, I want to walk home."

"It's still dark, babe. Why don't you go back to bed?"

"I won't be able to sleep. I'll wait until it gets light."

"Are you sure?"

I nodded and he said, "I'll ring you as soon as I can."

"Ring me from the airport," I said, choking up again. "I love you so much. This feels so awful."

"I know, but it's not forever. Good luck tomorrow."

"If I get kicked off the course, expect me in Italy tomorrow night."

20th ~ At home

The usual sluggish Monday blues switched gears after Sandi called me into her office. The good news is that I'm staying on the present course, however, there is one person who won't be graduating with us.

Being the sweet guy that he is, Carl suggested we take Louise out for a farewell drink. I feel sorry for her, but she's had a difficult time in class and struggled with the exams, so hopefully there's something better out there for her. I'm shocked she's been asked to leave and keep thinking how close I came to facing the same fate. A few drinks in, the conversation somehow turned to Ben.

Lorna, "While the cat's away…"

Lolly, "Chin up mate, you'll be alright."

Carl, "Supernumerary flights next week"

Meryl, "Sorry you're sad that your boyfriend had to leave."

Kimberly, "He doesn't seriously think you're going to wait for him, does he?"

Sam, with signature eyeroll, "Wallowing in self-pity does not become you."

Due to the detour (aka the pub) I got to Euston much later than usual and was surprised to find Lee on the platform. Leafing through a glossy brochure, he piped up, "Evening, Karen."

"Is this your usual home time?"

"On a Monday, yes." He continued flicking through the pages. "Typically, the most arduous day of the week." Closing the brochure, he turned to me. "You seem rather jovial."

I was about to tell him I'd just come from the pub, but the sound of a tinny announcement cut in.

"Did you catch any of that?"

Nodding, Lee said, "We've been informed that the train will be delayed for approximately fifty-three minutes, due to-"

"Ah, shit," I groaned, plopping on the bench before promptly getting up.

"Cold?"

"Frigid," I said, gritting my teeth, in annoyance.

"Would you like to go for a drink?"

"No thank you. I'm just going to wait here."

"Karen, I'm not insinuating anything by asking you to go for a drink. I know you're involved with someone. I'm merely offering a way to pass the time."

"Thank you for rectifying that, *Lee*," I said, with more than a hint of sarcasm.

The thought of waiting for the train wasn't exactly appealing, nor was the thought of listening to Lee's monotonous tone. As if reading my mind, he said, "I'll make a deal with you."

I cocked my head in question.

"If you join me for a friendly drink, during which we'll no doubt reminisce about our time at Stantonbury, I promise to save you a seat on the train. Every morning. For the remainder of your commute."

That got my attention. "How do you propose to do that?"

In an utterly deadpan manner, he raised his briefcase. "With this, of course."

21st ~ At home

The second I bolted out of the taxi, I heard the train huffing into the station, and with Sandi's voice ringing in my ears, *No running whilst in uniform*! I sprinted across the concourse. Halfway down the second flight of stairs, I thought I was going to throw up, but I knew if I stopped moving, I'd miss the train.

Trying not to look like I was using it for support, I leaned against the luggage rack until the piercing whistle stopped. Spread before me, a sea of drowsy commuters remained steadfast in their relationship with broadsheets and Styrofoam cups.

After trudging through several carriages, I'd just about given up any hope of a seat, when I spotted Lee's square rimmed glasses looking up at me. I couldn't help but smile when I saw the seat across the table from him was vacant. Not daring to break the silence in the stuffy carriage, I fell into the seat, and mouthed, "Thank you." Lee continued putting numbers in columns, before scribbling something he slid in my direction. *I doubt wearing sunglasses on the train is in keeping with uniform regulations.*

Smirking, I wrote, *I feel like death warmed up. You wouldn't happen to have anything for a raging headache, would you?*

With a level of discretion that failed to garner any attention from the trenchies in the window seats, Lee clicked open his briefcase, removed a small brown bottle and shook four tablets onto the notepad. I popped two in my mouth and swallowed, which, given I had zero saliva, was pretty impressive. From behind my sunglasses, I watched Lee do the same.

How bad is your hangover? I wrote.

Shocking! Now I understand the expression, "never again."

And yet...

I'm serious. Never again. Nor have I ever caught the midnight train home.

First time for everything!

I don't know how I'm going to make it through the day.

Stay hydrated and eat frequently!

Will that help?

I have no idea! I need to sleep, see you at Euston.

I imagine snoring is against uniform regulations. I'll wake you at the first sound of it.

Thank you!

Sweet dreams.

22nd ~ At home

Shortly after going to bed just after eight last night, I thought I was dreaming when I heard the phone ringing. I hate that feeling when you realise it isn't a dream and are forced to snap back into the real world. Hoping it might be Ben, I sprinted downstairs.

"Okie dokie, here she is," mum smiled, handing me the receiver.

"McGarr! What are you doing in bed at this hour?"

"Last night was a bit of a late one."

"With that wild bunch from your training course?" "Something like that."

"Listen, I have a meeting tomorrow, it's not far from where you train. I was wondering if you'd like to meet for lunch. I imagine they allow you to eat?"

"We usually break for lunch around half twelve, depending on what we're doing."

"Excellent, I'll be there to pick you up."

"Hold your horses, I didn't agree to meet you!"

"McGarr, it's lunch. Lunch is food. You love food. I already know it's a yes!"

"That's rather presumptuous," I laughed. "And accurate."

"Half twelve it is, see you tomorrow. Sweet dreams."

The morning dragged, and it was close to one when we finally finished the section on Hijacking. When Lorna and Lolly asked if I was going with them, to uniform stores, I said I was meeting a friend, and when I stepped outside with them, a horn beeped. From the car, Jon waved and when I waved back, Lorna said, "*That's* your pal?"

"Uh-huh, see you after lunch," I said, turning to scurry away.

Grabbing my arm, Lorna said, "Oh no you don't, who is he?"

"His name is Jon."

Lowering her head, Lolly said, "*Friend*?"

"And ex," I grinned, practically running away.

Had the weather been nicer, we'd have sat outside but it's not quite there yet, so we grabbed a table inside, by the roaring fire.

"McGarr, you can't possibly be refusing a beverage of an adult nature," Jon said, after I asked for a lemonade.

"I can't go back to class sozzled."

"Fair enough. I won't have a drink either, which, after last week is probably a good idea."

"Too many stints in the pub?"

"Nah, I went skiing, with the boys. It was brilliant, especially the apres-ski."

"You mean snow bunnies?"

Peering at the menu, he mumbled, "Of the French variety."

"I heard that," I laughed. "Et bon pour tu."

"You'd love the resort," he enthused.

"I love anywhere in France."

"No, not France, we were in Italy."

"*Italy?*"

Hearing Jon name the resort where Ben works, I caught my breath and wondered if their paths had crossed, on the piste, or elsewhere.

"You alright, McGarr? You've gone a bit quiet."

"Sorry, I got a bit lost on the slopes, there."

Back in class, I was flipping through my notes when Carl came sauntering in my direction with what I call his cheesy grin. "Who was that bloke with the nice wheels? The one you just snogged."

"That wasn't a snog, it was a friendly kiss goodbye."

"Why's your face so red?" Lorna asked.

"She was snogging some bloke a minute ago," Carl said.

"Uff, I'd have done more than snog him! I was going to suggest Alistair's brother for you doll, but you seem to be doin' alright for yourself."

"Yeah," Carl continued, "Between getting drunk with an old mate from school-"

"And mister hot wheels," Lorna chuckled.

"You have it all wrong," I pleaded.

"Maybe so, doll," Lorna grinned. "But from the looks of it, you could teach me a thing or two."

23rd ~ At home

When the phone rings, I secretly hope it's Ben and when the post arrives, I look for Italian stamps. The last time Ben was away, his letters took up to two weeks to arrive so I won't hold my breath, but a phone call, even a quick one, would ease my mind.

Met Lee on the train, and true to his word, he saved me a seat. As usual, the trenchies had taken a vow of silence, so on a sheet of British Airways letterhead, I scribbled, *You look engrossed in your numbers, so I'm sorry for interrupting but I have a late start tomorrow so no need to save me a seat.*

I slid the paper across the table.

Ok was his reply.

I won't be on the train next Monday, Tuesday or Wednesday either.

I expected a lengthy reply, but all he came back with was a question mark.

Sunday is my supernumerary flight.

Lee pulled a blank sheet of paper from his clipboard and started writing. Then he twisted the clipboard so I could see. *What on earth is a supernumerary flight? Sounds like you're off to space.*

An extra body on the flight, not key cabin crew, so I'll probably be working down the back.

Another question mark.

Crew speak for the economy cabin.

Where are you off to? Actually, let me guess. First letter?

J

I watched him write *Jakarta*, and shook my head no.

Johannesburg?

Another no.

Juba?

I gave him a questioning look.

Did I guess correctly?

Quickly, I scribbled, *No, but where is Juba?*

Sudan.

Oh ok. Guess again.

I watched his hand glide across the paper, pausing only for my response.

Juneau?
Jackson?
Jacksonville?
Jamestown?

Joplin?

After rolling his pen on the paper, Lee wrote, *Can't think of any others in America.*

It's not in America.

Now you tell me!

I shrugged and tried not to laugh.

This is more difficult that I thought.

You can't imagine my intense pleasure at knowing I stumped the numbers man!

Without looking at me, he scribbled, *I am NOT admitting defeat. Yet!*

That prompted him to write even more furiously.

Jubail?

Juan Mateo?

Jalandhar?

Jerusalem?

No, no, no, and NO! I wrote, gleefully. *Are you throwing in the towel?*

I have no desire to, but I can't think of any others.

When I mouthed, "Quitter," he responded enthusiastically, with, "Jordan?"

I shook my head and watched as he very slowly placed the pen on the paper.

Wait, I wrote. *My mistake, it doesn't start with J.*

Leaning forward, Lee scanned the page, then released a throaty growl that almost snapped a few trenchie heads. Shielding the paper with my hand, I wrote, *Just kidding! Sorry if that raised your blood pressure.*

Your cruel nature knows no bounds, he penned, trying not to smile.

"I win!" I mouthed, before filling the entire page with *JEDDAH.*

Dry, correct?

I nodded.

Perfect for me because I'm never drinking. EVER AGAIN!

You reached that conclusion based on one night of recklessness?

Once was enough for me.

Not me…I continue to make the same mistake over and over. Just to make sure.

Lee's deep laugh was cut short after a few trenchies tutted.

For example, I wrote. *I have a niggling headache.*

Dare I ask?

Friend's birthday celebration last night at Ye Olde Swan. Indulged. Ever. So. Slightly.

Can't say I know it.

Beautiful old Tudor pub, right on the village green in Woughton. One of my favourites. I'll let you get back to your work.

Not work, personal finances. I'm looking to buy a pad in London, somewhere around Euston, close to where I work.

I know a good pub close to the train station!

He looked at me and smiled, then wrote, *Good luck on Sunday. How very exciting.*

I'd be more excited if was going to…New York.

Too obvious. I don't know anyone who's been to Saudi Arabia.

I'll tell you all about it next week.

I shall look forward to that.

Sorry you lost the J game.

Sorry you're going to a dry place.

24th ~ On the train

The couple seated across from me have literally not stopped kissing since they got on the train. In the event either of them keels over from lack of oxygen, I shall deny any, and all knowledge of CPR.

It's interesting being on the viewing side of such a glaring display of affection (slurping) and it makes me wonder how Ben and I come across, whenever we steal the odd kiss or two in public. It's something I've never given much thought to but observing slobber mouths in action has given me a new perspective.

I wonder if Ben is asleep (it's 1240 here, so 0640 in Italia) or if he's already at work. Saturday is his busiest day, when the guests arrive, so it's highly possible his day is already in full swing.

I didn't expect to go out after class, but Carl suggested we celebrate our upcoming supernumerary flights, so it was off to the Green Man for most of us (only a few missing and only because they're flying first thing tomorrow). When Carl and I got out of his car, a Boeing 747 with BA's Landor livery flew over, and we both let out a loud cheer.

Tonsil hockey has come to an end, and *les amoureux* are now in a disagreement over who loves who more. This might be worth a watch.

25th ~ At home
I should be packing, but I'm on the couch with Lucy, watching, *Platoon*, which is intense to say the least. Lucy is spending the night (back to London tomorrow) and when she arrived, she was in one of her quiet moods, but I know she hates being prodded, so I've learned to wait for her to share what's on her mind.

Spent the morning with mum, birthday shopping (gorgeous shoes from Ravel) then she treated me to lunch at Café Rouge, which always makes me long to be in France.

Meryl rang in a panic about what to pack for temperatures well in excess of one hundred degrees (nothing?). She said she feels sick every time she thinks about; The briefing, the long flight, the passengers, the crew and being away from home. I told her not to worry and that everything we covered in training will kick in. What I didn't tell her is I'm feeling equally anxious.

Tried getting through to Ben but no answer. He sent me an Italian birthday card (no idea what it says!) and a four-page letter I, thankfully, understood. Lucy seemed amused when I told her I'd already memorised every word of the letter and asked how things are going. I didn't mention anything about the Helena incident because there's a chance it might not have been her. Ben could've been talking to someone about her, anything's possible. What I do know is that Ben and I agreed to a fresh start and that means leaving the rotten stuff in the past, which I'm prepared to do. I think.

"Do you still feel the same about him as you did when you two.." Lucy's voice trailed off.

"You and I have never really talked about that, have we?"

"Not really," Lucy said, averting her eyes.

"Do you want to?

"Do you?"

"I do. I'm sorry for the way it all…unfolded. All I can tell you about back then is that I felt like I'd been hit by a bolt of lightning."

"I think it was like that for him as well," she said, taking me by surprise. "I remember sitting in the sixth form common room, and Ben came in. I expected him to come and sit next to me because he was…"

"Your boyfriend."

"I tried not to get angry but when I looked over, the two of you were facing each other. Talking. Laughing." She paused. "It was as if you were in your own little world."

I was unsure whether to speak, but I thought it was probably time to take the bull by the horns. "You must've hated me."

She nodded, slowly, and there was so much I wanted to say but I stopped myself.

"But here we are," she continued. "I think the fact it's lasted this long means it's meant to be."

"I truly love him."

"You always have," she smiled. "Do you think you'll marry him?"

It was my turn to smile.

26th ~ LHR – JED
Jeddah, Saudi Arabia

I woke up with butterflies in my tummy, thinking about how the day might play out and went downstairs to find Lucy and mum chatting up a storm. Mum made poached eggs on toast, but I was too nervous to eat. Lucy said she was excited for me and even hugged me, which is out of character for her.

Worse than dragging my new Samsonite on and off the train and several tubes, was being stopped by tourists and locals alike, mostly asking for directions. Buying a car has become a priority.

In TriStar House, the first order of business is dropping off our luggage. With trembling fingers, I attached the yellow crew label to the handle and drew a complete blank, not only about the flight number but the three-letter code.

"Supernumerary?" asked one of the baggage handlers. When I nodded, he grabbed a pen, asked where I was going and offered to, "Take it from here." I was so relieved I could've kissed him.

In the canteen, I bumped into Lolly and Henry. Lolly was a bundle of energy and Henry was as cool as a cucumber, but seeing their familiar faces helped calm me down. Looking utterly flustered, Meryl came into the canteen, and we waited there until it was time to go to the briefing room.

Alfie, the Cabin Service Director (CSD) made sure none of the crew were in possession of anything containing images of scantily clad women (for example, a magazine ad for underwear) that could cause offense and get confiscated on entry into Saudi Arabia, thereby delaying the crew and, to quote Alfie, "land us in hot water." We covered that extensively in training but again to quote Alfie, "There's always one."

By the time we stepped onto the TriStar I was eager to get going. Alfie suggested Meryl and I work in Club World together, so after stowing our bags, and getting acquainted with the galley, we went into the cabin. During boarding, the screen at the front of the Club World cabin plays the *Face* ad. The music gives me goosebumps and when Alfie announced passengers were on their way, I beamed, "Here we go!" in Meryl's direction.

Meryl and I were invited to sit on the flight deck for take-off and when she asked me to lead the way, I joked, "It's not hard to find!" but I think she was too nervous to get it. After the pre-flight checks were complete, the Captain welcomed us and asked if we were ok in the jumpseats. Meryl opened her mouth, but nothing came out. It seemed like only a few minutes later that the aircraft was barrelling down the runway. I felt incredibly excited to have a front row seat and loved everything about it.

During the first drinks round, I enjoyed interacting with the mostly business passengers and I even managed to remember all the wines we offer, without having to consult the menu. The rest of the crew were super helpful, which put me at ease.

Just under six hours later, after a very hectic flight, Meryl and I sat on the flight deck for landing. It was dark so not quite as exciting as take off, but still thrilling knowing we were landing in Saudi Arabia, where just after midnight it was eighty-two degrees.

Walking through the terminal, we were the only uncovered females, which felt odd. The crew bus was pretty lively, and Jenny (Club Purser) said Meryl and I were naturals. Alfie invited everyone to his room, and most of the crew showed up. They teased us about what we'd done to get sent to a dry area. Seems most trips start off in someone's room, or as someone piped up, "Or on the crew bus!"

This bed is gargantuan with the softest linens and enough pillows for every day of the week. If today is any indication of life as long haul British Airways cabin crew, I have a feeling I'm going to love it!

Goodnight from Jeddah, on the eve of my 22nd birthday.

27th ~ Jeddah, Saudi Arabia

Soft drinks with birthday dinner wouldn't be my first choice but the food was delicious, and the crew crooned *Happy Birthday* while I blew out the candles on a tiered chocolate cake.

At nine this morning, after a restless night, I met Meryl and most of our crew in the lobby. Within seconds of going from the heavily air-conditioned lobby to the outside, I thought I was going to melt. Last month in Florida I was on bad terms with AC, now she's my new best friend.

Wearing the abaya provided by the hotel, we piled onto the shuttle bus and headed to the beach club. With mostly desert landscape dotted with the odd building, there wasn't much to see. In contrast, the beach club was buzzing with cabin crew (mostly Lufthansa) and ex-pats, who looked crushed when Meryl and I confessed to not knowing what's happening in *Eastenders*.

The furnace only intensified as the day wore on and I was desperate to cool down but there was no way I was prepared to walk all the way down to the dock in my cozzy. Meryl is ultra-slim, so I'm surprised she never dove in. While we were hiding under a huge umbrella, Andrew the Flight Engineer came over.

"I hear you're the birthday girl. Happy Birthday," he said, filling our glasses with chilled water. "Sorry this is all I have to offer in celebration."

The three of us clinked our glasses together.

"Would either of you like to come sailing?" Meryl shook her head and looked at me. The thought of being out on the water if not actually in it sounded perfect, so I said I'd go. "Have you sailed before?" he asked.

"No. Never."

"They sell hats inside; you might want to grab one. I'll meet you down by the water." Andrew left and Meryl said she hoped I had a nice time.

"Are you sure you don't want to come?"

Blinking against the sun, she said she had a headache from the glare but that she'd buy me a hat for my birthday.

Andrew proved to be a great instructor and I thoroughly enjoyed not only learning the basics but being out on the water. I kept my top on over my cozzy, so my legs got the brunt of the sun, but thanks to the cap from Meryl, my face was spared a serious sunburn.

Back at the hotel, I spent an entire day of allowances calling home. I knew mum and dad would appreciate knowing I was safe, plus I knew mum would be chomping at the bit to talk to me on my birthday. Something about the way dad said, "Ma lassie's spending her birthday in Saudi Arabia," made me a little tearful but I think it's just the fact I'm so far from home. When I told mum I'd been sailing, she started talking about how seasick she got when she sailed home from New York. In the sixties! I hated cutting her short, but I've heard that story a million times.

I'm about to write to Ben to let him know how lucky I feel to be in love with the best guy ever. According to Andrew, Italy is roughly two and a half thousand miles from here.

28th ~ JED - LHR

It was another sweltering day under the umbrella at the beach club and when Meryl dozed off, I couldn't help but notice how thin her ankles are. I don't exactly have cankles, but they're certainly not as slender as Meryl's. Nor are my wrists as dainty as hers. I hate the expression (excuse?) big boned, but maybe that's just my build. Regardless, I'd give anything to be part of the delicate wrist brigade.

Some of the more senior crew invited us to go to the souk and Alfie reminded us we'd have to cover our faces, which Moe, the Economy Purser, helped us with. The market was sensory overload, and walking in an abaya doesn't come naturally, so after tripping one too many times, I was happy to leave.

Reunited with AC, I slid under the covers and tried not to drool too much at the sight of River Phoenix, in, *The Mosquito Coast.*

Call time comes an hour before pick-up, and I wonder how long it will take before I get used to not chirping *hello,* after I pick up the automated call. Pick up is when our crew convene in the lobby before boarding the crew bus that takes us to the airport.

Due to a misunderstanding with some paperwork, there was a boarding delay, but we still managed to depart on time. Once again, Meryl and I were on the flight deck during take-off, but this time we knew the drill and Meryl didn't look quite as petrified.

Passenger load is only 48! Here on the TriStar, the crew rest area is a row of seats in the rear, cordoned off by a curtain, but even when it's drawn, passengers still manage to sniff us out.

MARCH

1st ~ At home

Meryl's deep sigh of relief on landing was audible enough that Andrew asked if she was ok, but by the time we reached the jetty, her rosy complexion had returned, and she was all smiles.

I got home just before eight and was surprised to see dad rounding the corner with Tini. He (dad, not the dog!) looked equally surprised and I held the leash while dad paid the taxi driver.

"Cheers, guv!" the cabbie bellowed, in acknowledgement of what I'm sure was a generous tip.

"Yer early," dad said, with a hug.

"Less commuters coming out of London than going in but still a nightmare with that bloody thing." I gestured to my Samsonite as dad effortlessly retrieved it from the boot. Suddenly, my thoughts went to mum. Hoping she wasn't having a bad episode, I asked dad what he was doing home in the middle of the day.

"I wanted to be here when ye got back. It's no every day yer lassie flies in fae the middle east."

Tini made a beeline for his water bowl and mum was halfway down the stairs, the elbow of her powder pink bathrobe scraping against the wood panelling.

"This is a nice surprise," she beamed. "We wurnae expecting ye tae much later." Wrapping me in a tight hug, she said, "Happy Birthday, hen! Oh, ye smell lovely."

"Eternity, by Calvin Klein," I breathed, mimicking the tv ad. "Don't worry, I got you one as well."

"Smashing. So, how was Arabia? Tom, did ye get the papers?"

"Yes, your majesty." Dad passed the newspapers to mum, then hung up his jacket.

"Saudi Arabia, mum." I followed her into the kitchen.

"Was it hot? Oh, and can ye put the kettle on, Tom?"

"Geez a wee minute, Liz." Dad said, rolling his eyes in a way that made me laugh.

"It was sweltering, too much for me."

"No for mum," dad said, filling the tea kettle. "Right, Lizzie?"

"The weather's been dreich here, roll on summer."

Dad asked what I wanted for breakfast.

"Do we have cheese? And mushrooms?"

Dad looked at mum, who nodded.

"Omelettes, it is," dad said, disappearing behind the fridge door.

Long after I'd scraped the last of the cheese off the plate, still buttering an endless supply of toast, mum and dad were still asking questions about Jeddah, a place I doubt they'll ever go.

2nd ~ At home

In the queue at the market stall that sells jacket potatoes, I thought back to when I worked nine to five, at Fennemores in CMK. Typing one boring letter after another, I'd wish the day away, looking ahead to the weekend, when I'd head to Freeman Hardy and Wills for yet another pair of shoes that I didn't need but had to have.

In my absence, I'd missed Ben's call, and wasted no time ringing him back. After twenty-seven rings, I hung up and tried Sarah.

"Come round tomorrow night."

"I can't, I'm going to Pamsy's."

"I haven't seen you for ages," she groaned. "And I want to hear about Jubail."

"Jeddah."

"Sorry, what?"

"Jeddah, I went to Jeddah, in Saudi Arabia."

"Oh," she uttered. "Did you have to dress like the women there?"

"Mostly, yes." I was expecting more questions, but Sarah started telling me about Simon's cousin, who, "Not only likes travelling but is very good looking. And he'll be here tomorrow night for pizza making."

"Sarah," I stated. "Did it slip your mind that I have a boyfriend?"

"He's not a *real* boyfriend. Just come over and meet Rob, you'll like him. I'm sure he'll be interested in hearing about Jubail."

I tried Ben again, this time giving up after it rang thirty-eight times.

Quick chat to Pamsy, but only because she was off to the dentist.

"I have so much to tell you." From her tone, it was obvious a family member was looming.

"Doesn't sound like you can talk freely. Besides, I want to see your face when you tell me who you snogged."

"You know me too well," she chuckled.

Tried Ben again. Slammed down the receiver on the eighteenth ring.

In my quest for a jacket potato slathered in beans and coleslaw, I'd also missed a call from Jon. Mum said he'd rang from work, so I waited until I knew he'd be home.

"McGarr! To what do I owe the pleasure?"

"You rang me!"

"No, you just rang me."

"Earlier, you rang earlier."

"I did?"

"Uh-huh," I muttered, feeling slightly confused.

"Are you sure it was me?" His laugh at the end gave him away.

"Stop it!"

"Admit it, McGarr, for a second there you were doubting yourself. Listen, I wanted to let you know that a few cars showed up this week-"

"I only need one."

"Choice isn't a bad thing."

"I don't need choices," I whined. "I need a car!"

"You really are utterly impossible."

"Just pick the one I can afford."

"It's not all about price."

I got him back by asking about the colour of the cars.

"I'm not answering that, but there's one I think would be suitable, with plenty of space for your suitcase. Why don't you come this weekend and see for yourself?"

Prompted by the recent memory of lugging my Samsonite up the broken escalator stairs, I asked when he was free.

"Whenever you want, I'll even come and pick you up if that makes it easier."

"You always make it sound like you live ten minutes away."

"I do," he laughed. "If you add eighty minutes!"

"Don't you have plans for the weekend?"

"My plan is to set you up with some wheels."

3rd ~ Pamsy's, Sussex

More than ready to crawl under the duvet but if I don't write, my recollection of the day's events will be blurry, and we can't have that!

Had to be at Cranebank early for Bar Plus training, BA's new onboard system for purchasing duty free items. The machine is easy to use and much more efficient than the present system which doesn't extend much past the abacus.

Fortunately, I remembered to change out of uniform before the trek to Pamsy's, otherwise I'd have been bombarded by tourists asking if they were on the right train, thereby interrupting Armistead Maupin's engaging, *Tales of the City*, for which I have Stephen to thank.

Pulling into the last parking spot at The Castle, Pamsy gestured to the beat-up sports car next to us. "Looks like le wave's."

"Sooo him," I drawled. "Pretentious pratt."

"You're the last person he'll be expecting to see," she grinned.

"Do you recognise anyone else's car?" I said, squeezing my way through the tightly parked cars.

"Why do you ask?" Pamsy said, casually.

"From the way your head just spun, I got the impression you might have spotted say, Ollie's car?"

"I can't get anything past you!" She chuckled. "This could prove to be an interesting evening, you might get drunk and end up snogging le wave, if only for old time's sake."

"No fear of that, I'm on antibiotics for a chest infection, so I can't drink."

Thrusting out her chest in an exaggerated way, Pamsy cooed, "Maybe le wave will rub it better."

4th ~ Pamsy's, Sussex

Pamsy's flight to Mahon was cancelled and she didn't have to twist my arm to get me to stay another night. I had to let Sarah and Jon know about the change of plans, so I rang Sarah first.

"Rob will be really disappointed."

I was only one cup of tea into the morning, so I let her go on for a while before I apologised and hung up.

After wolfing down a mars bar and two slices of raisin toast, I rang Jon who suggested he come and pick me up, tomorrow. The thought of getting halfway home without having to set foot on public transport was beyond appealing so I agreed.

In Hastings Pamsy and I used the rain as an excuse to pop in and out of a few cafés, and in one of the many antique shops I found a little trinket box to add to the stuff I already bought for Mother's Day.

In Boswell's in Eastbourne, we bumped into Guy D and Guy E but managed to lose them after they signed us into TJ's. As usual the place was heaving, but we found a great viewing spot at the edge of the dance floor, and when Womack and Womack came on, I jumped up and grabbed Pamsy by the hand. Narrowly avoiding flailing arms and heavily lacquered hair, we made our way to the middle of the dance floor.

Singing, "And the music don't feel like it did when I felt it with you," my eyes filled with tears and the lump in my throat put the kibosh on more singing. In response to Pamsy's questioning look, I mouthed, "Ben." Pamsy rolled her eyes comically and stuck out her tongue, which would usually make me laugh, but the pangs of missing him were too great, because without him, nothing feels right.

5th ~ On the M25

Plumping up the pillows behind her, Pamsy asked if I was looking forward to getting my first car.

"I s'pose," I shrugged.

"Why the hesitation?"

"I'm not sure how Ben will react when he hears Jon is helping me."

From across the room, she glared at me. "Ben's away. Jon's here. *And* he works with cars."

"Yeah, and he's also someone I used to go out with."

"And now he's a mate, willing to help, while your boyfriend is out of the country."

Because we were up early, there was time for a walk on the beach. Pulling her hair into a ponytail, Pamsy said she was glad I'd made it down.

"Me too, it's been great. And I got to meet Evan."

"Oh yeah, what did you think of him?"

"He's way more into you than you are to him."

"Ah, love stuff," she sighed.

In the car, singing, "Circle in the Sand," we tapped our chests, for maximum mimicking of Belinda Carlisle's voice.

Jon arrived a few minutes early (terrible trait) and after a brief chat with Pamsy and her mum, we hit the road.

"Do you want to look at cars first or stop at the pub for a quick drink?"

"To be honest, I've kind of lost interest in the whole car thing. At least for today."

Jon let out a hearty laugh and shook his head.

"What's funny about that?"

"Never a dull moment with you, McGarr."

"I'm just not in the mood for traipsing about a car lot."

"Fair enough. So, do you want me to take you home? We're about an hour and a half away."

Turning to look at him, I said, "I have an idea."

His eyes lit up and I swatted his arm. "Not that, you cheeky bugger!"

6th ~ At home

I usually dread Monday but knowing it's the last week of training made getting out of bed a little less painful. Taxi showed up early (what's up with all this early stuff? Don't people know that the last few minutes are when I pull it all together?) which meant I was at the station way ahead of my usual time.

On the chilly platform, I scanned the trenchies, looking for Lee, but he was nowhere to be found. I thought he might be running late but he never did show, which meant no seat on the train.

When I rolled in just after seven, dad was in the hall, phone in hand. I gave him a little wave and dropped my bag on the phone chair (unlike moi, dad never sits when he's on the phone) and with his hand covering the receiver, he mouthed, "Pamsy."

"Oh, goodie," I said, kicking off my shoes.

"Here she is Pamsy, all the best, cheerio, hen."

"Bon soir mademoiselle, comment ca va?" I slipped my arm free of my jacket.

"Do you want me to ring you back?"

"Maintenant c'est bien," I said, cradling the phone on my shoulder, slipping my other arm free. "What are you up to?"

Dad took my jacket and gestured, tea? I nodded enthusiastically and kicked my bag off to the side.

In what I call her saucy voice, Pamsy said, "I believe the question is, what have *you* been up to?"

"Not much, did your mum enjoy the surprise Mother's Day lunch?"

"Loved it. So, ehm, how was your afternoon with Jon. In London."

I slumped deep in the chair. "Really nice, actually."

"Is your dad still floating about?"

"He's in the kitchen, but I don't know where my mum is."

"She's at a church meeting." Pamsy's tone was matter of fact. "Your dad sounded well chuffed when he told me Jon brought you home yesterday."

"They'd love to see you again, Pamsy, you should come up soon!"

"Stop changing the subject," she rattled. "And tell me how you ended up in London."

"Hold on a sec," I said, as dad handed me a mug of milky tea, before going into the living room, shutting the door behind him (unlike mum!).

"Sorry about that, the coast is clear now. Eh...I wasn't in the mood for looking at cars, so we went to Primrose Hill and had a wander, not for too long though because I wanted to get home for Mother's Day."

"Did you snog him?"

"No, of course not."

"You should've! Even my mum said he's a hunk."

I laughed. "He's a big hit with women of a certain age. You should've seen my mum's face when he came in with a big bunch of flowers for her. I swear she was giddy."

"I thought he was lovely but the thing I liked the most was seeing how you acted around him. You were very much yourself."

"You only met him for ten minutes!" Knowing what was coming, I took a huge gulp of tea.

"Why don't you go out with him again?"

"I'll give you a clue. It starts with B."

"Did he even *try* to kiss you?"

"Absolutely not!" I exclaimed, almost knocking over the mug.

"It's obvious he still fancies you. My mum said the same."

"In that case, I can't be friends with him, doesn't seem fair to-"

"Stop worrying about capital B for five minutes and allow Jon-"

"Hey Pamsy," I said, interrupting her. "Will you do me a favour?"

"What?"

"Will you please stop making sense!"

7th ~ At home

In class we were filmed carrying out Club World service. Watching the playbacks was hysterical, with Carl getting the award for most amusing. I have more than a sneaking suspicion he'll be more than popular with crew and passengers alike.

I was disappointed to hear I'd missed Ben but ecstatic when he rang back.

"Hey you," he breathed. So much reaction to just two words.

"Feels like I haven't talked to you for yonks."

"You ok, babe? You sound a bit croaky."

"I have a chest infection, but the antibiotics are helping."

"Don't forget the pill isn't as effective when you're on antibiotics."

"Contraception isn't exactly a concern at the moment," I laughed.

"You sure?" He said, sounding unsure.

"One million percent!"

"Good, I just need to hear it."

"I'm madly in love with you, you know that."

When he returned the sentiment, my heart literally skipped a beat.

"Tell me again," I pleaded.

"I absolutely love you and can't wait to come home and-"

"*Dot dot dot*," I tutted, making him laugh.

"The season is just about over, so things should hopefully start slowing down."

He sounded wiped out, so I kept my tone upbeat. "I bet your skiing has improved."

"It has but I'm ready for it all to be over."

"Any word on when that'll be?"

"Nah, not yet," he groaned. "Your letter from Jeddah came today. Sounds like an interesting place. Where to next?"

"I won't find out until I get my Wings. This Friday!"

"You sound excited."

Unlike you, I thought, chiding myself because I know how exhausting the end of the season is for him.

"Hopefully I'll get to fly with some of the people I've trained with."

"That's highly unlikely."

"I know, but it'd still be nice." If he sensed my despondency, he didn't let on.

"I wonder where you'll go next."

"New York would be amazing-"

"We always talked about going there together. It'll be weird if you go first."

"Ben, we have our entire lives ahead of us, to travel and do what we want."

"What do you want, babe?"

"To be with you. And live happily ever after."

8th ~ At home

Spotting Lee on the platform, I zig zagged through the trenchies, in his direction. As usual, he was holding his briefcase, a copy of the *Financial Times* tucked under his arm.

"Morning stranger, have you been ill?" I asked, in almost a whisper.

"No, I was up in Scotland, at a conference in Glasgow."

"Ah, my hometown. Did it rain?"

"On and off. You look well," he remarked.

Touching my cheek, I said, "In between wearing an abaya and hiding under umbrellas, the sun still managed to find me."

"Two more days and your commute will be over," he said, glancing at me, as the train's arrival was announced.

"Actually, only one more, I'm staying with a friend tomorrow night."

For the first time ever, I embraced the brisk walk from Hatton Cross to Cranebank, allowing my thoughts to wander to the incredible events of the past six weeks, thankful for the amazing group I'm training with, a handful of who I imagine will remain friends for years to come.

9th ~ Lolly's, Middlesex

I'm in Lolly's room and Carl and Sam are sleeping in the living room. From the sound of it, they're not ready to call it a night, which I am, but first this, starting with this morning, when mum and dad waved me off with lots of good luck wishes.

On the platform, I was surprised to find Lee in a different spot.

"Morning," he quipped, handing me a train ticket. "A congratulatory gift," he explained with a smile. An actual smile! Scanning the ticket, the words First Class jumped out. I looked at Lee, but the train was already shunting into the station, and I didn't want to have to shout.

"Lead the way," he said, following me to the First Class carriage. With only a smattering of people, I chose a window seat and Lee sat across the table. Wasting no time, I staked claim to the vacant seat, draping my coat and jacket over my bag.

"I don't think you need to be concerned about anyone sitting there," he smiled. Another one!

"Habit! This is a lovely treat. Thank you so much."

"This way we can actually talk."

"Would you mind doing me a favour?" I said, passing a stack of notes from training, mostly pertaining to the location of the safety equipment. "Final exams this morning, my stomach's already in knots."

"Would you like a cup of tea first?" He asked, getting up.

"Yes please. Oh, and maybe a pastry if they have any."

Smile number three.

General Papers test, followed by Passenger Papers and we'll have our grades in about five hours! After class I came to Lolly's, with Sam and Carl. Lolly's delightful parents spoiled us rotten, and her dad played some of his favourite jazz records.

Thanks to Sam's elaborate routine getting dressed, we were the last to arrive at the restaurant. Out of uniform and the confines of

Cranebank, Ella, Jeremy and Sandi appeared incredibly laid back and had us in stitches with ample flying stories.

We were refused entry to Options nightclub because Vince was wearing cords, so we ended up in Cinderella's (in Purley?) with a non-existent dress code. With more meat on display than a butcher's shop window, sticky carpets and watered-down drinks, Cinderella's proved the perfect spot for an evening of sheer abandon.

10th ~ At home

Walking down the corridor to the final interview didn't feel quite as nerve-wracking as when I was summoned to meet with Sandi. The door was open a crack, so I popped my head in.

"Morning, Karen," Jeffrey clipped. The professional air was back and after a minimum of pleasantries, he asked how I'd rate my overall performance. I prattled on about how great everyone was (true) and how much I'd enjoyed the coursework (not true) and how excited I was to be getting my Wings (true).

Scribbling line after line, Jeremy ended by asking if I'm prepared to, "Embrace the BA crew lifestyle."

"One hundred percent," I beamed. "I can't wait to get on board."

"Most excellent," he said standing up. I followed his lead and shook his outstretched hand. "Thank you, Jeffrey."

"It's been a pleasure, Karen. I wish you luck and look forward to flying with you. Welcome to British Airways."

YES!!!!!

11th ~ At home

What I wouldn't give to be kissing Ben, but I'll have to be satisfied with our two-hour chat that found its way into *that* territory, which was more than stirring.

Mum and dad are at a dinner dance, and they looked a million bucks, with mum in a red peplum dress, all gold jewellery, and dad in a navy suit, sporting the silk tie I bought from the duty-free shop in T4, during a class visit. They were both in high spirits and kept expressing how thrilled they are that I got my Wings.

I've been so preoccupied with just getting through training that I haven't yearned for Ben as much, but after talking to him I feel an immense longing for us to be together again. For the first time ever, I got the impression he was feeling insecure.

"Some cocky pilot better not come along and sweep you off your feet."

"Don't be silly," I said.

"You never know."

"I know."

That will never happen.

12th ~ At home

I came home from a bike ride, to find mum in the phone chair, looking very demure, sitting up straight, with her ankles crossed.

"Aye come and see us soon," she cooed. "Ye know yer always welcome."

She handed me the phone, which I wasn't quite prepared for, so it took me a second to unclip my Walkman and roll up the headphones.

"Good God, that woman can talk!"

"How long have you been on the phone?"

"Twenty minutes, maybe more."

"You're getting off lightly today."

"Do you know, there is absolutely nothing I don't know about you, McGarr."

"I beg to differ, Jon," I joked. "What're you up to?"

"Just got back from the pub."

"Let me guess, Sunday roast and a few pints?"

"Had to be done," he chuckled. "Your mum said you start standby in a few hours?"

"Yeah, and I'm sure she explained it all to you."

"That and so much more! Exciting to know you could be going anywhere in the world."

"Routes are somewhat limited, until I get on the seven four."

"The *what*?"

"Sorry, the Boeing seven four seven. Also known as the jumbo, or the queen of the skies. I won't be licenced to fly on it for another few months."

"Hopefully you'll have a car by then!"

"This'll probably sound silly, but I'm really nervous about driving. The roads from here to Heathrow are some of the busiest in the country."

"It'll soon become old hat."

"I should just bite the bullet and do it, shouldn't I?"

"Only if you want to," he sang.

"It'll make life a lot easier."

"Put some time aside and come and take a look. But not today," he said, with a slight slur.

"No," I laughed. "Definitely not today."

13th ~ At home

Lucy rang early this morning to let me know she was coming home, so we met at the Beefeater. As usual, I overindulged so tomorrow my goal is to consume only liquid, which should prove interesting.

Still feeling stuffed, even after sitting through *Scandal* at The Point, we skipped the queue for taxi's and decided to walk.

"It's so nice coming home for the weekend," Lucy said. "Life in London can be really hectic."

"Well, I, for one, am glad you're here," I said, as we waited for a break in the traffic to cross the road. "I loved the film, didn't you?"

Legging it across the road, Lucy shouted "It's outrageous that two young women caused such an uproar in the government."

"And they seemed so innocent," I remarked, once we were out of harm's way.

"I don't know about that. I think Mandy Rice-Davis was a bit savvier than Christine Keeler."

"Which one did you relate to?"

"Good question," Lucy said. "You go first."

"I think I'm a little bit of both of them."

"I'd say you're more like Christine Keeler."

"That's funny, I was about to say the same to you."

"Actually, to be honest, I didn't relate to either of them."

"Why not?" I asked.

"They were both quite girly, especially Mandy. I think Bridget Fonda played her brilliantly. She's so pretty, how old do you think she is?"

"A few years older than us, mid-twenties?"

"Her English accent was spot on," Lucy said.

"She's not English?"

"No, she's Jane Fonda's niece."

"Oh, the workout queen. I bet there's nothing good to eat at her house."

Lucy laughed. "Only you would think of such a thing. But you're probably right."

"She looks amazing though, doesn't she? Especially for a woman her age. She must be in her fifties."

"You'd never know it. I guess there's something to be said for all the aerobics she does."

"Ugh," I grunted. "Just talking about Jane Fonda makes me feel fat."

"Don't be ridiculous," Lucy tutted. "You're far from fat."

As we neared Lucy's, she asked if she could come here.

"I was hoping you would, we still have too much to talk about. Plus, I have an idea."

Blowing her wispy fringe out of her eyes, Lucy asked what it was.

"We'll kick my dad out of the living room, and I'll dig out the *Buns of Steel* video."

"With Auntie Jane!"

"No, *Buns of Steel* is Greg Smithey, who's hysterical. My mum loves him, she gets well into the exercises and even sounds like him. Four, three, two, one," I yelled in my best American accent. "Press it out and push to the side. I'm proud of you! Good job!"

The sight of Lucy, doubled over from laughing only egged me on. "You know there's something happening down there! Ooh, that feels good! Squeeze those cheeseburgers outta those thighs!"

"No way," Lucy cried.

"Trust me, it's an experience."

"Well in that case we need to stop at mine first."

"Why?"

"I need leg warmers."

14th ~ At home

Being on standby is akin to being in a state of limbo and every time the phone rings, I lunge for it, hoping for news of a trip, but nothing yet.

Started a course of malaria tablets which taste vile but after what we learned in training about the dangers of being bit by a mosquito carrying the plasmodium parasite (if it finds its way to your liver, it matures!) I'm willing to do as instructed.

The pelting rain matched my gloomy mood, and my moments of missing Ben reached an all-time high around seven, which is when I came to bed. I couldn't sleep, so I filled eighteen pages with love and desire, but after reading my words, they seemed ridiculously over the top, so I scrunched the pages up and chucked them in the bin. There's a teeny tiny part of me that feels Ben doesn't deserve such a letter and a bigger part of me that wishes I didn't feel this way.

15th ~ At home

The postie showed up bearing not one but two letters from Ben, but that's not the only good news. While I was poring over Ben's heartfelt prose (feeling guilty that I'd binned similar sentiments) the phone rang.

"Good morning, this is Martha from crewing."

"I was beginning to think crewing didn't exist," I said, immediately regretting my outburst.

"Not only do we *exist*," she clipped, "but if you're Karen, I'm calling you for a trip tomorrow night. Do you have a pen?" I imagined her in her office, sitting ramrod straight, adjusting her pearls.

"Just a second please," I said, stretching the phone cord to its limit. "Ok, ready," I said, after biting the top off the pen (grrrr, dad always replaces the cap).

"Report time is twenty forty-five."

"Tomorrow night you said?"

"Yes. Flight number is the BA one six three. Returning on the BA one six two. March nineteenth. Did you get it all down?"

"I did, yes, thank you," I said, still scribbling.

"Do you have any questions?"

"Ehm no." Quick scan of my notes. "Wait, where am I going?"

"TLV."

Israel, here I come!

16th ~ LHR – TLV
Sheraton Hotel & Towers, Tel Aviv, Israel

Squashed like sardines on the tube during rush hour, my jangled nerves reached their peak, and by the time I checked in at TriStar House, I felt nauseous. In the briefing room, the stern looking CSD was more than diligent asking SEP questions, but safety is, after all, the reason we're there so I shouldn't have been surprised by such an extensive briefing.

I'm the most junior crew member so I didn't get to pick a working position. Consequently, I'm working in Economy with a purser called Leslie, who just rang to remind me to close the curtains, so the light won't wake me!

17th ~ Sheraton Hotel & Towers, Tel Aviv, Israel

Following through on Leslie's request to ring her the minute I woke up, I picked up the phone.

"It's Karen, sorry, did I wake you? It's ten past three."

"Local?"

"Yes."

"I remember when I first joined, I couldn't keep track of the time changes, so for years I wore two watches. You should probably do the same."

I'm not the one who was still asleep!

"I'll have a ring around but after a night out of bed, the first night here is usually quiet. I'll meet you in the lobby at four, oh and bring a cardi, it gets chilly here by the water."

I changed four times before finally deciding on black trousers and a striped top (both new from Miss Selfridge, thanks mum!) but with nothing resembling a cardi, I stuffed a light scarf in my bag, just in case Leslie insisted I wear it.

Leslie's neon outfit clashed heavily against the purple brocade chair that looked about to swallow her up (another one with delicate wrists). "It's just us!" She shouted, garnering the attention of several guests milling about the hotel lobby. I opened my mouth to speak but Leslie beat me to it. "I was going to suggest a stroll to Jaffa, or Joppa as it was known during biblical times. Did you bring a cardi? You might get cold in those short sleeves oh and are you wearing linen trousers? Fancy schmansy. You ready?"

To be alone!

"We'll stock up on oranges, you know, Jaffa and all that but not jaffa cakes." Her cackle was so loud, my hands reached for my ears. "The locals call them Shamouti and they're to die for. We'll take the beach route. You'll find the light from the Med absolutely mesmerising."

Will I now?

Bathed in luminous light, the Bauhaus architecture was stunning, but the rays did nothing to hide the cracks in Leslie's cakey foundation.

"I'll give you the same advice I dish out to all you newbies," she said, her gait gathering speed, as I made a mental note to stop wearing foundation after I turn thirty. "See the world! Save as much as you can, then get out while you're still young enough for the chance of a normal life, with a normal person." She turned to me. "*Normal*, as in someone who doesn't fly."

"Interesting," I uttered, side stepping through the crowd to keep up with her.

"No, not interesting," she stated. "*Fact*. Do you have a boyfriend?"

"I do, he's working in Italy-"

"Italian stallion?" she winked.

"Ehm, no, he's English. He's a rep-"

"I suggest you drop him! Relationships and flying *do not* go hand in hand."

18th ~ Sheraton Hotel & Towers, Tel Aviv, Israel

I skipped breakfast and met the crew outside the hotel. Decked from head to toe in hues of red, Leslie took it upon herself to, "Count those present." When the tour bus pulled up, she claimed the first row and made sure Kalmar, the driver, was familiar with the route she'd planned.

In Bethlehem, the queue to enter the Church of the Nativity showed no end in sight, but thanks to a prior arrangement Leslie made with, "a certain someone," we entered through the Door of Humility. Filled with huge, towering pillars, the space held an air of serenity rarely found in the presence of so many people.

As we approached the Grotto of the Nativity, hushed voices from across the world filled the narrow walkway, lined with exquisite, vibrant coloured tapestries. The only way to view the birthplace of Jesus was to get low to the ground. Many of the people around us kissed the ground and the sound of sobs and prayers mingled in the air as we huddled together, peering into the sacred space.

Stepping from that moment into the light felt intense and the cacophony of sound surrounding the market stalls thrust me back into the present. Crouched beside one of a great many children with outstretched hands, I was rummaging through my bag for something to share, when Kalmar yelled, "Get in the bus! Now!" I looked up to see a rock flying overhead, and instinctively reached for the boy, but he was already scampering away.

As the bus jounced wildly out of the square, a rock hit the front side window, shattering the glass. Someone screamed, "Brace for impact!" and I folded forward. After what felt like ages in that position, Kalmar announced we were out of harm's way. With a collective sigh of relief, head after head popped up as the Captain made his way down the aisle asking if we were ok, followed by Leslie, dishing out sweets, and wet wipes!

In Jerusalem, Kalmar parked on a steep hill and we slowly made our way outside. The view across the city was breathtaking and I don't know if it was the after-effects of what had just happened, but we were all silent, even Leslie!

From there we went to the Monastery of Temptation in Jericho, but it was at the Wailing Wall that I felt the most moved, from the sights and sounds of so much emotion, and evident suffering.

At Mary Magdalene Chapel goats and camels roamed freely and I wanted to linger and soak it all up but there was one more stop.

At the end of this incredible day, I threw caution to the wind and stripped down to my cozzy. Floating on top of the mud, in the Dead Sea, gazing up at the sea of frothy sky, I thanked my lucky stars.

19th ~ TLV – LHR
At home

I've been going back and forth on whether to grow out my hair but at half three this morning, while groggily getting dressed, short won the vote.

Flight was a hectic five hours, during which I only sat during take-off and landing. In TriStar House, I bumped into Sam, who looked ghastly after a "Not so tame evening at Madame Jojo's in Soho." He was off to Athens with a mature looking crew, so much so that he said he thought he'd mistakenly stumbled into a Concorde briefing!

Mum and dad were keen to hear about Tel Aviv and mum was especially interested in the Church of the Nativity, but it's the sort of place you need to experience in person. The little I saw of Israel was enough to make me want to return and explore more of its history and beauty.

Sarah invited me round to play cards and watch videos. *No thanks.* Jon offered to come up take me out for dinner. *No thanks.* Pamsy invited me to hers. *No thanks.* Ben rang. *Thank you.*

20th ~ At home

Woke from a dream, where I was with Ben, in a lush forest. He kept running ahead and whenever I'd catch up to him, we'd kiss, but then he took off and I couldn't find him. Tripping over twisted twigs and thorny branches, I ran until my feet were so cut up, I had to stop.

With stationery and pens of every description strewn across the kitchen table, dad looked surprised to see me up.

"Are ye jetlagged?"

"No, the time difference was only two hours."

If only to shake the bad dream, I thought about mentioning it to dad, but he was getting ready to leave for work, so I kept it to myself.

It was still early when the phone rang.

"McGarr! A cracking car came in over the weekend, by the way sorry it's so early but I just got into the office."

"How much is it?"

"Eleven fifty."

"I only have a thousand quid."

"Can you come and see it? Today?"

"I said I only have-"

"I know, I'll help negotiate the price. Can you come today? It'll get snapped up soon."

"Not today," I yawned.

"Why not?"

"I can't face British Rail or the London Underground."

"The sooner you get a car, the sooner you'll be done with-"

"Stop needling me," I growled.

"Sorry, I was only-"

"No, I'm sorry, what were you saying?"

"I know you don't want to hear this, but this is no time for faffing about. I've had one of the mechanics give it the once over, and it's sound. If you can't come today, what time can you be here tomorrow?"

"I don't know, I'll ring and let you know."

"You'll have changed your mind by then. Commitment, McGarr! I need a commitment, so I can hold the car for you."

"Fine! Tomorrow afternoon."

"What time?"

"Early afternoon."

"When?"

I let out a lengthy guttural sound.

"I'll be well impressed if you can do that again," he chuckled. "Give me a time."

"Two. I'll be there at two."

"I'll meet you on the platform."

21st ~ Jon's, Middlesex

"Only forty-three minutes late," Jon grinned, when I stepped off the train.

"Sorry, I got a late start."

"I would expect no less."

"Am I really that predictable?"

"I'm not touching that with a ten-foot barge pole. Come on," he said in an exaggerated cockney accent. "Let's go and get you a motor!"

Said motor is a Ford something or other. It's dark blue and there's plenty of space for my Samsonite. I was quite impressed with the way Jon negotiated the price, all the way down to just eight hundred quid, plus he offered to get it detailed, while I'm away.

To thank him, we went to his local for dinner, the spot of many a fun evening, where someone always bumps their head on the low beams. After a few pints, Rick made it known that he'd like to see Jon and I back together. The more beer Rick consumed, the more he let his wish be known. I pretended not to hear because as great as Jon is, my heart belongs to Ben.

22nd ~ LGW - BDA

Princess Hotel, Hamilton, Bermuda

Woke to the sound of Jon on the phone, rescheduling work appointments so he could drop me at TriStar House, for which I'm extremely grateful.

On the crew transport from home base at LHR to LGW, I sat with a girl called Annabel, whose plummy accent kept me entertained throughout the flight, and beyond.

"Your chap is simply *scrumptious*," she enthused, as I drew the curtain in the makeshift crew rest area.

Assuming she was talking about Ben, I tried to figure out how she knew him. Probing me with her piercing green eyes, she explained. "The chap in the rather tasteful car, from which you sauntered into TriStar House. Do keep up!"

I dunked a biscuit in my tea, then swiftly shoved it in my mouth.

"Well? Is he or is he not your boyfriend?"

"Not."

Slipping a velvet eyeshade down over her eyes, she tutted, "Poppycock!"

Most of the passengers were holidaymakers, so they were in good spirits, all except for one poor sod who was ill the entire flight. Shortly before landing, still ashen, he came into the galley and offered Annabel and me fifty quid each. Obviously, we refused, but when we took our jumpseats for landing, Annabel whispered, "Had we graciously accepted the dosh, we could have splurged on some decent champers."

Lovely surprise on arrival when Lolly boarded with her crew to take the flight to Tampa. We didn't get much chance to talk, but we agreed to meet up tomorrow, which I'm already excited about.

The driver on the crew bus had his work cut out for him, dodging brightly dressed tourists on scooters, weaving in and out as though they were the only ones on the road. Pastel painted houses with white roofs lined the narrow roads, beyond which turquoise water shimmered in invitation.

The hotel is pink! Opened in 1885, it retains a classic, elegant feel. No sooner was the door of my stately looking room shut, when I whooped an excited squeal, that only escalated when I opened the balcony doors to a view of the pool and harbour.

After luxuriating in the bath, I made good use of the lavish hotel toiletries, before wrapping my grateful skin in a cotton robe. With the evil AC shut off (another break-up!) I slid between the crisp white linens and drifted off to the steady thrum of vessels in the harbour.

Feeling refreshed from the loveliest nap, I waltzed around the room to George Michael singing, "You are far, when I could have been your star," and made a conscious decision to put Ben out of my mind, if only for the remainder of my time on this special island.

23rd ~ Princess Hotel, Hamilton, Bermuda

The day began early with Lolly and Suzanne (from my crew) who seemed content to play tour guide, suggesting we rent scooters. After a short stop in the charming town of St. George (and a heaping bowl of fish chowder) we made our way to a secluded cove. With only the three of us, there was no need to hide beneath my baggy t-shirt, so I quickly lost it and dove into the crystal-clear water.

Sadly, Lolly was operating the Tampa shuttle so she couldn't join us tonight. I jumped on the back of Suzanne's scooter (not easy in a skirt!) and in M.R.Onions, we enjoyed platters of seafood. Some of the crew were going clubbing but the appeal of the pink palace won out.

Desiring one last peek at the view before calling it a night, I popped out onto the balcony. Lost in thought, I jumped when I heard, "Evening, Miss M." Peering out from the balcony next door, Annabel giggled. "I almost refrained from disturbing you. You look rather contemplative."

"Hmm, just taking it all in. Where have you been hiding all day?"

"Unlock the adjoining door, and I'll tell you."

24th ~ BDA – TPA – BDA
Princess Hotel, Hamilton, Bermuda

The rum was stronger than I'd expected and after several of Annabel's wonderous concoctions, I switched to water. The entire time she was in my room, she grilled me, first about Jon ("that yummy chap who waited until you were inside before he drove off") and then Ben's name found its way into the conversation (so much for not thinking about him!).

"Family name?" she said, throwing me for a loop.

"You mean his surname?"

"Ya, of course," she said waving her not so delicate wrist.

After I shared Ben's last name, she shuddered. "Ghastly!"

"Annabel," I laughed. "You really are a dreadful snob."

"Thank you," she grinned.

Lovely time by the pool with Lolly today watching keen kite fliers, before jumping on the scooters. Stretched out on the warm sand at Horseshoe Bay, we laughed and yapped in equal measure.

Shuttle was full of ABP's (able bodied passengers) that were easy on the eye (some American football team I've never heard of.) Lolly and her crew boarded in BDA to take the flight to LHR and when the crew bus pulled up outside my favourite hotel, Annabel swore she, "Couldn't possibly sleep without bubbles in my bloodstream," so we walked into town to fulfill her wish.

25th ~ Shuttle from BDA - TPA - BDA
Princess Hotel, Hamilton, Bermuda

On turnaround in Tampa, I rang Miriam, and was surprised to hear the Orlando Police Department had been in touch. After a spate of thefts similar to ours, it was discovered that the housekeeping crew had a racket going. I can't wait to tell Pamsy, who will no doubt want to come back and testify!

Felt bloated all day and thanks to the soft water, my hair feels and looks limp. Not a good combination. On a brighter note, I'm getting paid to spend time, cavorting in paradise!

Because of the delay leaving Tampa it was after midnight when we got to the hotel. Suzanne was suffering from excessive sunburn, and none of the crew were interested in going out. Annabel invited me to her room, which is amusing, considering we have adjoining rooms. I was expecting her to suggest more mixers for what remained of the rum (not much) but she surprised me by ordering, "Tea and yummies."

"This is rather civilised," I said, removing the domed lid to reveal an assortment of delectable looking desserts.

"*Decorum*. It's what separates us from the animals," she stated, deadpan, while I picked up the teapot and said, "Shall I be Mother?"

"Ya," she nodded. "I've been mulling over some ideas for when you visit, and stay, of course."

"Stay where?"

"Well, there's the family estate in West Sussex, but I share a pad with my brother in Chelsea."

"You have a brother?" A look of horror flashed across her face as I clinked the teaspoon against the delicate cup.

"Two, actually. I share with the older one, Hugo, but not for much longer. Much to mummy's dismay, he's moving in with his latest squeeze."

"Is she nice?"

"To me, ya, but she and mummy are *constantly* at loggerheads."

"Over what?"

"Tamra is a divorcée. She has a child. She's eight years older than Hugo. *And* she's a shop girl. I'm not sure which one mummy is most upset about."

"Aha, so that's where you get it from!"

"Indeed," she said, throwing up her hands. "Dreadful snob, that's mummy for you."

26th ~ BDA – LGW
Somewhere over the Atlantic

I was on the bed reading when there was a *rat a tat tat* at the door.

"Darling!" Sam exclaimed, showering the air with kisses as he burst into my room. "Ooohh, your room is sooo much nicer than mine." Elbowing me, he grinned, "Who're you shagging?"

"How did you know I was here?"

"First thing I do down route is check the crew list. Don't you?"

"Never thought to. You just arrived?"

"Fresh off the aircraft, can't you detect the stale scent of *eau de TriStar*? Here 'til Thursday. Place looks ah may zing. Let's go to the pool and have a cocktail."

"I can't drink, I'm on the flight home tonight."

"Cocktails, mocktails," he sang, dancing his way out the door.

Stretched out on sun loungers, Sam uttered, "Two o'clock."

"What about him?"

From behind his angular, purple tinted sunglasses, I sensed a heavy eye roll. "Would you, or wouldn't you?"

"No chance. Too much hair."

"Meow. How about nine o'clock?"

"Nah, too flashy looking."

"Darling, you are picky."

"And in love."

"Ugh, we're not still harping on about *him*, are we?"

"Yes, we are actually."

"Oh, oh, four o'clock."

"Are you kidding?"

"I don't mean for a shag, check out the outfit. If she's not careful, she'll take off."

A minute later, kaftan girl tripped and was only saved from a dip in the deep end by Sam's rapid response, seizing as much fabric as his diminutive frame could handle.

"Are you alright?" He asked.

"I'd 'ave been a goner if you 'adn't grabbed me! Fanks ever so much."

"You're most welcome." Sam began unravelling his hand from the swath of butterfly print.

"It's these bleedin shoes innit?" She said, kicking off four-inch heeled platforms. "Me 'arts beating so fast, I fink I'm in shock."

"Would you...like a drink?" Sam stuttered.

"I fink I'd better, just to calm me nerves. Malibu and coke. Better make it a double."

Sam gestured to the waiter (anytime o'clock, phew!) who wasted no time coming over.

"Darling?" Sam winked at me. "Virgin strawberry daquiri?"

"Thank you, lovebug," I cooed.

"Awwww, ain't you two sweet. By the way, me name's Jade," she said, plopping on the edge of Sam's lounger. I watched in amusement as he squirmed to stop his foot from making contact with the butterfly wings circling Jade's not so delicate thigh.

"Rupert," Sam clipped, his hand outstretched. "And my wife. Clarissa."

"Bootiful names for two bootiful people." Noticing the tremble in Jade's hand, I asked if she was sure she was ok.

"Yeah, I'll be alright. I was just finking how sad it'd be if I drowned on me honeymoon."

"Where is your husband?" Sam sounded like he'd just come from an elocution lesson with Annabel.

"At the ho tell. He 'ad sum dodgy seafood last night and he's paying for it today. Not me," she said, wrapping herself in the extensive fabric. "I don't touch nufink like that."

"Are you staying here?"

Gesturing in the direction of the harbour, she said, "We're at the other Princess, the one in Southampton. I just popped over on the ferry to have a nose and compare the two."

"Tremendous," clipped my beloved.

Much to the waiter's amusement, Jade grabbed the drink and knocked it back in one. "I might need another." She fluttered her fake eyelashes at the waiter. "If you don't mind." I watched her eyes roam over our hands. "You must be one of 'em modern couples that don't wear wedding rings."

Without missing a beat, my lying husband said, "We indulged in a spot of snorkelling earlier and didn't want to risk losing our rings."

"Heirloom, I s'pose? You won't catch me doin' none of that. I'm petrified of the water."

"Fortunately, there are plenty of other *activities* one can enjoy on one's honeymoon. Isn't that so, pudding?" Sam grazed my hand with his, forcing me to look at him.

Pudding!

Leaning forward with her bosom resting on her lap, Jade said, "I've a little secret. We're only 'ere coz me husband works for BA, you know, British Airways. One of the perks," she looked around to make sure nobody was listening. "One of the perks," she continued, "is flying on the cheap, standby mind you, but-"

"We have friends who work…are *involved*…with British Airways," Sam said airily.

"It was touch and go whether or not we'd get on the flight, but Jay 's been with 'em for years so he's, you know, up there in seniority an that. The crew made a real fuss of us, we woz treated like royalty."

"Where is your husband based?" Asked my cotton wool mouthed husband.

"Gatwick, we live in Haywards Heath, he don't half work long hours. He's a bit of a boffin. Unlike me," she chortled. "How long you two been married then?"

"A very short, but sweet time," cooed Sam.

This time Jade allowed the waiter to put her drink on the table "Cheers, luv." Turning to me she said, "You still getting used to calling 'im your husband?"

I nodded.

"It's second time down the aisle for Jay but I already told 'im this is it for me."

"Here's to love and marriage," proposed my thoughtful husband.

"Cheers and fanks again. You're a lifesaver. I imagine my Jay will wanna come over and shake your 'and, he's that sorta bloke. He'll most probably insist on going out for a meal."

"Actually," Sam stated, with a slight squirm. "We're only here for the night."

"Wot a shame. We leave furzday."

I watched in glee as Sam's face contorted into a look of horror.

"We woz hoping to stay longer but, well with the cost of the wedding an that-"

"Thursday you said?"

Jade drained the glass. "Yeah, furzday night."

No longer afraid of the kaleidoscope of butterflies adorning Jade's kaftan, Sam motioned for her to move closer.

"From what we've gathered, from our dear friends here who, how do I say it, are some of the *higher ups*, is that Thursday is the worst day to leave the island. Given what *Lionel* has shared with us, I'd suggest you leave on Friday. It'd seem such a shame to get caught in a pickle at the end of your honeymoon."

Tapping the side of her nose, Jade thrust closer to Sam.

"Fanks for that," she whispered. "I'll mention it to Jay and see wot he says." Resting her hand on my lying sack of you know what's bony knee, she smiled, "Cheers, Rupert, mum's the word. You know," Jade said, getting up and gathering the remnants. "I knew when I spotted you two, you woz the sorta people who knows stuff like that."

Ah, Jade, if only you knew!

27th ~ At home

Pointing outside, as the crew bus pulled into TriStar House, antsy Annabel said, "Look! It's the chap you refuse to go out with."

I leaned across her for a better look. "Sorry, I couldn't resist," she said with a sly chuckle. "Nor is your so-called boyfriend coming to pick you up."

"Ouch Annabel, that was uncalled for."

"Sorry, poppet," she pouted. "I can be rather vile after a night out of bed."

"Finally, you're admitting you're tired!"

"Utterly exhausted. I'm more than ready for some quiet time at the country house. Such a pity you're not going in my direction, I'd have dropped you at home."

My laugh prompted her to ask, "What?"

"Annabel, I doubt I'll ever be going in your direction."

"I wouldn't be so sure about that," she grinned.

It wouldn't be Easter without mum insisting we roll the boiled eggs she decorates every year. After we'd rolled egg after egg down the grassy verge behind the house, dad dished up the leg of lamb he'd prepared, and I piled my plate high with roasted potatoes and veggies.

The evening was spent unwrapping endless Easter eggs, but even better than overdosing on chocolate, is going to bed under the same roof as nana.

28th ~ At home

Nana was first up, and we sat in the kitchen, nattering over a pot of tea, while I picked at what was left of the Simnel cake.

"When did ye say Ben's coming back?"

"According to his most recent letter, next Sunday. I can't wait!"

"Aye, I can see yer excited."

"Nana, did you ever feel like that about a boy?"

"Oh aye," she said, with a coy smile.

"Was it granda?"

"Now, now, that would be telling."

"Aw, go on, I'm twenty-two!"

"Och, yer making me feel like an auld wumin. Ye know sometimes when I look at ye, I still see a wee lassie wi long hair and a shy wee smile."

"That might be because I'm your first grandchild. And your favourite," I teased, with a questioning tone nana smiled in response to.

"So, was it granda?"

With her eyes downcast, she uttered, "Sometimes the first person ye love isnae necessarily the one ye marry. That first flush of love can be intense."

In my best French accent, I cooed, "And *passionate*, oui?"

"Aye that as well," she said, looking almost embarrassed.

"Do you think such intense love can burn itself out?"

Glancing out the window, she uttered, "Sometimes."

"I wonder if that's what concerns mum when it comes to how I feel about Ben."

"Yer a wise lassie…always have been."

While I poked at the last of the cake crumbs, nana poured us a fresh cup of tea, and said, "I think we, wumin, I mean, hold a lot in our hearts we don't always share."

"Who's the wise owl now?" I said, stirring more milk into my tea. "After granda died, did you have any desire to get married again?"

"Och no, none at all."

"But you've been alone all these years."

"And that's a choice I made." Her tone verged on stern.

"I don't remember much about granda. I wish I did."

"Ye were just a wee tot when he.. he-" Her voice faltered, and she dabbed her eyes.

"Sorry, nana, I didn't mean to upset you."

"It's fine, hen," she said squeezing my hand. "There are parts of life ye just keep tucked away and it's a surprise when they come oot again."

Through the glass wall, I spotted mum padding down the stairs.

"To be continued," nana whispered, with a knowing smile.

29th ~ At home

A few minutes into catching up with Pamsy, I said, "Guess what?"

"You're pregnant?"

"Can you imagine me telling Ben I got knocked up in his absence?"

"I'd pay good money to be a fly on that wall," Pamsy chuckled. "What did you want to tell me?"

"They caught the perpetrators who robbed us in Orlando. The police told Miriam they arrested several people."

"Ooh, do we have to go back and testify? We could saunter into the courtroom wearing big shoulder pads like they do on-"

"I doubt it's like that in real life."

"Regardless, if they need us, I'm there!"

Drove my car for the first time and must remember to thank Jon for dropping it off. It smells lemony fresh, and every inch of the interior is spotless.

While mum and nana were in the cinema at The Point, I met Sarah at the bar. It was so nice having her to myself (selfish, I know but just because she loves Simon doesn't mean I have to).

Mum hasn't stopped raving about Dustin Hoffman's performance in *Rain Man*, so I guess I'll have to go and see it.

30th ~ At home

Mum was full of the joys after seeing the news that Dustin Hoffman took home the Oscar. *Rain Man* also won: Best Director, Best Film and Best Screenplay. What an incredible feat for everyone involved. It'd be so amazing to write a screenplay.

Whenever I tell people I live in Milton Keynes, the concrete cows come up. Who'd have guessed that an art installation in the middle of a field would become such a prominent part of this place? Over lunch at The Victoria Inn, in Bradwell, we got chatting to a German couple, who came specifically to see the cows! According to the wife, the creator, Liz Leyh is Canadian. The husband argued she's American, so who knows.

At Willen Lake, we fed the swans and took a bunch of pictures by the Peace Pagoda. It's been a fun day playing tourist in the place I call home.

31st ~ At home

Didn't feel up to driving to Heathrow so once again it was the taxi, tube, train routine.

In my mail slot at work, was a monogrammed correspondence card.

Greetings Miss M,

I trust you've come to your senses and ended things with your faraway boyfriend? And, if so, are you going out with the car chap? (I do hope so!). I adored being flat mates and feel we ought to request a trip together. Thoughts on a postcard please, ha! Off to The Big Apple and wish you were on the trip. I imagine us finding our way into some fascinating territory, perhaps with the added benefit of a swift romance with some yummy yanks.

Please do get in touch!

Affectionately yours,

Annabel's cursive signature filled half the card.

After spending a small fortune on public transport, I walked through the front door.

"Whit happened?" Mum said, with a look of concern.

"There was a huge delay to the flight, so they had to call out a new crew."

"Whit happens noo?" Nana asked.

"I'm on standby, with twenty-four hours' notice of a trip, so not too bad, unless I get called out for a lengthy trip, and miss Ben."

I got up thinking I'd be going to bed in Nigeria but here I am, back in my own bed. I can't stop thinking about Ben and the fact he'll be home in a few days. When he's away, I try and put him out of my mind, if only not to get distracted, but knowing he's almost home propels everything I feel for him to the forefront.

APRIL

1st ~ At home

Mum and dad spent the last day biting each other's heads off, so when Sarah asked if I wanted to meet at The Point (again!) I jumped at the chance. Driving past the train station, it hit me that I was driving solo for the first time. My initial reaction was fear, but I just put it out of my head (much easier than I thought!) and lapped up the sense of freedom.

I was disappointed to find not only Simon, but two friends of his, whose names I don't remember (yes, they were that dull). My mind kept wandering to Ben so after one drink, I whispered to Sarah that I had to go.

"Noooo, you can't leave now," she pouted.

"I have to be up early in the morning, to meet Ben at the airport."

One of the nondescript friends piped up something about it being, "Alright for some," but I couldn't be bothered to engage, which I'm sure came across as unsociable but sometimes I just can't be arsed.

I wasn't quite ready to come home so I bounded down the stairs to the cinema foyer, grabbed the biggest bucket of popcorn and went to see *The Accidental Tourist*. Absolutely adored Muriel, the quirky character Geena Davis played. Kathleen Turner (oh that voice and that hair) was perfect onscreen but I'd be lying if I didn't admit the real appeal was William Hurt (oh that voice and that hair!). I loved it so much that I'll probably go and see it again.

2nd ~ Ben's, MK

In love.

With Ben, whose face is a few feet from mine.

Fingers entwined, with our legs tangled together underneath the blanket, we laugh until it hurts.

And suddenly, life is vibrant again.

3rd ~ At home

Several rapturous hours canoodling with Ben after his parents left for work, sadly, interrupted, with mum on the phone to let me know crewing were looking for me.

"Good news?" Ben asked, after I hung up.

"I just got called out for a four-day trip to Athens, but it's not 'til Wednesday."

"You'll be gone all weekend?"

"No, in between flights to and from Athens I'll be staying at a hotel near Gatwick."

"Paid for by BA?"

"But of course, dahling!" I chirped. "They are, after all, the world's favourite airline."

"You can't stay there alone," he said, melting me on the spot.

Walking my fingers up his arm, I said, "I wonder who I could ask to join me?"

"I'll need time to think about that," he grinned, pulling me to him.

I suggested we see *Scandal* because I knew Ben would love it (he did) and afterwards we went to our favourite Italian restaurant. Halfway thorough dinner, Ben became distant, so I asked if he was ok.

"Yeah, fine," he uttered, without looking up.

"You're awful quiet. Is your food ok?"

"It's not great."

"Do you want to swap? This tagliatelle carbonara is scrummdiddlyumptious."

"Scratching the back of his neck, he moaned, "Nah."

"I'm sure you had amazing food in Italy," I chirped, hoping to engage him but all he did was nod. We ate in silence (hate that) and my

109

insides were churning, but not from the food. By the time we left the restaurant, everything felt awkward and clumsy, like we hardly knew each other.

In the car I offered to drop Ben at his, hoping he'd say he wanted me to stay with him but all he mumbled was, "Ok." When I pulled up outside his house, he gave me a peck on the cheek and said, "See you tomorrow."

Still hoping he'd invite me in (pathetic, I know) I brushed my hand against the back of his leather jacket, but all he did was get out of the car. I waited as he unlocked the door and expected him to turn and wave but he went inside and shut the door with his foot.

Nana was on the couch with her arms crossed, her head dropped to her chest. Over the sound of the tv, I could hear her snoring. I was about to leave her in peace when she said, "Och is that you in, hen?"

"Sorry, I woke you up."

"I was just resting my eyes," she yawned.

I almost laughed because that's what mum always says, even when she snores loud enough to wake the dead.

"Yer mammy and daddy are at Janice at Terry's."

"You didn't want to go?"

"I don't mind a wee bit of time tae maself."

"Ah, that's where I get it from," I smiled.

"Is that ye in fur the night?"

"Uh-huh."

"Yer mammy and I took a wee walk over to the bakers this afternoon, there's apple pie and strawberry-"

"Strawberry tarts?"

"Yer favourite," she smiled, getting up. "If that's ye in for the night, I'll make ye a wee cuppa tea, and ye can tell me whit happened to make yer eyes red."

4th ~ Ben's, MK

No matter how upset I am with Ben, the second I hear his voice, all I want is to see him, so when he rang this morning, I chose not to mention yesterday. And when he came over, nana acted like she knew

110

nothing (how refreshing it felt, pouring my heart out in way I can't with mum) and made small talk.

We had dinner with Ben's mum and dad but when we came up to his room, he resorted to being quiet.

"You said earlier that we could talk tonight."

"What do you want to talk about?" His tone was gruff.

"This feels weird. I don't like it. Aren't you happy to be home?"

"In some ways yeah, in others, no."

"I hope the yeah part includes me."

"Course it does."

When he sat on the bed, I stood in front of him. "You don't sound very convincing."

"Why are you so cross?"

"I'm not angry, I'm confused. You're running hot and cold. One minute we're completely wrapped up in each other, which feels amazing, and the next, you act as if you don't even like me."

Standing to face me, he hissed, "Me, me, me."

I took a big step back. "That's cruel."

"There are things I want to share with you."

"Such as?"

"Stuff that happened while I was away."

"This time or last time as well?"

"All of it!" His voice was raised but there was no way I was backing down.

"I don't want to know," I stated, with my hands in the air. "I really don't want to know what you did or didn't do because it's not important. We can't keep going back to the past…it's d*estructive.*"

Staring me down, he said, "Are you saying that because there are things you don't want to tell me? Like Florida, for example."

"We split up before I left for Florida."

"So, you *did* sleep with somebody." He plopped on the bed. "I knew it."

"I didn't."

He glanced up at me. "You're a terrible liar."

I sat next to him, but not too close. "I'm not lying. The fact is, we weren't together then, so what I did or didn't do doesn't matter. Just like it doesn't matter what you did during that time. We're back together and that's enough for me. It truly is."

We fell back on the bed, but didn't touch or speak for a long time, until the silence got the better of me and I turned to face him.

"You know what I feel like doing?"

Suppressing a smile, he said, "What?"

"I feel like getting stoned."

Bolting upright, he said, "You've never said that before."

"I know, but right now, in this moment, that's exactly what I want to do."

5th ~ LGW - ATH
Hotel Athenaeum Inter-Continental, Athens, Greece

This bed is huge and I'm all alone without my beautiful Ben. I'm also a bit tipsy. And soooooo hungry. I just ordered room service so hopefully I'll still be awake when it shows up.

We arrived late afternoon and most of the crew met up at the hole in the wall bar in the square across from the hotel, where some evil person suggested ouzo…potent! After that, things began to get a bit blurry. The good-looking guys wandering through the square were not blurry. If I don't eat soon, I swear I'll die of starvation.

We carried a body today. As in, a dead one. The daughter of the deceased man came into the galley and through sobs, she thanked us profusely for being so kind to the family. I can't begin to imagine how they must have felt knowing they were coming home to bury their father next to their mother, here in Athens, where they were all born.

Life is so incredibly sad, and I am so incredibly hungry.

6th ~ ATH - LGW
Copthorne Hotel, Crawley

Ben is already asleep, and I love watching the way his smooth chest rises and falls…ahhhhh, be still my beating heart.

It's strange to think I was at the Acropolis today! The guide, a very appealing Athenian, was a wealth of knowledge, and I particularly loved the way he pronounced, "Byzantine." Sitting on the steps of the Acropolis with that incredible view and the warmth emanating through the ancient stone is one of the many reasons I love cabin crew life.

When we landed at LGW the ground crew paged me. The agent passed me a note I tore open to find a message that Ben was waiting for me. I had to get permission from Dennis, the CSD to skip taking crew transport to the hotel because Ben was waiting for me at Concorde House. I had no idea he was coming to meet me, so it was the most amazing surprise.

This hotel is where I spent six weeks during Air Europe training, but none of those nights came close to what I just experienced, with Ben.

7th ~ LGW - ATH

Presently on crew rest with just enough time to down two cups of tea, a jam roly-poly and a diary entry.

Found Dennis the CSD in a shaded area of the hotel garden, engrossed in some scandalous news item in *The Sun*.

"Morning, Dennis."

"Morning? It's almost time for Elevenses," he said, tucking his hands between his knees. "What're you two up to?"

"I was hoping to get permission to leave the hotel for the day."

Bowing his head in an exaggerated way, he tutted, "Oh you were, were you? To do what? And where?"

"We'd like to go to Brighton."

"Can you pop in and feed my cat?"

"You live in Brighton?"

As soon as he said, "Hove, actually," the three of us burst out laughing. I've yet to meet a Hove resident who doesn't add *actually,* after naming the town.

"I imagine you'll be driving?"

"Ben will probably drive. Right?" Ben nodded in agreement, and I blurted, "I hate driving!"

Swinging a hound tooth trousered leg from underneath the picnic table, Dennis declared, "I'm with you, sister! I've been flying for over twenty-five years, and I've yet to learn how to drive."

"Listen to you two," Ben chipped in. "You fly all over the place, but you don't like driving?"

Giving Ben the up down, Dennis said, "Some of us are more suited to speed and elevation." He smiled at me. "Soooo, this is where you reassure me that you'll be back in time for pick up and that you won't partake of anything that could be misconstrued as alcohol."

"No chance of that after that the booze-o overload in Athens!" I laughed.

"I know not what you speak of," Dennis teased, pushing his glasses up his nose.

"Funny, I could've sworn the person who suggested ouzo looked just like you."

"Middle aged with a paunch and slightly balding? We're ten a penny. Unlike you pretty, young things. Now off you go and have a fab time."

8th ~ ATH - LGW
Ben's, MK

The best thing about checking into crew hotels isn't crawling into bed. It's the sight of the little brown envelopes we receive. In addition to a basic wage, and overtime, we get paid cash allowances for the duration of the trip. Allowances are calculated on what it'd cost to eat breakfast, lunch and dinner in the upscale hotels we stay in. Typically, we don't eat in the hotel. Why would we when we can stash the cash and grab something cheap elsewhere.

Having said that, I didn't leave my room in Athens! After a heavy, much-needed sleep, I woke up feeling especially esurient, so I ordered a Greek salad and chocolate mousse from room service. Once the dishes were clean and I'd placed the tray outside the door, I got back under the covers and dozed my way through several crappy movies.

Ben was waiting outside TriStar House and I was elated to see him. His parents are away for the weekend, so the evening began magically, but as the night wore on, he became detached. I was too tired to ask questions so we went to bed but I couldn't sleep, hence the reason I'm up. Life was a whole lot easier in Greece.

9th ~ At home

Watching morning tv, eating sugary cereal (Ben) and buttery toast (me) I made what I thought was an innocent comment about how awful tv ads are.

"You know something," Ben growled. "You're too opinionated for your own good."

Without a word, I got up and left, making sure to slam the door behind me. Of course, I forgot my car keys, so I had to ring the bell. Ben made me wait a few minutes before opening the door. In a soft tone, he said, "You don't have to leave."

I held out my hand for the keys, turned, got in the car and drove off. I could feel the tears coming but I was so riled up, I shouted, "Don't you dare!"

Mum and dad were in the garden, and I was tempted to go and hide in my room, but I knew if I did, I'd only dwell on my misery.

Talking about Athens was a good distraction, and when the phone rang tonight, I knew it'd be Ben, especially since I hadn't heard a peep from him all day.

"Where've you been hiding? You've been off the radar for ages."

"Hi Pamsy, what's going on?"

"What's the matter, mate? You sound down in the mouth."

"Hang on a sec." I stretched the cord as far as it'd reach and plopped on the bottom stair.

"My mum and dad are in the living room, and I don't want them to hear."

"Tell me about it," Pamsy sighed. "Try adding a little brother and sister into the mix. So, what upset you?"

"The usual…I had a bit of row with Ben this morning, over something silly."

115

"Are you on leave this week or next?"

"Next, and we'd planned on going away but-"

"If it doesn't work out, come here. I'll ply you with chocolate and we can sit on the beach watching the hunky windsurfers. How does that sound?"

Perfect.

10th ~ Ben's, MK

In the moment, when you're upset with someone, it can feel like the world is tumbling down but there's resolution to everything, which is what I prefer to any kind of conflict. So, when Ben rang this morning, I acted like nothing untoward had happened and he appeared to do the same.

Consequently, we ended up in London, where I spent a small fortune in The General Store, then more in The Body Shop, stocking up on my favourite banana hair conditioner. Hand in hand, we wandered the streets, all the while talking about our plans and how amazing it'd be to live in London.

On the way home, Ben asked if I wanted to stay at his, so we stopped to let mum and dad know. Back in the car, I commented that it wasn't that late, considering how much we'd packed into the day.

"You hungry, babe?"

"When am I not hungry?"

"What are you in the mood for?"

In response to my answer, Ben grinned and slapped my thigh.

"Actually, scrap that. I want popcorn, slathered in butter!"

"Kinky," he joked. "But I'm up for it."

"Speaking of kinky, *Dangerous Liaisons* is playing at The Point."

"Who's in it?"

"Glenn Close. John Malkovich. Michelle Pfeiffer."

He shrugged his shoulders.

"And…." I waited for him to look at me. "Uma Thurman."

Sold!

11th ~ Ben's, MK

Another Ben bombshell.
He's leaving again.
Ten days from now.

12th ~ At home

With the news of Ben's much earlier than expected departure, I woke up with that unsettled feeling you get after a bad dream, or when something is looming over you.

We went shopping, for nothing in particular (the worst time to go shopping) and after traipsing through John Lewis, I suggested lunch. Everything was going great, until Ben asked if I wanted dessert, which annoyed me, because he should know me better than to ask the obvious.

"Let's at least look at the menu," I said.

"You already know everything they have."

"There might be something new."

"There won't," he snipped. "But you go right ahead."

"Forget it!" I pushed the chair back so hard, it tipped over.

Without a word, we stomped to the car park and when I went to the driver's side, Ben said he would drive.

"Can you hand me my keys?" I knew I was being ridiculous, but I couldn't seem to help myself.

Halfway home, he said, "Is this all because I'm leaving so soon?"

I was too exhausted to explain, so I just nodded.

13th ~ At home

I know I should be strong and not let things (Ben) affect me so much, but why wouldn't I be upset about Ben's departure, when all I want is to spend all my time with him.

14th ~ At home

Ben went to the Spanish embassy in London for his work visa and looked mightily surprised when I said I didn't want to go with him.

You keep saying you need space, I wanted to say but instead I offered no explanation, which didn't exactly feel great, but I thought given time to stew in his own juices, he might see my point of view.

Spent a chunk of the afternoon huddled in the phone chair and was getting up to make tea when the phone rang.

"McGarr! I caught you at home. Shocking! Listen, the guys and I have a gig tonight, you should come and hear us play."

"Sorry, I'm going to a party."

"This'll be much better than any party. I guarantee it!"

"Possibly, but I've made a commitment."

"McGarr, please, you and commitment do not go hand in hand."

"Hey, that's enough of that."

"Sorry, I was only joking. Ditch the party and I'll come and get you. This is your chance to scream for the best band ever."

"Thanks, but I really can't-"

"Suit yourself, "he said sounding despondent.

Ben rang and said he'd had a long day in London and that he wasn't in the mood for a party, but with Jon's words ringing in my ear, I insisted we go. Big mistake. Not only did Ben spend most of the night sulking and refusing to dance (I agree the music wasn't the best, but it was an anniversary party, average age 40 something so what did he expect?). On the walk home, he accused me of being selfish and condescending and when I asked him to explain why he thought that (is that considered selfish?) he said he didn't have the energy to get into it, so the minute we got to his, I jumped in my car and came home.

15th ~ Torquay, Cornwall

After the past few shitty days (Weeks! Months! Years!) with Ben, I wasn't sure if we'd still come away but as he pointed out, this is his last hurrah before he goes to Spain and I don't know when I'll be granted leave, so it might be a while before we see each other again.

After driving for a few hours, Ben said he needed a break, and without thinking, I asked for how long. Scowling, he pulled onto the hard shoulder, and we swapped places.

"I'd rather avoid anywhere with narrow roads," I said, my heart already racing at the thought of driving in unfamiliar territory.

"I really don't understand you sometimes," Ben tutted.

"I could say the same about you," I retorted, adjusting the mirrors.

"About what?"

Pulling out into the lane, I said, "All sorts that I don't want to get into. This isn't the time."

"I disagree, this is a perfect time."

"Don't distract me," I said. "I'm trying to drive."

"*Trying*," he muttered under his breath, but the word filled the entire car.

"That was mean," I said, trying to sound calm.

"What was?"

"You know what!" I yelled, hitting the indicator.

"What're you doing?" He shouted, as I pulled across two lanes, onto the hard shoulder.

"I need encouragement, not-"

"Just drop it," he said, unbuckling his seatbelt.

I got lost in *A Far Cry from Kensington*, (loving it but then again, I love everything Muriel Spark writes) and before I knew it, we were in Cornwall!

The hotel was last outfitted around the time the guests were born, and we're the youngest by at least half a century. Bundled up, we braved the elements and ambled our way along the seafront, for Cornish pasties (heavenly) and a bounty of snacks and drinks to enjoy in the comfort of the room, which has two twin beds (the woman who checked us in made a show of glaring at my bare ring finger!).

Ben just turned on the tv and it seems there's been a disaster at the Hillsborough football stadium, in Sheffield, during a match between Liverpool and Nottingham Forest.

That was two hours ago…the latest reports are saying seventy-four people are dead.

16th ~ Torquay, Cornwall

The conversation over breakfast was dominated by the horrific news from Sheffield. Most of the guests are old enough to be our grandparents and were keen to ensure we didn't have any family/friends at the match. The newspapers reported varying versions of what transpired, but one of the guests believes the stands collapsed from the weight of too many people.

Still reeling from the news, we got in the car with no destination in mind. We talked at length about how life can change so quickly and how sad it is that so many lost their lives.

In Exeter, we strolled hand in hand, taking in the sights and I especially loved the thatched roof cottages, with bright painted doors. Shops and cafés were plentiful and after a cream tea, we meandered through the winding sunlit streets.

"You ok, babe?" Ben asked, planting a kiss on my cheek.

"It's lovely here," I smiled. "So twee, and I love all the swirly glass windowpanes."

"Swirly glass?"

"The heavy glass that makes everything appear distorted and kind of magical."

"I don't think that's what it's called, but from hereon in we shall refer to it as..." After making a drumroll sound, he boomed, "Swirly glass! Ooh, look up ahead."

"What is it?"

"A fudge shop."

"*Noooo*," I whined. "I'm stuffed, I couldn't possibly eat anything else."

"I bet they have clotted cream fu u udge," Ben sang, stepping up his pace.

"Just a bite, then," I laughed, catching up with him.

17th ~ Newquay, Cornwall

With Radio One playing in the car, we sang along to everything Simon Bates played, but when the *Our Tune*, segment came on at eleven, Ben groaned and reached for the dial.

"I like the soppy stuff," I said, with more than a slight pout. Ben refrained from changing the station but soon got me back.

"Ugh," I groaned, when this week's number one came on

With an exaggerated flourish, Ben pressed my hand against his heart and sang, "Close your eyes, give me your hand darling, do you feel my heart beating…"

Feigning a shudder, I batted his hand away. "That shaky voice of hers reminds me of Belinda Carlisle."

"She does *not* have a shaky voice."

"Yes, she does. What's her name again?"

"I don't remember," he grinned.

"You're such a liar!"

"Yes, yes, I am." He was trying not to laugh but his mouth was already curling up. "Susanna Hoffs."

"Must be a Californian thing," I tutted.

"The sex appeal?"

I rolled my eyes. "The whole *quivering* voice thing."

"Could that be jealousy I'm detecting?"

"Not even," I said, flicking my hair, theatrically.

Walking his fingers up my leg, Ben said, "Not even a teensy-weensy bit?"

In my most tremulous tone I sang, "Am I only dreaming, or is this burning, an eternal flame?"

Reaching out his hand, Ben asked, "Is it?"

"Yes," I breathed, brushing my lips against his knuckles.

18th ~ Salisbury, Wiltshire

Our morning in Newquay consisted of breakfast in our room, with a clear view of the windsurfers, which made me think of Pamsy and the number of times we've spent watching le wave and his mates attempt to outperform one another.

I drove the first of the three-ish hour drive here, accompanied by Steve Wright, whose voice I could listen to for hours, which is probably why he's a radio personality!

We're spending the night in the epitome of old-world charm, with beams galore and a view of Salisbury Cathedral (built in 1220) but as amazing as that is, the newly refurbished bathroom is hogging all the attention. From behind a sea of bubbles in the double slipper (no fighting over who gets the crappy side with the taps!) Ben mumbled, "Do you think it'll be like this when we live together?"

"Only if we get a claw foot tub like this one."

He flicked a handful of bubbles in my direction.

"I think it'll be better," I said, easing closer to him.

"Why is that?" he said, opening his arms to me.

"Because we won't have to leave."

19th ~ At home

Thanks to the torrential rain, we skipped touring Salisbury and drove to Stonehenge, but unlike the last time we were there, there's no direct access to the stones, so we gave it a miss and headed to Oxford.

In Sweeney Todd's we had a disagreement about something petty (of course) but instead of getting huffy like I usually would, I bit the bullet and told Ben I had no intention of ruining the end of our time away.

"I don't know when or if I'll be able to visit you in Spain," I said, tears springing to my eyes. "Or how long you'll be gone but-"

Scooting his chair closer to mine, he said, "So, what are you saying?"

"I love you and I don't want to spend our last forty-eight hours together, arguing."

"So, you're apologising?"

"I didn't say that!"

With his cheek pressed against mine, he whispered, "What exactly are you trying to say?"

"Shut up and kiss me."

By the time we strolled out of the restaurant, all was well with the world, so much so that I drove home. It should've taken about an hour but in rush hour it doubled. I still wasn't ready to go our separate ways, but I thought I'd better show face at home.

Spent the night with mum and dad, watching the news about the Hillsborough disaster, and mum lit candles for, "The poor souls who lost their lives."

20th ~ Ben's, MK

Today is dad's 45th birthday and he was thrilled with the watch I purchased from duty free on my way back from Bermuda. Dad doesn't have a sweet tooth, something mum has failed to notice throughout their marriage, so all he had was a few bites of the chocolate cake mum smothered in candles.

Once again, Tracey got carried away with her shears. I like the cut, and colour, but Ben said it gives George Michael a run for his money!

After the phone rang (here, at Ben's) about twenty times, it was Susan who got up off the couch to answer it.

"For you, Ben," she said, looking none too happy.

Untangling his legs from mine on the couch, he asked who it was.

"What did you say your name was?" Susan's tone verged on abrupt, which is what got my attention. At the sound of Helena's name, I felt my stomach lurch.

"Would you like a cup of tea, Karen?" Susan asked, with a forced smile.

"That'd be lovely, thank you," I said, looking past her to where Ben was on the phone, his back to us.

The news was all about the London underground strike (workers protesting plans for driver-only operated trains), but my ear was tuned in Ben's direction. From the kitchen, came an almighty clattering sound that made me jump.

"You alright, love?" Stan called out.

"Fine, thanks," came Susan's reply, followed by another clang.

"Mother!" Ben yelled.

The cacophony continued until Ben hung up (approximately three minutes and half minutes later) and came and sat next to me. I kept my eyes fixed on the tv.

"Karen, tea's ready, love."

In the kitchen, I mouthed, "Thank you," as Susan passed me the mug, with a heavy wink.

21st ~ Pamsy's, Sussex

Watching the person you love meld into the crowd, to the point where you lose sight of them is one of the worst feelings and it was at that point at Gatwick today, when I burst into tears.

"You made it!" Pamsy shrieked, as I climbed out of the car, cheeks still streaky from too many tears. Squeezing me hard, she said, "If it's any consolation, your hair looks fab. Very Wham!"

Le wave was in The Castle with his girlfriend, Cressida, or Cress, as she likes to be called (appropriate given that she looks like she exists on watercress). She's nowhere near as posh as Annabel but I got the impression, she'd like to be. Eyeing me with a look of utter disdain, her fake smile revealed tiny teeth that reminded me of a rat, and when le wave came over and hugged me, she looked ready to gnaw me to shreds.

22nd ~ Pamsy's, Sussex

The second I closed my diary last night, Pamsy's eyes shot open.

"I thought you were asleep."

"I was pretending to be so you could write." She plumped up the pillows behind her, and enunciating each word slowly, said, "I did not desire to disturb your recollection of events on this rather fine, albeit amusing, evening."

"Has to be done," I chirped, nudging my diary into a tiny spot on the bedside table. "More stuff to add to the already huge pile of cards and letters I can't bear to part with."

"Do you keep anything I send?"

"Your cards and letters are some of my most treasured possessions."

"Aw, if you keep it up, imagine how much stuff you'll have when we're like, fifty. We could sit and read them all over again."

Slipping my feet under the duvet, I groaned, "We have a very long way to go before we reach fifty. Maybe we should say forty?"

"When we're fat and bored and our kids and hubbies are driving us up the wall!"

"Ah, our bright future," I joked. "But no matter how life plays out, it'll all be in the pages of my countless diaries."

"What did you write about tonight?" Pamsy asked. "Or would you rather not say?"

"I wrote about my fantastic best friend."

"Aw, thanks mate," she cooed.

"Her name," I said, ducking under the duvet. "Is Cressida!"

23rd ~ At home

Pamsy woke me with a cup of tea and as usual, we dissected the events of the previous evening, which wasn't much different to the one prior, with le wave and Cressida, who I can't seem to warm to.

Le wave was in the pub again (lunchtime) but this time he was alone. When he went to the loo, Alton (who for some unfathomable reason just got a perm) said le wave is much happier when Cressida isn't on the scene. Another confusing relationship!

Le wave invited us to the flat he and Dickie just bought and when Pamsy clocked the French dresser, she flashed me a knowing look. Years ago, in a panic after I was a day late, I took a pregnancy test, and laid it to rest on *grandmama's* cherished antique. While I paced the room, Pamsy reassured me I had nothing to worry about, and that the combination of the pill and condoms would produce a negative result.

Awaiting my fate, some of my urine dribbled onto the dresser, leaving several stains I tried, in vain, to remove. I was dying to see if any trace of my relationship with le wave remained, but the dresser was piled high with books.

On the couch, Dickie and Shaza were draped all over each other and with their heads so close together, it's clear they use the same shade of hair dye. Our presence did nothing to deter their lust.

Lust is loud. And messy.

24th ~ LHR - CDG - LHR
At home

On my way to the crew car park, I spotted Lolly at the bus stop. She'd just come in from New York and couldn't stop gushing about how fantastic it was. Now, more than ever, I'm desperate to get there. After I dropped her off at Hatton Cross, I went to Paris, then came home!

Dad was feeling poorly so he went to bed early, leaving mum and I to pore over some old photo albums, which I always enjoy. Somewhere in the summer of 1974, mum asked if I miss Ben.

"I do, but I know this present set up with him working abroad won't be forever."

"No?"

"No, not at all."

"Whit d'ye foresee, ye know, in the *future*?"

Trying not to sound too serious, I mentioned marriage. When mum didn't respond, I said, "You don't see us getting married?"

Closing the album, she turned to me. "No. I don't think ye will."

I was shocked, not only by her candor, but with the conviction in her voice. Feeling my chest tighten, I uttered, "You've never said that before."

"Don't get me wrong, I've nothing against Ben." I was anxious to hear more but she stopped talking.

"I think we sometimes get our lines crossed," I explained. "And when he winds me up, I get annoyed when I should probably just try and, I don't know, be calmer?"

Mum's disapproving look was one thing, but it was her silence that spoke volumes.

25th ~ At home

Tipsy on a Tuesday! Sounds like a book I might enjoy. My writing is all over the place and phew, my head is spinning. Must try and keep it raised, which makes writing rather difficult.

I felt fine leaving Dukes so I think my present state started in the Zoo Bar while Jon and I were engrossed in a chat about life, love and where we think we might end up. Jon predicts I'll marry a Frenchman and live in both Paris and New York (ooh la la and awesome!). I see Jon married to an English girl (of the delicate wristed variety) and have two children. Come to think of it, he didn't mention anything about me and kids. Need to stop writing, the room is spinning faster than a disco ball.

26th ~ At home

Mum was full of the joys when I finally surfaced this morning (is half eleven considered morning?).

"Whit time did you roll in last night?"

"I don't know," I yawned. "Late?"

Filling the tea kettle, I heard her mutter, "Jist after one."

"Why are you asking if you already know?"

"I was in the bathroom," she fibbed.

In an effort to steer mum away from one of her favourite subjects, I said I was glad dad is feeling better.

"Aye, it was jist a wee bug. I think seeing Jon perked him up," she smiled. Widely. "Dad regards him highly."

In the event I'd suddenly lost my ability to understand English, she added, "Dad thinks Jon is *smashing*. And I have to agree."

Knowing there was no point trying to get mum to change the subject I filled her in and watched her eyes become saucer like when I spilled more than I usually would. Rubbing my temples, I groaned, "I think I drank too much."

"Uff, ye were just caught up in the moment, nothing wrong wi that at your age."

Smiling at the memory of the conversation Jon and I had about feeling sloshed/tiddly/plastered, I smiled.

"Whit?" asked mum.

"I was just thinking about how funny Jon is, and how he never runs out of things to talk about."

"Like you," mum smiled.

"Look who's talking!"

27th ~ At home

I was hoping to hear from Ben, but I fear he might be reverting to last year's behaviour, when he seemed to lose all memory of my existence. I hated how little we were in touch and when we finally talked, it felt strained and unnatural, which was so upsetting. I love him so much, but when we're together I sometimes feel I'm not as easygoing as I'd like to be. He winds me up something rotten and I know I need to learn how to brush things off and not be as sensitive. That's something I'm going to make a huge effort to change.

28th ~ At home

Mum said nana's been feeling down but when we rang her tonight, I thought she sounded ok. I wonder if she gets lonely living alone. I think initially, it'd be nice to have the freedom to do what you want and eat what you want (no, that would not be good for me, especially after the food bender I've been on all day). I don't want to live alone when I'm old like nana, which I can't imagine ever being, nor can I imagine what it'll be like to be thirty.

Spent this Friday night in my room, writing an epic letter to Ben. Sometimes I write reams and other times, the words come in fits and starts. I'm feeling the distance between us, and not just geographically. This time tomorrow night I'll be in Bermuda, putting even more miles between us.

To console my sad little heart, I watched Sting's *Bring On the Night* video. The opening scenes in the French chateau never fail to take my breath away but it's Sting's onscreen presence that makes me positively swoon. Given the number of times I've rewound it, I'm surprised it still works!

29th ~ LGW - BDA
Somewhere over the Atlantic

Presently on crew rest with tea and choccie biscuits that I quickly discovered are unsuitable for dunking, ugh, what a mess! We're almost five hours into this hectic flight and the pax are lovely but none of that matters because Neil, the purser, is a misery guts. Clearly disgruntled with every card he's ever been dealt in his five or so decades, he feels the need to spread negativity with anyone unfortunate enough to be in close proximity (working on a plane doesn't exactly allow a wealth of freedom!).

If only to escape Neil's *woe is me* attitude, I've spent ample time in the cabin. I guarantee there's not one passenger beyond this curtain who's remotely hungry or thirsty.

30th ~ BDA-TPA-BDA
Princess Hotel, Hamilton, Bermuda

Average age of this crew is under thirty so the fact we got back from operating the shuttle, close to midnight was irrelevant. We started at one end of the street with the intention of hitting every bar but after the karaoke started up, Alison and Pina refused to leave bar number three.

Moving at a snail's pace, Alison eased her lithe frame out of the deep stuffed couch we'd nabbed, in the dimly lit corner. With her glassy hazel eyes staring down at me, she smoothed down her red halter dress, and in a series of slurs she named several songs she was going to request.

With Alison gone, I sank deeper into the cushions and felt my eyes closing. I must have drifted off because the next thing I heard was a deep, slow drawl. "Man, this things's reeeaallll soft."

"Be careful, or it'll eat you alive!" As soon as the words were out, I felt embarrassed, and turned to explain that wasn't what I'd meant to say.

"Wow," uttered the stranger from less than six inches away. "Where's that accent from?"

"Ten a see," I said, trying not to laugh.

"How 'bout that?" He smiled, holding out his hand. "Travis."

Alison came teetering back, a frothy cocktail in each hand. At the sight of Travis, her eyes lit up and when she handed me the drink, I took a giant gulp. The brain freeze was immediate, and I was about to go and lock myself in the loo 'til it passed, when the British DJ announced, "Next up, we have Alison and Karen!"

Giving Alison the evil eye, I hissed, "I am *not* going up there."

"Come and give it a whirl," she sputtered, tugging at my arm, spilling half her strawberry daquiri on my new white eyelet skirt.

"Come with us, Travis!" I blurted, my tone verging on flirty.

With the crew cheering us on, Travis climbed up on stage, and pulled me up. Squashed between us, he whispered, "First timer here, go easy, huh?"

The three of swayed in time to the piano intro and sang loudly into the microphones, "Why do you build me up, buttercup baby, just to let me down and mess me around." By the end of the first verse, we had a dance routine down.

MAY

1st ~ Princess Hotel, Hamilton, Bermuda

Regardless of where in the world we are, or the hour we arrived, you'll find cabin crew, in the lobbies of the world's finest hotels, for breakfast, at nine.

The sight of Alison in her aviators told me how she felt.

"Ace night, but I think I'm losing my voice," she croaked, looking past me. "Travis not coming?"

"I don't know," I said cockily." Did you invite him?"

She slid her sunglasses down her nose to reveal bloodshot eyes. "He didn't spend the night with you?"

"He left the bar shortly after you and Pina did, and I went to my room. Alone."

"Oh, ok," she stammered, clearly not convinced. "I don't usually go for the brooding type, but I have to admit, I quite fancied him."

After breakfast, a handful of us caught the ferry to the Southampton Princess and spent most of the day lolling on the beach. In a bikini I never thought would see the light of day, I drowned all negative thoughts about my weight in the deep end, and relaxed.

Walking into town tonight, with Pina and Alison, I commented on the size of the cruise ship that came into view as we rounded the bend.

"You didn't see it last night?" asked Pina.

"We were too blotto to see anything," Alison chirped.

"They'll let us on," Pina said. "Do you have your ID on you?"

I nodded and Alison patted her fake quilted Chanel handbag.

Sauntering around the Lido deck, we sipped cocktails and chatted to some of the guests, most of whom are regular cruisers. Just as we were about to head inside, I stopped in my tracks when I heard someone call my name. From the other side of the pool, Travis waved as he made his way towards us.

"Did you know he'd be here?" Alison asked, sounding more than suspicious.

"Hey y'all," Travis beamed.

"Hello, southern boy," Alison purred, lunging at him for a hug.

"Hey, Pina," Travis smiled, breaking free from Alison's clutches.

"What are you doing here?"

"I'm on vacation with my family," he replied, kissing my flushed cheek.

"We wanted to see the lurrvvv boat," Alison cooed.

"I'm fixin' to go to dinner with ma family. Have y'all eaten?"

"Not yet," Pina pouted. Alison was clearly rubbing off on her.

"Come on, y'all, let's go surprise ma family."

What Travis failed to tell us is that his family are twenty-two strong ("Like our crew," joked Alison.) They were beyond welcoming and insisted we join them for dinner, after which we ended up in one of the plush lounges, where a band played sixties music.

Just like last night, Travis walked back to the hotel with us and the four of us went to the bar. After Alison and Pina took their leave, Travis asked if he could walk me to my room, but I didn't think it'd be a good idea, so I followed him outside. Overhead, palm trees swayed in the balmy fragrant air, and I won't lie, I wanted to kiss him, but all I could think about was Ben and how awful I'd feel if I found out he'd kissed a girl with eyes like mine.

2nd ~ Princess Hotel, Hamilton, Bermuda

Too tired to write but suffice to say it was another beautiful day in paradise.

3rd ~ BDA – LGW

35,000 feet

Enjoying some finger sandwiches Alison acquired from the Club World galley on her way back from a flight deck visit, with a doting dad and his twin daughters. We still have three hours to go and because of the hour, the cabin lights are dimmed so I have no excuse to be lurking in the cabin, which means I'll be stuck in the galley with Neil. The beautiful Bermuda weather did nothing to lift his spirits, in fact, he seems even more miserable tonight.

Alison, Pina and I went back to the Southampton Princess and got so caught up talking, we missed the last ferry and had to take the bus, which was crammed full of school kids, chatting animatedly, in much the same way we were. When the bus rounded the corner in Hamilton, Travis's ship came into view, giving Alison the perfect excuse to start talking about him.

Nudging me, she said, "You should've asked for his address."

I didn't tell her he asked for mine.

Knowing it'd be a night out of bed, I tried to sleep before pick-up but all I could think about was how close I'd come to kissing Travis. Meeting him made me see how things can escalate, especially when you're in the moment and far from home. It was different with Gabriel, because Ben wasn't my boyfriend, but now that he is (again!) I need to know I can trust him and be trustworthy in return. Having said that, the desire to kiss Travis was strong, but had he ended up in my bed, how would I feel? The good girl in me thinks I'd feel awful and would never forgive myself for betraying Ben, but the other girl, the one I'm slowly getting to know (I refuse to label her as bad!) shrugs her shoulders and winks before throwing back another dark 'n' stormy.

4th ~ At home

"That's ten years we've been putting up wi the iron lady," were mum's first words, when I walked in the door.

"*What?*"

133

"They were just saying on the radio that Thatcher's been in fur ten years, making her the longest Prime Minister of the twentieth century."

At the kitchen table, in a state of exhaustion with mum firing questions, I let slip, "American," and "Travis," in the same sentence, and watched mum's face open in question.

"So, this Travis was American?"

Gazing at the toast as though it held the secret to life, I said, "From Tennessee."

"Oh, that's where Elvis came fae."

"Actually, Elvis was born in Mississippi. He moved to Tennessee when he was a teenager and of course he died there, at Graceland."

"How d'ye know that?"

"You know what dad's like when he gets into something, he gives you every last detail."

"Whether ye want it or not!" she laughed.

"Anyway, getting back to Elvis, did you know that-"

"Och," mum clucked, dismissing me with her hand. "That's enough aboot Elvis the pelvis, whit aboot this Travis boy?"

"He was on a cruise with his family, celebrating his grandparents wedding anniversary."

"I've always fancied going on a cruise, but I don't think it'd be dad's cuppa tea. How many years?"

A deep stretch followed my yawn. "How many years for what?"

Sounding impatient, mum grumbled, "How many years have his granny and granda been married?"

"I don't know! It's not something I thought to ask."

"Probably golden."

I looked at her with a combination of bewilderment and annoyance, drained the last of my tea and went to get up.

"Whit age was this Travis?"

"His name was Travis," I snipped. "Not *this* Travis."

"Don't be crabbit! Older than you?"

I shook my head. "Same age."

"Really? Ye made him sound older, och well it disnae matter. Yer only as auld as ye feel," she chuckled.

Not only could I feel my eyes closing but my patience was wearing thin.

"I'm going upstairs to take a bath then I'm going to bed," I said through another yawn. "I'll probably sleep all day."

If only for some peace and quiet!

A look of hurt and disappointment flashed across mum's face as she pushed her chair back.

"Thank you for the tea and toast," I uttered.

"Aye," she huffed, immediately making me feel guilty.

"You know what, with another pot of tea I'm sure I can stay up a bit longer."

"And tell me more aboot yer trip?"

"Only if there's biscuits involved."

5th ~ Pamsy's, Sussex

Wasn't expecting to be here tonight but after mum and I went shopping (vivid pink off the shoulder top to clash with loud green shorts!), Pamsy rang.

"Guess what? I got through standby without being called out. If you leave now, you'll avoid rush hour. Pretty please."

It wasn't the traffic I was concerned about; it was the possibility of missing a call from Ben. As though reading my mind, Pamsy said, "He's not going to ring on a Friday night, or for that matter, over the weekend, which you know is his busiest time."

Much to my surprise, I was out the door in no time, and glad I did because we made it onto the dance floor in TJ's just in time to sing, "Tell it to my heart, tell me I'm the only one, is this really love or just a game."

6th ~ At home

Pamsy was on the phone when I woke up, so I sleepily made my way downstairs.

"So, I can change it?"

She raised a finger gesturing, wait a minute.

"Thanks Ahmed, that's brilliant. Cheers!" Grinning, she hung up.

"What was all that about?"

"I started standby at six and obviously didn't want to get called out, so I rang crewing to see if they needed me for anything later today."

"I thought you finished standby yesterday?"

Looking sheepish, she said, "Don't be mad but I knew if I told you about it, you wouldn't have come down."

"Your crafty little trick worked!"

"And it paid off, because we now have a Zurich night stop."

"*We*?"

"You're coming with me! We'll grab a staff travel ticket at the airport."

At the beach we watched le wave and company windsurfing, then Dickie invited us to theirs for a barbeque, but when we went back to Pamsy's to change, I discovered I'd forgotten my passport. And that's the reason I'm home alone, and not in Switzerland, with my best friend.

7th ~ At home

Taking a break from packing for a trip that might never materialise, to an unknown destination, the art of which I've yet to master.

Pamsy rang and I had to laugh when she said she was doing standby from the pub. She reminded me, how during Air Europe days, I'd *accidentally* knock the phone off the hook until standby was over. The aircraft went tech yesterday and they sat on the ground for hours, after which the flight to Zurich was cancelled, so I guess forgetting my passport was a stroke of luck.

8th ~ Carl's, Surrey

It's been a lovely day here at Carl's and he just reminded me our freedom officially ends six hours from now, when we begin the dreaded standby. I got to meet his brother Connor, who seems a bit full of himself but that might be a cover for his insecurity (I'm reading, "Gifts Differing: Understanding Personality Types," as recommended by Florence).

After dinner, I drove (thanks Carl for being a brilliant help) to Hounslow, where we met up with Lorna, Meryl, Kimberly, Lolly and Sam. It was mobbed in the pub, so after just one drink, we left and went to the flat Kimberly, Lorna and Meryl just rented.

When Carl was in the loo, Lorna cornered me. "What's going on with you two?"

"With Carl?"

"Aye, Carl, who else would I be talking about?"

"Nothing's going on, he offered to let me stay at his during standby, because he lives a lot closer to-"

"Aye, right."

"I'm fond of him but not in that way, he's more like a brother."

Mid eye roll she said, "What's been happening with bad boy?"

"*Ben* has been gone for almost three weeks and I haven't heard a peep."

"I met a gorgeous American guy on my New York trip. Wined and dined me all over the city, amazing. Very successful businessman, I'll see him next time he's in London. Keep your eyes peeled onboard, doll, they're everywhere!"

"Thanks, Lorna, but I'm not interested in meeting anyone else."

9th ~ Carl's, Surrey

After lunch, Carl and I stretched out on towels in the garden. Each time the phone rang, I expected it to be BA, looking for at least one of us.

"I'll wake you, if crewing ring," Carl whispered.

"Sorry," I said, embarrassed that he'd caught me dozing off. "I'm a bit stuffed."

"My mum likes everyone to be well fed."

"Same as mine, is it ok if I ring my mum later?"

"You looking to find out if Ben's been in touch?"

I hoped my cheeks didn't look as crimson as they felt. "How did you know?"

"You've mentioned him a few times, I got the impression you're missing him."

"Sorry, was I going on a bit?"

"No, he's your boyfriend, it's normal to miss him."

"Feels like he's been gone for months."

"Will you go and see him in Spain?"

"That depends on whether or not I can get leave."

"Might be difficult, considering we're so new."

"That's what I'm worried about," I sighed.

"How long have you known him?"

"We met when I was sixteen, he was seventeen."

Carl's eyebrows shot up. "I didn't know it'd been *that* long."

"There's been a lot of on and off," I sighed.

"Is that when you went out with the bloke with the nice wheels?"

"Yeah, Jon."

"What's the deal with him?"

"I don't think he's seeing anyone, if he is he hasn't mentioned it."

Carl laughed. "I meant with you and him."

"Oh, nothing. We're just friends. He's the one who helped me find my car."

"Sounds like a sound bloke," he smiled. "Would you say the same about Ben?"

Slightly taken aback, I stuttered, "Actually, no, I wouldn't."

"Why not?"

"Carl! You're killing me!"

He propped himself up on his elbow and I looked up at him. "Ben and I have a very, what can I say? *Intense.* We have a really intense bond and an extremely passionate relationship."

Carl smirked.

"Not just in that way," I explained. "But there are times when I feel he brings out a side of me that I don't like."

"Like what?" he urged.

I rolled onto my side to face him. "He makes me so furious that I literally lose the plot. I think I need to change-"

"Change what?"

"Everything," I laughed, rolling onto my back.

10th ~ Carl's, Surrey

I woke up thinking about Ben (what's new?) and rang mum.

"Is that ye off on a trip?"

"No, neither of us has been called out yet."

"Well, make sure ye phone, just so we know where ye are."

"I can't stay on the phone long, mum."

"How is Mrs. Flanders?"

"She's been feeding me like there's no tomorrow."

"Make sure ye thank her for letting ye stay and don't forget tae clean up after yerself."

"Of course," I tutted.

"And whit aboot Carl? Has he been behaving himself?"

"It's nice getting to know him better. I should probably go, just in case crewing are trying to get through."

"It was scorching here yesterday, we had dinner in the garden under the wee fairy lights."

"Mum, I can't stay on-"

"I jist hope it lasts."

It was clear mum had no intention of hanging up, so I asked if anyone had been looking for me.

"Aye, Stephen phoned last night. Whit a scream he is, he was on the phone for ages."

How surprising!

"Anyone else?"

"That posh lassie you met on the Bermuda-"

"Annabel. What did she want?"

"I never thought to ask her. What a voice, eh? I told her she should be oan the telly."

I laughed. "Is there anything else before I go?"

"Ben phoned yesterday, at teatime."

My heart leapt into my mouth.

"He said he'll try and phone this weekend."

"Did you tell him I'm on standby and-"

"Listen, I won't keep ye any longer. Tell Carl I'm asking fur 'im and don't forget to thank his ma and da."

"Mum, what else did Ben-"

"And phone if ye get called oot. Cheerio, hen."

11th ~ At home

When the clock struck noon, Carl and I cheered in unison. To celebrate the end of standby, we popped down to the pub, nabbed a picnic table and munched our way through the menu.

12th ~ At home

Snoozed on and off in the garden to the sound of the Pet Shop Boys. I love all the songs on, *Introspective*, but "I Want a Dog," always makes me smile.

By afternoon, I was bored so I started an epic letter to Ben that morphed into a not so short story about a girl who loves a boy (because that's never been done!). It was too maudlin to keep, so I binned it and rang Sarah. The words, "Simon's mates," ought to have been enough to deter me, but the thought of another dreary night at home, watching something along the lines of *Rab C. Nesbitt*, felt depressing.

The *mates* was a guy called Randall (who names their baby Randall?) who insisted I call him Randy. Sporting a dodgy haircut and a shirt that looked slippery, he said, "I've heard a lot about you." From his smarmy expression I knew his preferred response would be a shy giggle, the ever original (not!) "All good I hope?" or anything that falls under the heading of coquettish, so I didn't answer.

140

"Whassamatter, kitten?" He tutted, making my blood curdle. "Cat got your tongue?"

I tried to get Sarah's attention, but she and Simon were in a heated discussion over whose turn it is to feed the cats...tomorrow!

Randy ordered a pint of Carling Black Label and started prattling on about his naff job.

"One pound, twenty, mate," the barman said, precariously placing the pint on the bar. You can call me Randy made a great show of producing a fifty pound note he slid slowly across the bar. Fingering it like it was monopoly money, the barman flashed a sympathetic smile and asked if I wanted a drink.

"Didn't think to ask!" Randy boomed. "You don't want anything, do ya?"

With my sweetest smile and an eyelash flutter, I purred, "Just a small bowl of milk."

13th ~ At home

Stephen invited me to Brighton for the weekend but I'm back on the dreaded standby so that put the kibosh on catching up with what he calls, "Trolley Dolly Tales."

Mum bought me a beautiful ecru skirt I paired with all sorts during our fashion show tonight. I cranked up the acid house and we used the upstairs hallway as the catwalk. Mum cracked me up with her pouty pivot, as she stared into the fake camera. "Work it, baby!" I shouted above the din.

14th ~ At home

Great evening at Florence's, reminiscing about our secretarial days at Fennemores, where, despite our fifteen-year age difference, we bonded over tea and the lofty demands of our horrendous boss who treated us like dirt.

I'll never forget the day Florence brough in an ad she'd carefully cut out of the newspaper. Britannia Airways were looking for cabin crew to be based at Luton Airport. After much encouragement from Florence, I applied and made it through the first two interviews, but didn't get invited to the third round, which, in hindsight, was good because I was much better off with Air Europe at Gatwick (things you don't know at the time when you're crying over getting "rejected!").

It's interesting how friends play different roles in your life and can lead you in a direction you hadn't given any thought to.

15th ~ At home

Massive surprise when I opened the door to find Stephen, grinning from ear to ear. From out behind him, stepped his new beau, whose name is Sebastian. We wasted no time getting acquainted and after dad came home from work, he joined us in the garden, happily doling out beers and laughing at Stephen's jokes.

At The Point we bumped into Sarah. She was on a works night out and was beyond tipsy, as were her co-workers, one of whom invited us to a party in Tinkers Bridge, but Stephen had already made it clear he was ready to leave so we could, "Go and strut our stuff in London."

"It'll take at least an hour to get there," I said, hoping that would deter him.

"I'm well over the limit," Sebastian said. "Do you mind driving?"

"Not at all," I lied.

Being Monday, the drive wasn't too bad, but parking was another story. I've yet to conquer reversing so Sebastian took it upon himself, not to park, but to find someone that could! He managed to flag down an obliging bloke, on his way home from work, who seemed more than happy to assist. With the car perfectly parked, we made our way to Bang, on Charing Cross Road. In the old ballroom in the basement of what was once the Astoria theatre, I danced myself silly to Adamski, without the worry of being pursued by anyone wearing a slippery shirt.

16th ~ At home

Because I didn't get to bed until half five (I came in just as dad was getting up for work!) I didn't wake up until after lunchtime and when the phone rang, I just knew it was Ben. At the sound of his voice, I burst into tears.

"Sorry I haven't had a chance to ring much, babe."

"*Much?*"

"You know what I mean. I missed you a couple of times and it's been nonstop since I got here."

"It's sooooo good to hear from you."

"You sound tired."

"I went clubbing with Stephen and his new guy last night."

"In Brighton?"

"No, London."

"Don't," he groaned. "I'm already homesick. All I do is work around the clock and this bunch are nowhere near as chummy-"

"Guess what?" I said, cutting him off.

"You love me?"

"I do. So much so, in fact, that I booked a flight to come and see you!"

"When?"

"In just over two weeks. Is that ok?"

"I can't take time off but-"

"I know but at least I'll get to see you. Can I stay with you?"

"My accommodation is sparse to say the least, but yeah of course you can. Just send me the details and if I can't get you at the airport, I'll send someone to meet you."

17th ~ At home

The expression, "Out of sight, out of mind," resonates, because whenever Ben is out of touch, I tend to think about him a little less (ok maybe just a smidgen, but that's still less!). But when I hear from him again, I can barely think about anything other than how much I miss him.

Sarah asked if I wanted to go to one of my favourite pubs, The Swan, but better than that was discovering Simon was going out with his mates. I could tell from Sarah's tone on the phone there was something she wanted to share, and lo and behold, the second I picked her up in the taxi she said, "I wanted to wait and tell you in the pub but I'm too excited!"

I gave her a questioning look.

"How would you like to be a bridesmaid?"

"Yes!" I squealed, leaning over to give her a hug. "Simon proposed?"

"Not exactly."

Unsure how to respond, I kept quiet and let her explain. "We had a chat about maybe getting married. One day."

"Oh, I'm sorry, I thought you meant-" I stopped short when I caught the cabbie's knowing expression in the mirror.

"But he will, propose I mean," she continued. "And when he does, will you be a bridesmaid?"

"Of course," I chirped. "I'd love to."

"It's not official yet," she whispered. "So don't tell anyone."

I won't tell a soul, but I might write about it!

18th ~ At home

Loving this streak of great weather, which is perfect for reading in the garden. Enjoying Peter Carey's, *Oscar and Lucinda*, winner of last year's Man Booker Prize, and recommended by Lucy. It's about two gamblers but of course there's so much more to the story than their addiction. It's one of those epic tales that would make a great film.

19th ~ At home

Carl rang with, "A friendly reminder not to forget to pack hangover cures." When I assured him that I won't be requiring anything of that nature, he stressed, "There's just something about Cairo." I told him I'll ring him when I get back, if only to prove him wrong.

"McGarr!" Regardless of how many times Jon has boomed my name through the phone, it still amuses me. "How's tricks? What's on the agenda for this weekend?"

"I'm off to Cairo tomorrow."

"That's one place I have no desire to visit."

"Why not?"

"Not sure, just not somewhere I'd shell out money for."

"I'm not paying to go; I'm getting paid to go."

"Go ahead and rub it in McGarr! I've got bugger all planned and you're off to the pyramids."

"Just stating a fact."

"You are simply horrible," he quipped.

"That's why you like me." No sooner were the words out when I regretted them.

"One of the many reasons." He paused. "I think you know the others."

Without acknowledging his remark, I said, "I'll send you a postcard."

20th ~ LGW – CAI

Flight is chock-a-block and it feels good to have a chance to slip off my shoes. Before me is a cup of Earl Grey and several chocolate biscuits I'll hopefully get to enjoy *en paix*, but that's probably wishful thinking.

Mushy letter from Ben that I tore open right after the postie slid it through the letterbox. In the hall, I heard dad laughing. Pointing to the post that'd landed on the carpet, he said, "I wish I was that enthusiastic aboot the bills. Is Ben awright?"

"Yeah, he sounds good," I said, clutching the letter to my chest.

"I'm sure he's looking forward tae ye getting tae Spain."

"I do believe so," I said, barely able to contain my smile.

"C'mon Tini, time for a wee walk."

Tini came scurrying out of the living room, stopping short at dad's hand command.

"I wish I could teach Ben that," I said, making dad laugh.

"Is yer case ready to go in the car?"

"Not yet. I'm still deciding what to pack."

Dad shook his head and smiled. "C'mon, Tini."

I haven't spoken to Kimberly much since training, so this'll be the perfect opportunity to catch up. We're working with a stunning girl called Melissa who is incredibly confident, and with legs that go on forever and piercing green eyes like Annabel's, how could she be anything but. Cairo is one of Melissa's favourite places and she's promised to show us around. Starting tonight.

23rd ~ CAI – LGW
At home

Two blank diary days tells the story of Cairo, but for now I'm leaving it at that because all I'm fit for is bed.

24th ~ At home

As promised, I rang Carl, hoping he'd be out, but of course he picked up right away.

"Sis! You survived Cairo?"

"Barely," I croaked.

"Told ya!"

"You were spot on!"

"Sorry, what was that?" he teased.

"You weren't kidding, it was…eventful."

"Did you make it to the club close to the crew hotel?"

"I think so, but we went to so many, I lost track."

"Who's we?"

"Kimberly from training and a total man magnet called Melissa, who I'm sure you'd love."

"Oh yeah, what does she look like?"

"Just shy of six feet, best legs and hair ever and really huge, like ridiculously huge…eyes!"

"Yeah, thought so," he chuckled.

"But lovely all the same, and great fun."

"What nationality was the guy you snogged?" He said, catching me totally off guard.

"How did you know?"

"Busted!" He yelled.

"Shit, I didn't mean to give that away. Ugh, I don't know how I'm going to spill the beans to Ben."

"You're not seriously considering telling him, are you?"

"You don't think I should?"

"Nah."

"That doesn't seem right, but it was just one of those trips."

"Oh, I know, I know… you were in a club, enjoying yourself. You drank a bit too much. Some good-looking bloke asked you to dance, and you ended up snogging."

"Shit, Carl! Were you there?"

"So that's what happened, eh?"

On the first night.

25th ~ At home

I was in the bath when the phone rang and counted nineteen rings before it stopped, only to start again, which is when I shot out of the bath, wrapped the towel around me, and dashed downstairs, my sopping wet hair leaving a trail.

"Babe," Ben breathed.

"Ah, it's you. I was in the bath."

"Don't tell me that, I'm surrounded by people."

I laughed. "How are you?"

"In dire need of you."

"I'll be there really soon," I cooed.

"Not soon enough, babe." He sounded weary. "I wanted to let you know there's been a few changes."

"To what?" Shivering, I reached for my uniform jacket, hanging under the stairs.

"My location. I'm in France."

"For the day?"

"No, I'm working here now."

"But I booked a flight to Spain!"

"I know, don't worry, I'll sort something out-"

"How?"

"I don't know yet, just let me-"

"There's no time to-"

"Calm down," he said in a tone that's been known to knock me over the edge.

"Don't tell me to calm down!" I yelled, squirming so much the towel fell to the ground.

"I already told you I'll sort something out." He sounded like he was explaining something to a child. I grabbed the towel, inhaled deeply and waited for him to continue. "Anyway, how was Cairo?"

Feeling the bloom in my cheeks, I stuttered, "It was ehm, good."

"Just good?"

"It was hot. You know how much I dislike extreme heat."

"Did you enjoy *anything* about it? Did you see the pyramids?"

"Uh-huh, and I had fun with some of the girls on my crew."

"Just the girls?"

"Yep," I chirped. "Just the girls."

And the guy from Sweden.

26th ~ LHR – CDG – LHR
Kimberly, Lorna, Meryl's flat, Richmond upon Thames

Lorna is a born storyteller, Kimberly's sarcasm knows no bounds, and Meryl's innocence ties it all together, which is why I am literally sore from laughing.

27th ~ Pamsy's, Sussex

There something wonderfully uplifting about singing in the car, when the sun's out, and you're heading to see your best friend.

Saturday night in Sussex was dance free, because Pamsy's dad fired up the barbeque and we decided to stay in. Much later tonight, her mum came outside. "Just checking to see if you two are alright."

"We're fine, thanks, mum. Just having a good ole natter."

She handed each of us a blanket and in unison, we cooed, "Aw, thanks."

"You can stay out longer, now. Dad and I are off to bed so just make sure you shut off all the lights."

"Will do, night mum."

"Night you two."

Pamsy shook out her blanket and peered behind her to make sure her mum was inside.

"So, this Swedish guy you snogged, what was his name?"

"Melvin," I said, wrapping the blanket around my shoulders.

"Are you pulling my leg?"

"No, that was his name."

"Was he drop-dead?"

"Not in the least, he was a bit on the pudgy side."

"Now you *are* pulling my leg."

"I'm not. He wasn't what I'd usually go for but there was just something about him."

"Could he dance?"

"Oh, yeah."

"Then there you go, that was the attraction."

"Either that or I was ovulating!"

"Only you," Pamsy chuckled. "Keep going."

"We just kind of started dancing together, then we got a drink at the bar, and another, and I knew I should probably stop, but the music was throbbing. It was sweltering. We were in Egypt!"

"The whole atmosphere thing, love it."

"We went outside to the patio area, chatted for yonks-"

Smacking my knee, Pamsy said, "I can't stand it, fast forward to the kiss. Puhleez!"

"Ok so fast forward about two hours."

"Blimey!"

"We were outside, on sort of a bean bag thing, not sure what else to call it. Melvin said something funny, and I laughed and threw my head back."

"Floozy," she laughed.

"I closed my eyes for a split second and when I opened them his face was right here." I held my palm up to my face. "With his brown eyes-"

"Hmm, brown, not your usual."

"Nor were they anything special, but there was something about the way he moved his hands when he spoke, that did something to me, and when he cupped my face-"

"Wait, what?"

"Smooth or what, huh? It was quite the moment. His hands slid to the back of my neck-"

"And then you kissed," she sighed.

"And then we kissed."

28th ~ LGW – ATH
Hotel Athenaeum, Athens, Greece

Spent the morning on the beach with Pamsy, watching the windsurfers, all of whom we know, including le wave, who came over to say hello. His neoprene wetsuit left nothing to the imagination and when he was back in the water, Pamsy burst out laughing. "You are sooo bad!"

"I don't know what's gotten into me, but I actually still find him quite dishy."

"He obviously feels the same, I mean, that was a major flirting fest if ever I saw one."

"That bad?"

"Oh yes it was, very, very, bad," she said in one of her many, amusing voices. "Now you've got me in a tither because if I remember correctly, you told me le wave is rather, ehm, gifted, in a certain department."

"Stop it," I shrieked. "You're making me blush."

"You're the one who said it!"

"I did. And it's true. He's incredibly *gifted*."

And now I'm back in Greece, not only with Kimberly, but also Annabel, who looked positively crestfallen when I told her I'm going to Spain, I mean, France, to visit Ben.

29th ~ Hotel Athenaeum, Athens, Greece

Oh dear, another late night with scribbly writing. This one I'm blaming on Kimberly. Annabel. And Ouzo!

30th ~ ATH – LGW

Presently in the back row of the TriStar with my staples, longing for bed. We left Athens when we should have been going to bed but fortunately the flight isn't as busy as the outbound, which is good because it's been a zero-sleep trip.

When the phone shrilled, I lazily reached for it.

"Rise and shine, Miss M!"

"What time is it?"

"Time to get up! Open your door!" Annabel demanded. "I'm coming to your room."

I crawled out of bed and attempted to open the curtains, but the light was blinding, so I left them shut.

"You look *ghastly*," were Annabel's first words.

"Thanks, friend," I said, sorely tempted to slither back under the covers.

"I've already seen Kimberly and believe it or not, she looks even worse than you. She positively refuses to leave her room, so we shan't be seeing her today."

"How come you're so full of beans?"

"My new chap just rang. From Paris."

"Français?"

"Goodness, no! Mummy would disown me. He's there on business."

"Do tell," I said, sitting on the bed.

"He's *utterly* winsome," she enthused, smacking her plump lips together. "And he's desperately in love with me," she said, tossing her mane from side to side.

"You have the best hair."

"Rat's nest," she whistled, with another toss.

"How did you meet?"

"He rows with my brother, has done for years. Speaking of…you must join us at Henley for the sesquicentenary."

"The what?"

"Miss M!" she shrieked, placing her hands on her not so slender hips. "Go and splash some water on your face. You need to wake up!"

"Annabel," I groaned, heading for the bathroom, "You are by far, thee bossiest person. Ever!"

Leaning over the sink proved a bad idea so I cupped my hand and filled it with water.

"It's the one hundred and fiftieth anniversary," Annabel called out. "Of the Henley Regatta."

"I'd love to go," I said, patting my face dry with the super soft towel.

"And you shall! Where's your Filofax?"

"Beside the bed," I said, coming out of the bathroom.

"Gosh, this thing is *tatty*; you must get a proper one. I'll pop some dates in it, ya?"

"Yeah, go ahead."

"Now, hurry! Get dressed! We're meeting up with some chums of my cousin, Willoughby."

"To do what?" I groaned, opening the wardrobe.

Scribbling furiously, she said, "We're being escorted on a guided tour of the city. With two of Athens' most eligible bachelors."

31st ~ At home

First person I rang, when I should've been catching up with my zz's, was nana.

"Hullo hen, how are ye getting on?"

"Fine, I just got back from Athens. Two of my friends were on the trip, which is always nice."

"I'm sure that makes it easier being away. Was it warm?"

"It was scorching but we still managed to get out and about."

"That sounds smashing, what did ye see?"

"Quite a lot, all off the beaten track. The guys who arranged the tour did a brilliant job. Plus, they were quite charming."

"Uff, don't be telling me yer interested in Greek boys noo."

"Actually, they were English."

"Och, I don't know which is worse."

"Nana!"

"Aye, well I'm still getting used to ye having an English boyfriend."

"I'm going to see him soon."

"Yer mammy mentioned that. Maybe ye'll meet a nice Scottish boy in Spain."

"Actually, Ben's working in France now."

"Ooft, I canny bear the thought of you with a Frenchman."

Oh, nana!

I was much too comfortable to get up and was about to ring Pamsy when the phone rang.

"McGarr, how the devil are you?"

"It's Wednesday afternoon, aren't you at work?"

"I am, but I just heard The Proclaimers on the radio, and they always remind me of you."

"Will there ever come a time when you don't associate me with gawky Scottish guys?"

"Never!"

JUNE

1st ~ At home

Mum and I are still sobbing after seeing, *Beaches*, with Bette Midler and Barbara Hershey. I was holding it together quite well, until the final scene, then it was one giant gulp after another, with not a dry eye in the house.

2nd ~ Flight to Girona, Spain

It's 4.25am (on the 3rd) and we're on the tarmac, awaiting clearance. Ironically, we've been sitting on the ground longer than the actual flight time. The crew announcement mentioned two words that cover a multitude of possibilities: *Technical issue.*

I'm wedged between two burly guys I spotted stumbling through the terminal. That was hours ago, and the booze they consumed is seeping through their shell suits. One of them is already out cold and hopefully, after the other one follows suit, his head will loll towards the window, and not me.

3rd ~ Ben's, Cote d'Azur

It's the most beautiful evening, with beaucoup d'étoiles, sparkling across the sky and the sort of balmy breeze that calls for bare shoulders.

I knew I was missing Ben big time but until I laid eyes on him this afternoon, I didn't realise just how much. To say our reunion was spectacular gives no credit to the word.

Landing hours after the scheduled ETA, I was relieved not to have to find my own way here. One of the reps Ben works with was waiting to meet her guests for the week (ah, the beauty of a package holiday!) and I boarded the coach with them. Once we crossed the border into France, I desperately wanted to stay awake and take in the sights, but sadly I conked out.

When we arrived at what is essentially a campground, I scanned the crowd, but no Ben. After gathering up my stuff, I stumbled off the coach and was about to grab my suitcase when I felt a hand circle my waist. My gorgeous, sun kissed boyfriend's smile matched mine and we held each other's gaze for what felt like ages, but I imagine it was only seconds before he said, "Come here, you," and pulled me tight to him. Breathing him in, I thought I might burst with happiness.

Ben wasn't kidding when he said the accommodation is sparse. It's basically a caravan, but he doesn't have to share with anyone (except me!) so before he was due back at work, we made the most of every precious second.

4th ~ Ben's, Cote d'Azur

Sunday is typically one of Ben's busiest workdays, but he managed to wrangle a few hours off. In Canet-en-Roussillon, with the sun warming my back, we gorged on the flakiest, most delicious pain au chocolat, and all was well until I asked the surly waiter for, "Du thé."

Raking his fingers through his hair, he made a disdainful sound. "Thé? Avec croissants?"

"S'il vous plaît," I said sheepishly, wishing I knew how to explain in French that I'm allergic to coffee. Not that he'd care. Reaching across the table, I rubbed my buttery fingers over Ben's. To that point, he hadn't said much, and as usual my mouth got ahead of me.

"What are you thinking about?"

"Just stuff," he shrugged.

"Like what?"

"It's been suggested I go from here to Italy."

"But you hated it there!"

"I didn't *hate* it."

"I'm only repeating what I heard," I scowled. "You're not thinking of saying yes...are you?"

He nodded.

"Yes, you're thinking about it or yes, you've already agreed to go back?"

"The latter."

I blew out a long, steady stream of air.

"Now what?" His tone was so insolent, I almost got up and left, but I know that type of behaviour never leads to anything good, so I took a deep breath, before I said, "It's just a bit of a shock, that's all."

The waiter returned and placed a cup of frothy tea in front of me.

"Merci, monsieur," I croaked, and waited until he was gone before I said, "I've had my heart set on you coming home and maybe getting a place together, like we've talked about. A lot."

"There'll be a break in between, I can come home then."

"After this, I don't have any more leave. I don't know if you understand that."

"You're overreacting babe, you need to calm down."

Feeling the opposite of calm, I blurted, "You know my job takes me away for days, sometimes weeks at a time-"

"Oh yes, I'm perfectly aware of that. And you know *I* work abroad for months at a time. Right?"

"I'm perfectly aware of that," I hissed, mimicking Ben's tone. "I just don't know how we can have a relationship with me constantly flying and you living outside the UK."

"So, your job is more important than mine?" He sounded irate so I busied myself with the tea and nibbled on the last of the croissant, that suddenly tasted like cardboard. In the lull that ensued, the acid in my stomach swirled so much, I felt sick, and when I could no longer bear the silence, I kept my tone pert, and said, "We can work this out, right?"

With his eyes downcast, Ben shrugged. "I don't know."

5th ~ Ben's, Cote d'Azur

After Ben went back to work yesterday, I did what I do best; Eat. And when Ben popped in and out throughout the day, I acted as though nothing major had shifted. But it has. I can feel it. I want to be wrong. I desperately want to be wrong but his tone, his certainty that this is what he wants. It's all there, just like it is for me when it comes to what I do.

Sunbathing, with my headphones on, I sensed a passing cloud and opened my eyes to find Ben looming over me, so I clicked off the cassette.

"Whatcha listening to?" His tone was cheery, and his smile was enough to make me want to leap into his arms and kiss him forever.

"Ancient Heart."

"Tanita Tikaram?"

"Uh-huh," I uttered, re-adjusting my boob tube. "Are you done for the day?"

"Yeah, until tonight, and if you want, you can come with me. There's an excursion, to a restaurant."

"Ooh, nourriture."

"Heaps of it," he laughed. "I'll be performing a few skits after dinner, with some of the other reps. You still wanna come?"

"Absolutement!"

6th ~ Ben's, Cote d'Azur

The excursion wrapped up in the early hours of this morning, on a nearby beach, after which a dozen or so of us stumbled merrily back to the campsite, singing Kylie's, "Hand on Your Heart."

Ben wasted no time jumping into bed, where I quickly lost him to the land of nod. I crawled in beside him, but the room was spinning from too much sangria and jumbled thoughts about what it means for us if he goes from here to Italy, so I placed my hand on his smooth chest, hoping the rise and fall would lull me to sleep.

Next thing I knew, my eyes were opening to the sound of raised voices, coming from right outside the caravan. I expected Ben to wake up, but he didn't stir, so I got up, slipped my dress on and went to see what the hullabaloo was about.

I was surprised to see a girl about my age, sitting at the plastic table, beer bottle in hand, but more surprising was the sight of another girl, with flaming red hair, flat out on the ground.

"Are you two ok?" I said, inching closer.

In a broad Glaswegian accent, the girl at the table shouted, "Who're you?"

"I should you be asking you that!" I retorted, sounding much bolder than I felt.

"Where did you come fae?" slurred the redhead.

"Next door," I said, pointing to the caravan. "What's all the racket about?"

"Racket? Ye accusin' us a makin' a racket?" The blonde attempted to stand up. She was doing ok until she stumbled against the plastic table, toppled forward and landed on top of her friend. In between piercing shrieks of joy at being reunited, they finished what was left of the beer. From a nearby tent came a disgruntled, "Keep it down!" which only had the opposite effect. When the redhead rolled from under her friend, I reached out my hand to help her up.

"Whit's yer name?" she slurred, looking up at me.

"Karen. What's yours?"

"Am wee ish a bell."

"Easy does it, Isobel," I said, helping her into the seat.

I turned to help her friend, but she was already on her feet. "Urr ye here by yersel?"

"No, I'm with my boyfriend. He's one of the reps." I pointed to where Ben was hopefully deep in slumber. "I'm just visiting."

"Och, that's nice, sure it is ish a bell?"

"Brilliant," Isobel nodded, looking like she might throw up. Eager to get away, I pointed to two overstuffed canvas holdalls. "Can I give you a hand taking them inside?"

"Naw, it's awright," Isobel said, waving nails that matched her hair. "We'll sort them oot the morra."

"Alright, well I hope you get settled in ok," I said, slowly inching away.

With half her bulky frame dangling over the side of the chair, blondie shouted, "A like yer hair, Kathy."

"Thanks, but can you do me a favour and try and keep the noise down? Ben, my boyfriend, has to be up early, for work."

"Ben's the wee rat Michael Jackson sings aboot," chirped the blonde. Jabbing the air, swaying, she said, "D'ye know the song I'm talkin' aboot Kathy?"

"I do," I said, trying not to laugh.

Waving her hand in my general direction, she sang, "And you ma friend will see, you've got a friend in me e."

"C'mon you, it's time fur yer bed," Isobel said, pulling her friend by the sleeve.

"Goodnight," I whispered, hoping they'd get the message.

"Cheerio Kathy," they roared.

7th ~ Ben's, Cote d'Azur

"Hey sleepy head," Ben said, gently brushing my hair off my face.

"What time is it?"

"Just after two."

"In the afternoon?" I asked, through a deep yawn.

"Eh, yeah," he nodded.

"Sorry, I'm all mixed up. What are you doing back?"

"I'm done."

"For the day?"

"Yup," he grinned, slowly peeling back the bed sheet.

"Fantastique," I breathed, as his eyes trailed the length of my body.

Late this afternoon we caught the bus to Perpignan. With each passing mile I sensed a change in Ben, that I thought I'd detected earlier in the day, but sex tends to cloud my judgement (that must surely qualify as the understatement of the century!) so I thought I might be way off the mark.

I had just popped a generous spoonful of crema catalana in my mouth, when Ben looked at me and said, "I've been thinking about where we're going."

"You mean after lunch?"

He shook his head in a way my stomach instinctively reacts to. Filled with a dreaded sense that my appetite wasn't the only thing about to diminish, I shoved another spoonful of dessert into my mouth, as Ben said, "I just don't see a future for us."

Feeling woozy, I gripped the table, and shut my eyes, but the tears still trickled down my cheeks.

8th ~ Ben's, Cote d'Azur

I awoke to, *I'll be back late tonight. Hope we can talk then x* scribbled on an envelope, on Ben's crumpled pillow.

Shuffling about senselessly, it felt like the caravan walls were caving in. I thought about leaving, but I don't know where the closest airport is or how I'd go about getting there. I scoffed the rest of the wagon wheels I'd brought for Ben and at the bottom of my bag, I found a crushed packet of prawn cocktail crisps, that I ate, crumb by crumb (not my finest moment). Eyeing a packet of French biscuits, the voice in my head got so loud I could no longer ignore it.

Stop wallowing!

Get dressed!

Go to the beach!

And maybe buy some wine!

I did three of the four things, before finding my way to the beach. The vivid blue sky was smattered with defiant puffy clouds that gave not one flying you know what for how I was feeling.

Trudging through the hot sand, looking for a quiet spot to host my pity party, I heard, "Kathy!"

It was a few steps before I made the connection between the accent and the name and when I turned, Isobel was jogging towards me.

"Urr you deef?" She chuckled.

I couldn't help but smile. "Sorry, I was miles away."

"Where's yer boyfriend? By the way, sorry aboot the other night, ooft, a don't know whit happened. Lorraine said I was steamboats."

"Lorraine was right," I laughed. "Is she with you?"

"Aye, she's havin' a wee kip behind that big umbrella. Sum day sure it is. Where's yer boyfriend?"

"He's still at work."

"Come and sit wi us?"

I was about to say no but there was something about Isobel's open expression that told me I should say yes.

I pulled the wine out of my canvas bag and Lorraine wasted no time filling the plastic cups she and Isobel had the forethought to pack. When the bottle was empty, Lorraine produced another, it is France, after all.

I didn't plan on spilling the beans about my personal life to two people I barely know but plied with plonk and a need to digest what's been going on, I poured my heart out to them.

By early evening, I admitted defeat in the drinking department and used the dip in temperature as an excuse to leave. Walking in a not so straight line, I headed back to the caravan, hoping to find Ben waiting for me, with open arms. And a change of heart.

With all hopes dashed, I fell on top of the bed and only woke up a short while ago. It's almost midnight and still no sign of Ben. I can hear Isobel and Lorraine's laughter, over the sound of tinny techno music, and tinkling glass. Surely, they're not still drinking. I might just pop over and see.

9th ~ Girona Airport, Spain

Ben returned in the early hours of the morning to find me slightly worse for wear, after an extraordinary amount of Pernod and black, with Isobel and Lorraine. Without saying a word, he went inside, and when I finally called it a night, he was out for the count.

When the alarm buzzed, the first thing I felt was regret, swiftly followed by an overwhelming sense of sorrow that this was it. Without speaking, Ben and I skirted around one another getting dressed and when it came time to leave, the sight of him carrying my suitcase outside was one I'll never forget.

Snapping into work mode, Ben rounded up the guests and got everyone onto the coach, without a hitch. I sat at the front and whenever Ben made an announcement, he'd sit beside me, otherwise, he was up and down the aisle, answering questions, as we headed to the day's excursion, a water park, in Spain.

Winding through one bucolic village after another, I made a promise to return, under happier circumstances, and at the water park, wearing a high cut swimsuit, I lost all inhibition and experienced every slide, including the tallest one, with so many twists and turns that I screamed all the way down.

Worn out from the day's activities, there was only the odd murmur on the dimly lit coach. We sat up front again, and when the driver turned and said we were ten minutes from the airport, Ben grabbed my hand and squeezed it tight.

While the driver retrieved my suitcase, Ben reached for me, and from inside the coach, a loud cheer went up when we kissed goodbye. With my heart thumping against Ben's, the little voice in my head urged me to *keep it together*.

Oblivious of the fact they were witnessing the end of our relationship, the amiable crowd tapped on the windows, blew kisses and mouthed words to the effect of *safe flight*. When the coach pulled away, the horn beeped, but I never looked back.

10th ~ At home

The jovial sound of laughter woke me and the sound of granda's voice gave me a reason to get up. In the kitchen, with mum and dad, granda sat with his back to me.

"Hello, granda," I said, planting a kiss on his ruddy cheek.

"Och, it's yerself, hen," he said turning. "Yer looking braw."

"As are you. You never age!"

"That's me eighty-four next month," he stated proudly.

"What's your secret?"

"The odd wee goldie," he chuckled, gesturing to the empty Glencairn in front of him.

The rest of the day was spent in and out of the garden and it took everything I had to hold it together, especially when dad asked how Ben was and if I'd had a nice time. I felt mum's eyes on me and when she said they were going out for dinner, I breathed a sigh of relief.

No sooner were the three of them out the door when I collapsed on my bed and let the dam burst. The reality of life without Ben is hitting hard, and I'm filled with so many conflicting emotions, none of which I know what to do with.

11th ~ LHR – PIT
Somewhere over the East Coast of America

"So, yer saying ye can get a wee bevy on the plane?" Granda asked, with a look of surprise.

"Uh-huh, we carry several brands of whisky, not that I've tasted any of them," I tried to wink but for whatever reason, I can't.

"How would ye like to go on a flight wi Karen's sometime, Jimmy?" mum said.

"It'd be my first time oan a plane," Granda marvelled. "Imagine that at my age."

"I'd spoil you rotten, granda."

Granda released a throaty chuckle. "Och, yer sum lassie. And ye look bonny in the uniform."

"Thank you. Is there anything you'd like me to bring back from America?"

"Ye'd do that fur me?"

"Of course. What would you like?"

"Wit aboot a cap? You know, the ones I mean?"

"A baseball cap?"

"Aye, that's the one."

The girl I sat next to in the briefing room talked ten to the dozen, and when boarding was announced, she still hadn't come up for air. Her name is Frankie.

163

12th ~ Pittsburgh, Pennsylvania

Frankie said she'd meet me at the room party but when I shut the door, the gloomy feeling washed over me. After my suitcase showed up (CSD said to tip $1) I took a shower, crawled into bed and turned on the tv, but with so many ads, I soon lost interest and shut it off. I thought about getting up and writing by the window but when I pulled back the heavy curtain, the view was a dimly lit courtyard, filled with dumpsters that I was still staring at when the phone rang.

"Where are you?" Frankie asked.

"I think you know," I joked.

"Hurry up, we're leaving in two tics!"

The bed was taunting me but the thought of empty hours with nothing to think about but Ben, was not, so I quickly got dressed and made my way up to the CSD's room.

Frankie greeted me with a glass of wine, filled to the brim. Foisting it towards my mouth, she said, "Knock it back, we're leaving. What took you so long? I'm so glad I rang, otherwise you'd have missed going out. Isn't this your first time here? Cora suggested we go to the place next door, just to get the night going, but after that I think we should take a cruise on the river. At least I think it's a river, is it a river? Gosh, I'm not sure but it's pretty and I think it'd be a lovely way for you to see the buildings, especially at night." With no idea how to respond I guzzled down the wine.

Cora's suggestion was a sports bar, with giant tv's dominating every square inch of wall space. Each screen showed a different sport, none of which I was interested in, but I enjoyed people watching. For about the first four minutes. Frankie asked if anyone was interested in joining us, but with the Monday night special on drinks and nosh there was zero impetus for anyone to leave. Out on the street, I shook my head when Frankie asked if I have a boyfriend.

"I do," she chirped. "His name is Rutherford, but everyone calls him Ruts. He works in finance in the City, and when I say *the City,* you know what I mean, don't you? It's funny how people assume it's-"

Stopping mid step to get her attention, I said, "Can do you me a favour?"

164

Frankie cocked her blonde bob in question and her eyes widened.

"Can you ask one question at a time?"

"Oopsie daisy," she chuckled. "Why don't you have a boyfriend?"

"It's a long story."

"There's a lush wine bar coming up in about two secs, save it for there."

13th ~ PIT – LHR
35,000 feet

There's not enough time on this crew rest to:

a. Finish this Hero sandwich, named after columnist Clementine Paddleworth (now, there's a name!) who described it as, "a sandwich so large, you had to be a hero to eat it!"

b. Explain how Frankie and I met up with our crew again last night, but suffice to say, we had a fantastic time in the city of bridges. I'm still laughing about Frankie's advice to "Get back on the bike as soon as possible!"

Had I not promised granda a baseball cap, I'd have been happy to remain in hibernation, recuperating with tons of room service and trash tv but that wasn't an option. Besides, I managed to find a few boxes of Chips Ahoy! so all was not lost.

14th ~ At home

After a few restless hours in bed, I found mum and granda in the garden.

"Here she is," granda said, starting to ease out of the chair.

"No need to get up," I said, kissing his rosy cheek.

While granda fiddled with the tape on the box, mum tried prying details of the trip out of me.

"Would ye look at this!" With a look of sheer delight, granda held a cap in each hand.

"Try the American flag one on first, Jimmy," mum suggested.

"The other one is the Philadelphia Eagles," I said. "They're an American football team."

"The ones wi aw the padding?"

"Yeah, unlike when you played football, eh granda?"

"Skint knees and black eyes," he chortled. "And that wiz afore the match!" Twisting each cap for a better look, granda said, "I cannae believe ye've been all the way tae America and back."

"My feet say otherwise! Do you want me to show you how some of the American boys wear theirs?"

"Oh, aye," granda nodded enthusiastically.

Placing the cap on his still thick hair, I spun it backwards, and in a poor attempt at an American accent, I shouted, "Gimme some attitude, Jimmy!"

Clutching the elbow patches on his brown woollen cardigan, granda jutted out his chin and tilted his head in a way that left mum and me roaring with laughter.

15th ~ At home

Spent the afternoon with dad and granda, two peas in a pod, especially when it comes to talking. And whisky. When the pair of them get going there's no stopping them. From the way they reminisce you'd never know how impoverished life was. They didn't have much but when it comes to a sense of humour, they're rich beyond belief.

When mum let it slip, that Ben rang in my absence, I just nodded and didn't let on we're no longer together, but inwardly I felt everything churning in sadness. In my heart, I know it's over, but I'm finding it hard to acknowledge, because I still love him and wish he was still mine.

Stephen and Sebastian are on their way over. Stephen wants to go clubbing in London, which is honestly the last thing I feel like doing, but he claims, "Dancing the hurt away," will help.

16th ~ At home

Rolled in from Heaven (the club, not the other one!) after five and passed dad on the stairs!

With all the dancing last night (Sylvester's, "You Make Me Feel," is one of the best dance songs ever) and the little amount I've eaten recently, the scale finally shifted (YES!) and when I zipped up my shorts, there was a noticeable gap. Hold up, delicate wrists, I'm coming for you!

17th ~ LGW – BDA
Hamilton Princess, Bermuda

Good flight, good crew, and we wasted no time heading into town for the obligatory Dark 'n' Stormy. Docked in port was a Cunard ship that made me think of Travis.

"Penny for your thoughts," said Graeme, who I'm only just getting to know because he worked the A position. On the crew bus, he kept poking his head into my chat with Lyndsey, whose easy manner was perfect to work alongside. Our Purser, Fiona, is the spitting image of Emma Thompson, so much so that several passengers commented on the resemblance.

After a lovely evening in town, Fiona invited everyone to her room for a nightcap. Perched on the armrest of Lyndsey's chair, with the thin curtains billowing around me like skirts, the cocktails went down a treat.

When I got up to leave, Graeme sidled up beside me and offered to walk me to my room. I didn't invite him in, but we arranged to meet for breakfast, four hours from now.

18th ~ BDA – TPA – BDA
Hamilton Princess, Bermuda

While I was on the phone, there was a knock at the door, so I told Lyndsey I'd meet her in the lobby and hung up.

Grinning widely, Graeme said, "Morning," came inside and made himself comfortable in the wing back chair. With the balcony doors open, and the slanted light on him, I must admit, he looked pretty good. I excused myself and went into the bathroom, but it was only to add the final touches (ha, like I'm that kinda girl!) so I didn't bother to shut the door. Conscious of the fact that Lou Lou isn't for everyone, I sprayed a small amount behind each ear.

"Karen, are you seeing anyone?"

"Nope," I said, pulling my new Mason Pearson brush through my hair (the definition of *splurge*, but I love it!).

"Why not?"

"Bee coz I'm not," I said, unbuttoning a couple of extra buttons on my cheesecloth shirt, before mouthing, "*Single*," in the mirror.

After breakfast in town, the three of us meandered back to the hotel. Scooters galore, bougainvillea bursting from endless planters and no shortage of handsome men in Bermuda shorts and knee length socks.

Lyndsey wanted to rest before the shuttle and when Graeme asked what I was doing, I said I was going to the pool. *To read.* My book bag has been the butt of many a crew joke, but I'd be lost without it.

Ready to sink my teeth back into the happenings at 28 Barbary Lane, I opened, *Tales of the City*, and waited, and waited, and waited, for Graeme to stop talking. After reading the same line over and over, I finally gave up and jumped in the pool (a bold move, made in an act of desperation for a few moments of peace).

When the crew taking the flight back to LGW boarded, I was thrilled to hear Frankie trill my name. "I've been keeping a low profile," she groaned, tapping her temple. Clapping eyes on Graeme she cooed, "Now *that* is perfect bike material."

In Emma's room (Fiona has been renamed) we mixed cocktail after cocktail, and when I left with Graeme, Lyndsey bit her fist in a theatrical way that made me laugh.

Crossing the pool area, Graeme slipped his hand into mine, and in his room (I know, I know but hey, I'm single and we're in Bermuda!) there was much kissing, before he walked me back to my room.

19th ~ Hamilton Princess, Bermuda

On the phone with Lyndsey, a mere few hours after shutting off the light, she said, "Soooo?"

"Marathon kissing sesh in his room. Not too shabby!"

"Good for you," she giggled.

After a day on the beach, it was dinner for sixteen! Graeme, Lyndsey and I weren't the last to leave, which probably translates to hangover remedies being shared around the pool tomorrow.

In my room (oopsie!) Graeme helped me check for sunburn, and after I did the same for him (it was only fair!) we enjoyed a Bailey's nightcap on the balcony.

20th ~ BDA – LGW

After my first-time snorkelling (parrot and cocoa damselfish were my favourite) Graeme and I rented lilo's and watched streaky clouds sail through swaths of blue sky. Keen to catch the last of the rays, we decided to skip taking the ferry, and on the bus, he asked if I'd like to get together sometime, at home.

"Ehm," I started to sputter. With the windows open, the sound of the whipping wind gave me a chance to ponder, allowing Graeme to continue.

"Why don't I give you my number? That way you'll have it, if you fancy meeting up."

21st ~ At home

Landed to a drizzly, grey morning (so much for summer solstice!) at LGW, that only seemed to worsen as the crew transport crawled to LHR. From across the aisle (I sat with Lyndsey) Graeme talked nonstop and at the crew car park he pressed a piece of paper, with his address and phone number into my hand.

"Give me a ring," he said, gently kissing my lips.

No kissing in uniform!

Dad's knowledge of the places I visit never ceases to amaze me and tonight over dinner (mum went to Scotland, with granda) I learned that Bermuda's pink sand is due to pulverized coral, and shells. There followed a history lesson, but my mind kept wandering to Ben, so I didn't retain much.

Sam rang and I'm thrilled to hear he's seeing Xavier, who I met at Air Europe. Xavier is fabulously French, speaks five languages, and has a wicked sense of humour. Sam asked what's happening in my love life, but dad was milling about so the details of my unexpected trip fling will have to wait.

22nd ~ At home

Seems I can't even watch the news without being reminded of Ben. Story about the hordes of people who got arrested for trying to enter the grounds of Stonehenge before dawn, to celebrate the solstice. Made me think back to April, when we made a brief stop there.

23rd ~ Pamsy's, Sussex

While I was rinsing out my breakfast dishes, I jumped when I heard a noise outside the kitchen door.

"Hello?" I called out, my stomach knotting in fear.

"Karen!" Janice said, looking surprised to see me. "Sorry, I never knew you were home."

In mum's absence, Janice has been coming over to feed Tini. The extra food explains why he's been sleeping more than usual!

When Janice asked how my time was with Ben, I burst into tears and told her we split up.

"Seeing you reminds me of when we'd babysit the girls," I sniffed, my mind wandering to happier times. "We used to let the girls stay up late," I said, trying to lighten the mood.

"Aye, I know," Janice smiled. "They still talk about it. What did your mum say about you and Ben splitting up?"

"I haven't told her yet."

For most of the drive here, I cried those horrible noisy sobs that leave you feeling listless but when Pamsy came out to meet me, I perked up. Surrounded by friends tonight, at The Lamb, in Hooe,

Pamsy looked the picture of happiness, as we celebrated her 23rd Birthday.

24th ~ Pamsy's, Sussex

Gorgeous sunny afternoon on the beach, where Pamsy mentioned more than once how much she likes le wave's mate, Ollie. Her interest in Ollie has been ongoing, so after we came back to the house, I rang him. "Hi Ollie," I chirped confidently. "I just wanted to let you know it's Pamsy's birthday weekend, so maybe we'll see you in TJ's tonight."

I hated how disappointed she looked when he didn't show up.

25th ~ At home

Continued Pamsy's birthday celebrations lounging in the garden, accompanied by tea, cakes, tea cakes, tea and cakes.

Left just after one am and it's now almost four, so I should probably go to bed before dad gets up for work.

26th ~ LHR – CDG – LHR
Excelsior Hotel, Heathrow

Today I went to Paris and tonight, I re-read Ben's letter that arrived today. Every word tugs at my heart, but I won't respond. Not after the way he treated me.

27th ~ LHR – CDG – LHR
Excelsior Hotel, Heathrow

After another jaunt to the city of light, on a plane filled with impeccably dressed passengers, Carl arrived at the hotel, and suddenly it was party time. Fresh from a trip romance with a girl he really likes ("no name," he insisted) he was more jocular than usual.

Stephen was next to show up, and the three of us drove to Richmond. In a trendy wine bar on the High Street (so many to choose from!) we met Sam, Lolly, and a bunch of her friends and family. Wearing a black sheath dress, with a paisley scarf tied in her hair, Lolly was the belle of the ball, as we celebrated her 21st.

Stephen and I accompanied Sam to his flat in Kensington (only Sam changes clothes twice in one evening!). Underground parking, with security gates, in a leafy setting. Stephen joked that he hoped we'd be invited back and that he wouldn't mind, "Padding about here every morning in my housecoat and slippers."

At The Fridge in Brixton, we met up with Xavier, and not once, did any of us sit down!

28th ~ LHR – CDG – LHR
Excelsior Hotel, Heathrow

Call came two hours after I crashed on top of the bed, and I stumbled around the room, getting dressed, but Stephen never stirred, not even when I blasted the hairdryer.

With the duty day over, I crept back into the dark room, crawled into bed and promptly passed out. I had to laugh when Stephen finally woke up, oblivious to the fact I'd already been to Paris!

Tonight, we met up with some old faces from Air Europe days, and after I dropped Stephen off at Crawley train station, I drove home alone. Being single allows me to do exactly as I please, which sounds better than how I feel about it.

29th ~ LHR – CDG – LHR
Excelsior Hotel, Heathrow

Almost twenty-four hours ago, I groaned in response to the shrill of the alarm but knowing all I had to do was a quick flight to and from Paris, made getting up slightly less painful.

With work over, I slept all day and woke up gasping for tea. More than annoyed to find I'd run out of teabags. I contemplated ordering room service but that seemed excessive (and expensive) so I quickly got dressed.

I spotted him as soon as the lift door opened. He was talking animatedly to the guy at reception and my initial reaction was to hit the button and go back to my room, but he turned before I had a chance to.

"Karen!"

"Oh, hello Graeme," I said, feigning surprise. "How are you?"

"Much better now," he grinned. "Standby?"

"Paris dailies, and you?"

"Same," he sighed. "Have you eaten?"

"Not yet, I was actually just popping out to buy teabags."

Making a show of glancing at the Tag Heuer dominating his wrist, he said, "It's well past five, let's grab a drink somewhere."

Lonely girl drinking tea in a dated hotel room versus girl plus one, sipping cocktails in pleasant surroundings? Option two, please!

In Chelsea, with Graeme slathering overpriced *beurre* on some poncy creation posing as bread, he said, "Was it something I said? Did? Didn't do?"

"None of the above," I answered.

We caught the last tube back (aka the drunk one) and grabbed a taxi from Hatton Cross to the hotel, where I discovered Graeme's room is on the floor below mine.

30th ~ LHR – CDG – LHR
At home

Feeling weary ce soir, no surprise given that I crept back to my room right before call time. Sixty minutes is usually ample time to get ready, but not this morning.

Graeme was operating a later flight and when I was getting ready to leave his room, he said, "I'll ring you." Then, with a smirk, he added, "Oh no, I don't have your number."

I flashed a smile and left, but waiting for the lift, I did wonder at who I'm becoming.

Over tea and strawberry tarts, in the garden with mum, I told her I'd bumped into a guy I met on a Bermuda trip and that we went to London for dinner, but I failed to mention anything else.

"D'ye like him?"

173

"I do, actually. He talks a lot, but he's quite fun to be around."

"Janice told me about Ben," she blurted. "She said she hated seeing you so upset and thought I should know."

"And now you do."

"Are ye ok, hen?"

Shrugging, I choked back the tears I'm sick of shedding. "He doesn't want to be with me."

"But ye still want to be with him?"

"I think you know the answer to that, but I just have to get on with it."

"That's ma lassie," she said soothingly. Without having to ask, mum re-filled my cup. "Oh, by the way, Jon phoned last night."

"Did you talk his ear off?"

"Not at all, he did all the talking."

Highly unlikely!

"What's he been up to?" I asked between mouthfuls of strawberry tart number two.

"He jist got back fae South Africa. He was on holiday in Cape Town, said the scenery was stunning."

"I didn't know he was going to South Africa."

And how would I? It's not like I make any effort to keep in touch with him.

JULY

1st ~ **Jon's, Middlesex**

I wasn't expecting to be here tonight but fuelled by nothing other than guilt, I rang Jon first thing to let him know be over after I dropped mum off at church, where Billy Graham (no idea who he is) was scheduled to speak. He must be popular because two hours before the event, the car park was already overflowing.

Driving here was super stressful, so we went straight to the pub, where the usual suspects lined the bar. Rick and Ralph spilled the beans on their recent holiday to South Africa, where it seemed Jon was rather popular with several French girls. It's Rick's birthday, and Jon threw an impromptu party that only wound down a little while ago. In the kitchen, washing up after everyone had left, there was an awkward moment when we turned at the same time and bumped into one another. There was a split second where I thought Jon was going to try and kiss me, but I quickly stepped to the side, and we carried on as if nothing had happened.

With only a wall separating us, I can hear Jon moving about his bedroom. With Frankie's words echoing, I'm left to wonder; *Does it count if you have previous experience on that particular bike?*

2nd ~ **At home**

Early this morning, Jon popped out and returned with a stack of Sunday newspapers and danish pastries (he even remembered raspberry is my fave). At the pine kitchen table, we scanned the latest headlines and whenever either of us found something of interest, we'd read aloud, in silly voices. However, we ended up laughing so much that neither of us made it through a paragraph.

3rd ~ At home

Spent the morning poring over newspaper ads for property in France, that I've been saving for the past couple of months. Most of the offices I rang are based in London, but two were in France, which only confirmed my penchant for French accents. I've been house hunting in and around Milton Keynes but for the same price, it seems I can afford something decent in the North of France (sadly not the South). I know several crew that commute, so it's entirely doable.

Florence popped over tonight and was all ears when I told her about my possible French escape plans. A married with children friend offers a different perspective to that of my single amies, and our chats always leave me with something new to ponder.

4th ~ LHR – MAN

It felt odd checking in, in civvies, but we deadheaded here so no uniform requirement.

Lovely Lyndsey lobster (named after she got scorched on our Bermuda trip) left a bunch of fab pictures in my mail slot. Tucked behind, them was a note.

Sending a big hello! Don't forget to let me know if you need my number. G xxx Ah, Graeme.

For my first trip to…wait, where are we going tomorrow??? NEW YORK! With that in mind, I was thrilled to see Frankie in the briefing room. She's been to New York countless times so I'm relying on her to show me the ropes, and the hot spots. We arranged to meet up half an hour after we checked in, but Frankie showed up at the door much sooner. Brightening up the drab décor in a cerise top and orange skirt, I said, "Get you," as she twirled through the door.

"I thought we could go clubbing."

"It's Tuesday," I said.

176

"So?" she giggled, grabbing a handful of vodka miniatures from the mini bar.

5th ~ MAN – JFK
Lexington Hotel, New York

I conked out on the couch in Frankie's room, and when I woke up the sandwiches we ordered last night from room service, were still hiding beneath the dome shaped plate covers. We were so ravenous, we started picking at them and before I knew it, we'd polished them off. Disgusting, I know, but that's what hunger does to a girl.

Frankie and I were in high spirits throughout the flight and went more than the extra mile for everyone in our cabin. It was so exciting knowing that when we landed, we'd be in the place mum has talked about for as long as I can remember.

It was lively on the crew bus and the crawling traffic allowed us time to enjoy plenty of brown milk (a yummy alcoholic concoction) which is pretty standard, unless the CSD is a stickler for the rules, in which case we're more discreet. Peering through the rain-streaked window at what is possibly the most iconic skyline in the world, I felt my heart racing at the thought I'd be right there, in the middle of Manhattan, soaking up all the action.

The hotel is outdated but who cares, it's New York! According to the wiry guy who checked us in, Dorothy Lamour lived here, as did Marilyn Monroe, when she was married to Joe DiMaggio, who I think had something to do with baseball.

My room is on a higher floor with a better view than Frankie's, so she decided to move in. She wasted no time setting up the ironing board and scattered her lotions and potions around the black and white tiled bathroom.

Down on the street, the buzz was electrifying, and we took a cab (an actual yellow cab!) to a converted church, now the Limelight Club. It was dead so we left and hailed another cab (already using the local lingo) to a place on 54th Street, recommended by the chisel jawed concierge.

The Iguana was much more our scene, and out of the corner of my eye I clocked two guys that seemed to mirror Frankie and me. The shorter one was talking at warp speed, arms flailing, totally animated, while the dark haired taller one (reminded me of Gabriel) nodded but looked distracted.

When a guy the size of a fridge offered to buy me a drink, I politely declined, and when I caught the eye of the taller guy, he mouthed, "Ballet dancer." Frankie was so engrossed in the story she was relaying about her, "Latest in London," she failed to notice me chuckling. From that point on, the dark-haired guy mouthed comments about anyone who offered us a drink, and in between we each turned our attention back to, in my case, Frankie (who was still banging on about "Barclay's soulful eyes") and in his, his compact friend.

When a bald guy ("Hair model," mouthed tall friend) asked Frankie if she wanted to dance, she gestured to the three deep crowd padding the bar. "Dar..ling," she tutted. "Take a good look around. Do you see anyone dancing? No, nor do I. There is no dancing here. Only drinking, and yes, champagne would be lovely, thank you!"

Slinking away, he muttered a string of words, mostly starting with f and y. When I caught dark haired guy's eye again, he opened his mouth, but nothing came out. Shaking his head and laughing, he made his way over. "Hi," he said, hand outstretched. "I'm Christopher."

"And how would you describe yourself?" I joked, as Frankie looked on, mystified.

Shooting out from behind, his friend said, "Hil'mRoberthowyouguyzdoingyouwantadrink?"

The word intense sprang to mind as I watched Robert drink Frankie in, much slower than he spoke. Within a minute of chatting Frankie up, a bottle of Veuve Clicquot in an ice bucket, with four flutes, appeared on the bar.

"Did you really grow up here?" I asked Christopher, after falling into an easy chat with him.

"Manhattan, born and bred," he beamed, revealing ultra-white, perfectly straight teeth.

"I just love it here!" I gushed. "I don't imagine there's anywhere like it."

"You live here?"

"No, it's my first time here," I laughed.

In a club called MK's (I'll check the box of matches I nabbed, but I think it was in Chelsea) the four of us danced our way through each floor of the club that had the feel of an art gallery. The vibe was ultra-cool, as were most of the patrons and I felt totally out of place in white trousers and a flimsy Top Shop top that was on sale for a reason.

Robert works on Wall Street and Christopher works for MTV. They live in the same apartment building, but how I know that seems to have slipped my mind.

6th ~ Lexington Hotel, New York

Peering out from the coverlet, I gasped at the sight of Frankie, balancing on the dresser, her head not far from the ceiling.

"What on earth are you doing?"

"*Ta-da*," she announced, arms outstretched as though she were about to take flight. On the wall behind her, was a giant poster of Jason Donovan, wearing not a lot.

"Blu-tac," she chirped. "Don't leave home without it!"

"That's American Express," I said, as she leapt onto the bed.

In Bloomingdales we drooled over designer togs that got more expensive the higher the floor and in Bergdorf Goodman, we slipped our little piggies into shoes that cost more than we make in a month.

Back at the hotel, I planned to rest before hitting the town, but Frankie had other ideas. When Fine Young Cannibals came on the radio, she jumped up and down on my bed, belting, "She drives me crazy."

Smoothing down my frumpy navy and white dress (what was I thinking?) in the lift's smoke glassed mirror, I mentioned how underdressed I felt next to Frankie's sparkly creation and laughed when she said I looked chic.

We hadn't been in the lobby five minutes when Frankie said she was bored and wanted to wait outside for Christopher and Robert. Using the revolving door, we went from cool, controlled air, to a blast of humidity that left me with a bouffant. When a stretch limo pulled up,

Frankie said she wished she had her camera, which is exactly what I was thinking.

"Karen and Frankie?" Asked a dressed for the part chauffeur, moving in our direction.

"That's us," Frankie chirped as though we'd been waiting for him to show up. I hesitated but Frankie was already climbing in.

At Alo Alo (gorgeous interior with huge ceilings and glass walls) the guys were already seated but when they spotted us, they stood.

"Hi again," Christopher said, kissing each of my cheeks, allowing me a woodsy whiff of what I'm pretty sure was Dior's Fahrenheit (to be confirmed, after a quick nose through his bathroom cabinet, ha!). When Robert edged his chair closer to Frankie's, Christopher gave a little nod I interpreted as *watch out*, and so began their tete-a-tete.

The food was sublime (we were there for dinner, but they serve supper from 11pm – 2am) but Frankie seemed more interested in imbibing than eating. When she started slurring her words, I kicked her under the table and slid the water glass closer, but she soon cottoned on and moved her wine glass out of my reach.

Halfway through dessert (oh, Tiramisu, I'd like to meet you every day for the rest of my life!) Frankie whined that she was ready to go clubbing, but the guys said they were, "Heading outta town for the weekend" (something about Hampton?) but that the limo was ours for the night. As if that wasn't fab enough, Christopher made a call to a club they frequent, because "The line to get in might be crazy."

Auber was upmarket, and in the subdued comfort of all things silk, we lounged among men straight out of a Ralph Lauren ad, sipping flute after flute of champagne, all acquired thanks to Frankie's magnetic charms.

In the limo, when Frankie asked Anton to swing by the apartment building where the guys live, I reminded her they'd gone elsewhere but even if they hadn't already left town, I doubt they'd have appreciated us showing up at four in the morning.

7th ~ JFK – MAN

"How's your noggin?" I asked Frankie.

"Fine, why?"

"I thought you might be feeling a little worse for wear."

"Last night was tame!" she squealed, jumping out of bed.

The crowded streets did nothing to lessen Frankie's chatter as we navigated block after block on our way to the Empire State building. From that vantage point, with the sun glinting against skyscrapers and lines of yellow cabs eighty-six floors below, I was filled with a sense that anything is possible.

From the giddy heights of the Empire State, we found our way to Central Park, passing hot dog and salty pretzel stands, and sighing longingly when we passed The Plaza hotel. Frankie said we must pop in for a cocktail on the next leg of the back-to-back.

We were delayed by three hours leaving JFK and, except for the vile woman in 42E (which I agree is a terrible seat) the passengers are mostly low key. Because of the delay, we got the meal service out of the way on the ground, so when we finally got airborne, most of the pax fell asleep, all except for 42E, who is clearly nocturnal. I just heard a call bell ding ding dinging so I should probably slip on my ruby slippers and go attend to the witch.

8th ~ Manchester City Centre

I love that drowsy feeling just before you drift off into a deep slumber and thanks to the super comfy bed, I woke up feeling refreshed. I knew mum would be anxiously awaiting news of the trip so far, so I rolled over and picked up the phone.

"Finally! How was it?"

"Absolutely amazing, what a place. Can't wait to go back!"

"How's yer crew?"

"Fine but Frankie's on the trip so we did our own thing."

"Is Frankie the one wi all the sparkly stuff? I get mixed up wi all yer pals. Och, I'm sure the two of you were oot painting the town red."

"More like scarlet," I chuckled.

Now that I've experienced New York, I understand why, decades later, mum still talks about her time in the city that never sleeps (kinda like Frankie!) and why it made such an impression on her.

Saturday night in Manchester started out with dinner in Amigos, before going to the pictures. Several films were already sold out, but we managed to get tickets for, *Skin Deep*. The lead character, Zach, was played by John Ritter, an American actor I've never heard of, but he was good. In one scene, all shot in the dark, he and another guy were wearing glow in the dark condoms. The scene itself was funny but listening to Frankie's hiccup sounding chuckles as the condoms bounced across the screen was even better.

9th ~ MAN – JFK
Lexington Hotel, New York

Perched on the edge of Frankie's bed (we're staying in her room because she likes the robin egg blue painted walls) I held the handset while Frankie dialled the number Robert had scribbled on the back of the Alo Alo matchbox, after stressing it was his car phone number.

"I'm headed back to the city from the Hamptons." From his matter-of-fact tone, I got the impression he was with someone. Female.

We'd planned on checking out the Surf Club (recommended by Frankie's, Latest in London) but according to the dour faced concierge (bring back the hunk with the chiseled jawline) it was, "Way uptown," so we ended up at the Iguana.

After a couple of glasses of wine, I felt myself fading and suggested we come back to the hotel. I expected Frankie to protest but her only request was that we stop at the deli. Laden with junk food that cost more than a day's worth of allowances, we made our way to the hotel. I said I'd be right up, after I grabbed a few things from my room.

When I opened the door, I groaned at the sight of the flashing red message light illuminating half of the dingy room. The only time we get messages is to inform us of a delay to the flight or a change to the trip, neither of which I wanted to hear, but knowing Frankie would have the same message, I hit play.

"Hey Karen, how ya doin? Robert said you guys are back in town. That's crazy! I'd love to get together before you leave again. Oh yeah, you've probably already guessed (he let out a little chuckle) but this is Christopher. How does tomorrow sound?"

He proceeded to leave his office and home number (both of which I already noted in what Annabel calls my fakeofax) but, if only to hear him chuckle again, I replayed the message.

Frankie is asleep and unless I remove it, she'll wake up with a cream cheese filled bagel smooshed against her cheek.

10th ~ Christopher's, New York

Woke up with the phone ringing (*where am I?* is always my first thought). Switched on the lamp and watched in amusement as Frankie, with eyes still shut, banged her hand across the night table, searching for the phone.

"It's Robert," she mouthed, through a deep yawn. Uttering, "Uh-huh," and lolling her head repetitively, she shot me a questioning look as she peeled what remained of the crusty bagel, from her cheek.

"Seems he's too busy to see me," she snarled, after slamming down the phone.

"No, you're too busy to see him," I said, swinging my legs out of bed.

After clothes shopping (I bought way too much to mention) we joined the lengthy queue at the ticket booth in Times Square and managed to score seats for Shirley Valentine at the Booth theatre. My humidity hair was worth it to witness Pauline Collins in such a fine performance.

Humming the showtunes they'd just heard, theatregoers spilled into Times Square, so Frankie and I walked a little, before grabbing a cab. I'd arranged to meet Christopher at Coconut Grill and expected Robert to be there, but when he didn't show face, Frankie seemed more than disappointed. When she asked Christopher where Robert was, he shrugged and said, "Robert does his own thing."

We (yes, I'm including all of us) should probably have stopped drinking at Coconut Grill but Christopher insisted on, "One more, at

Juanita's." It slipped my mind that my disastrous relationship with tequila came to an abrupt ending, after a riotous, unscheduled night stop in Tenerife, during Air Europe days.

Christopher said Frankie and I were welcome to spend the night and offered us his bed (the guest room is teeny and has no bed) but I insisted we'd be fine crashing on the oversized couch. Christopher gave me a shirt to wear (beautiful, brushed cotton) along with a pair of what he called, "Workout pants." When I explained what pants are in the UK, he blushed a little.

Frankie swiftly fell asleep and in Christopher's miniscule kitchen, we kissed, but more on that later because I need to sleep.

11th ~ JFK – MAN

The gurgling, churning sound of Christopher's coffee maker woke me.

"Sorry," he whispered as I stepped into the tiny square where we'd kissed only a few hours before. "This thing is noisy."

"Not that noisy," I said, gesturing to Frankie, sprawled on the couch, her blonde locks plastered across her angelic face.

Christopher filled a mug with tap water, before popping it in the microwave. After it beeped, I watched, aghast, as he removed a teabag from a paper sachet, dipped it in the tepid water and handed me the mug.

"Do you have any milk?"

"There might be some half and half," he said, waiting for me to move, so he could open the fridge door. "This good?" He said, shaking the carton from side to side.

"Only if it hasn't been living in there too long," I said with a mock shudder that made him laugh.

"Next time you're in town, come over and show me how it's done," he said, leaning in to kiss me. It was a decent enough kiss, but just like last night there were no sparks.

"I gotta get going," he said, nodding in Frankie's direction. "Stay as long as you want, ok?"

"Thanks for everything," I said, turning my head so his kiss landed on my cheek.

I thumbed my way through shelf after shelf of Christopher's books and after reading the dust cover for *The Remains of the Day*, I was tempted to borrow it but thought that might be a bit forward. He has a great CD collection and *Naked* (love Talking Heads) proved the perfect CD to rouse Frankie back to life.

"Stripes really suit you, darling," were the first words out of her mouth.

I boiled water in a saucepan (surely, they must sell tea kettles in NYC?) and when the phone rang,

I turned down the music, while Frankie answered. With her hand covering the mouthpiece, she mouthed, "Robert? Lunch?"

I nodded and tried not to listen as she made kissing sounds into the phone.

On our way out we had a little chat with Michael the doorman (Frankie said she wouldn't kick him out of bed) who offered to get us a cab. "Actually, I think we'd rather walk, but thank you so very much," Frankie clipped in a flirty tone. I reminded her that one of us was still wearing the clothes she went out in last night.

Stepping out of a cab was a much more civilised way to arrive at the hotel, where we walked straight into our CSD. "Oh, hello Jasper," Frankie chirped, mascara smeared halfway down her face. The girl has no shame, not that I can talk, I was still wearing Christopher's shirt (the one I'd slept in). With an exaggerated step back, Jasper looked the pair of us up and down. "I'll see you two at pick up," he sneered, glancing at his fake Rolex. "Four hours from now."

Give us a break, Jasper we're in New York, having the time of our lives!

Fortunately, Jasper wasn't around to witness us skipping out again, twenty minutes later.

Over lunch, Frankie seemed inhibited and after being subjected to the appalling way Robert treated the wait staff, I concluded that Christopher is, by far, the nicer of the two.

Flight is totally chocka tonight and crew rest is just about up. I got so carried away writing that I forgot to drink my tea, and now it's stone cold. Back I go to attend to the passengers, who seem to have, as Robert said, regarding his clients, "A stick up their ass."

12th ~ At home

When I stumbled into the hall, dragging my overloaded Samsonite, mum was on the phone.

"Wait a wee minute, ma," she said. "She's right here."

Mum shoved the receiver into my hand and made a mad dash for the loo.

"Hi, nana."

"Hullo hen, is that ye just in? Ye must be exhausted."

"I feel quite good, considering I've been up all night. How are you?"

"Och, no too bad." Her tone was flat. "It's been scorching here the past few days and it disnae seem to be letting up."

"I'm sure it will soon. It was humid in New York, oh, I can't wait to go back!"

She let out a hearty laugh. "That's exactly what yer mammy said when she came back, many moons ago."

"Yet she never returned-"

"I'm sure you and yer mammy will go the gither."

"We should all go. You'd absolutely love it!"

"Oh hen, I think I'm a bit past that."

"Never, plus you've never been to America, so when I get staff travel concessions, we should go together. Three generations! Mum would love that."

"Ohhhh, that'd be something, sure it would?"

"It will be, we'll go. Definitely!"

Whiled the afternoon away, getting lost in French property brochures that have more than piqued my interest in buying something old, which shouldn't prove difficult to find around Normandy. Good chat with dad about the logistics of commuting from France and he agreed it could work but suggested I start planning some viewing trips.

Going to bed with my head floating somewhere between the Empire State, France, and wherever Ben might be.

13th ~ At home

Busy day on the phone:

Carl – Had me in stitches over some of his recent romantic entanglements down route. When I told him about Christopher he laughed and said, "He has an apartment in New York? Don't mess this one up!"

Lolly – Poor thing, she's not enjoying flying and is considering leaving. I think it takes a while to get into the groove of the cabin crew lifestyle. It's not easy being away from home for long stretches, and Lolly is very close to her family.

Florence – I should have gone over because we ended up talking for over two hours! Florence is a great listener and I always feel better after we chat.

Jon – If I had a job where I was always here, things might be different between us but having said that, we already dated and it didn't last, so I'm probably only thinking that because I'm feeling a bit lonely.

While I was cleaning out my old dresser (ordered a new one from Habitat) I found a picture of Ben from our first holiday together, in Spain. The sight of him still stirs me.

14th ~ At home

Friday night was spent at the pub with Sarah, Simon and a not so drippy mate of theirs called Sean, but more on that after I start at this morning, when I played table tennis with mum, in the garden.

The only time mum's competitive streak rears its head is when she plays table tennis. Her expression turns deadly serious, and nothing distracts her from the game.

True to form, Sarah and Simon showed up late. Simon's always having a go at Sarah about her tardiness, it drives him barmy, but I'm so used to it that I'd be shocked if she showed up on time. Besides, we were only going to the pub.

It was a lovely stroll down to The Vic, but it was packed so we sat outside. Sean arrived shortly afterwards and right off the bat, he seemed friendly and easy going. We sat across from each other at the picnic table and when the guys went to the bar, Sarah leaned across the table and asked if I fancied him.

"Sarah, I just met him!"

"I know but he's really chatting you up. I think he fancies you."

"You say that about every member of the opposite sex I come into contact with."

I expected her to pull a huffy face, but she surprised me by asking if I'm still gutted about Ben.

"I'm trying really hard not to be."

"Do you think you might get back together?"

"No," I said, shaking my head as the guys returned.

"Sean," Sarah chirped. "You do know Karen's single, don't you?"

Sean's eyes crinkled in a smile. "Snap," he said, handing me a glass of wine and sitting next to me. Whenever his leg brushed mine, I made no attempt to move and much to Sarah's delight, he asked for my number, but I doubt I'll hear from him.

15th ~ Angie's, Surrey

Mum woke me this morning with a piping hot mug of tea (ah, the perfect ratio of milk to tea!). Dad was gardening, something he has the patience for, unlike mum who expects everything she plants to grow overnight. Every so often, mum would stick her head out the window and call down to dad, asking what he was doing. The sound of his laughter echoed up through the window and it made me hope that if I ever get married, it'll be just like that.

I was in the hallway, sorting out my cabin bag, when the phone rang.

"Hello?"

"Karen, hiya, it's Sean. From last night?"

"Oh, Sean," I said, barely able to hide my surprise. "How are you?"

"Fine thanks, you alright?"

"Yeah good, actually."

"I was ringing to see if you're ehm, free. *Tonight*?"

"Sorry, I'm not," I said, feeling genuinely disappointed.

"Oh, ok then." His tone prompted an explanation.

"I'm going to a party at the house I used to live in. They're a mad bunch but I love them."

His laugh was so melodic the thought of inviting him crossed my mind. There was a slight pause before he said, "I really enjoyed meeting you last night."

"You as well."

"You and Sarah are mates from school?"

"Yeah, we met on my first day, after we moved down from Scotland."

"My mum's Scottish."

"Really?"

"Och aye," he burred, in a terrible accent. "Do you get back up there much? Sorry! Too many questions!"

"Not at all, I'm usually the one asking all the questions. I'm going up to Glasgow soon to stay with my nana. Where do you live?"

"Crawley."

"Oh, I thought you lived close to Milton Keynes."

"I used to, that's how I met Simon, but I recently moved. Work and that," he offered.

"The party I'm going to is in East Croydon but I'm driving to Gatwick then taking the train."

"The long way," he laughed. "How come we never talked about this last night?" After a slight pause, he said, "If you're going to Gatwick, maybe we could meet for a quick drink, before you go to the party. I'd be happy to drop you off afterwards."

"That might work."

"Excellent," he said, sounding much more confident. "Just give me a time and I'll meet you at Gatwick."

It's been an amazing night, with ridiculous amounts of dancing and libations galore. There's something very special about this house and all who inhabit it. All due to the fact Angie is the best landlady ever. Her kindness knows no bounds and she always makes everyone feel welcome. This might be the cocktails talking, but I almost wish I'd invited Sean.

16th ~ Jon's, Middlesex

Pamsy rang to let me know her flight to TFS had a major delay, which unfortunately changed our plans. Thought about going home but I have ample days off before my next trip, so when Angie suggested we ring Jon (she always had a soft spot for him) I did.

"Who died?" he joked.

"I'm at Birch Road, there was a party-"

"Thanks for the invite!"

"Sorry I've been away a lot and-"

"Yeah, yeah, yeah. You comin' over?"

"Funny you should ask. Angie and I were just talking about you, and she suggested-"

"Brilliant," he said, interrupting me. "I'll let the lads know you're both on your way over."

Watching Jon's sense of ease around his friends makes me think of mine and how different they are. When I mentioned to Ralph how happy Jon was, he said, "Course he is, you're here."

Jon came over and threw an arm around each of us. "What are you two whispering about?"

"Just having a catch up, mate," Ralph said, patting Jon on the back.

"McGarr! Promise you'll come and spend more time with…us," Jon said, motioning to his friends. Before I had a chance to respond, Angie sidled up to me, and whispered, "You really ought to."

17th ~ Flight from Gatwick to Brussels
Brussels, Belgium

Angie dropped me off at Gatwick, and my jovial mood soon turned sour after doling out fourteen quid for parking. I know you can't put a price on not feeling stressed from driving, but that seemed excessive.

Pleasant drive South, with the windows open and the company of *Steve Wright in the Afternoon* blaring through the speakers.

"You made it!" Pamsy shouted as I pulled into the driveway. "Quick, come inside, I have a surprise for you!" Filling the tea kettle, she said, "Everything got messed up with the delayed Tenerife so I thought you could come with me…to Brussels!"

"Yes!" I squealed, but if we're going to Belgium for the night, I need to take a nap."

"Go ahead," she said. "I'm going to watch *Neighbors*."

She chuckled when I told her about the Jason Donovan poster Frankie plastered on the wall in New York.

In the car, on our way to Gatwick, Pamsy played the Johnnie Hates Jazz cassette, and we strained our vocal cords singing, "And now you've given me, given me, nothing but shattered dreams, shattered dreams." During the instrumental parts we talked at rapid speed, before singing again.

Our fab night in Brussels started in the FO's room, after which we went to La Grande Place, where we popped in and out of lively bars, bursting at the seams with delectable guys, some of whom we chatted to. Is there anything better than a guy with an accent? Yes, yes there is! Spending time with your best mate. That wins, every time.

18th ~ Flight from Brussels to Gatwick
Pamsy's, Sussex

Call time was 4.40am, and Pamsy and I were up and dressed in record time. We even managed a cup of tea and a jam roll before heading to the lobby. Such pros!

In no time, we were back at Pamsy's with a big decision to make, Beach or bed?

Bed won and the lengthy nap put us in the right frame of mind for a night out on the town. In Eastbourne, we found the usual suspects in the usual hotspots but after a while it got a bit tedious, so we decided to call it a night. On our way back we popped into The Denbigh, fully expecting it to be dead on a Tuesday night but a girl Pamsy went to school with was there, celebrating her engagement. Christine welcomed

Pamsy with open arms and insisted we, "Stay for cake." We were introduced to Christine's fiancé, both sets of parents, siblings, cousins, aunts, uncles, friends, and ended up continuing the celebrations at Christine and Dean's new flat, but still, no cake!

"Look at all the stars," I said, craning my neck towards the inky sky, on our way back to Pamsy's.

"This is something we should be doing with guys, not each other," she laughed, swinging into the parking lot at the Cooden Beach hotel.

Still gazing up, I said, "Who would you like to share with romantic moment with?"

"Ollie. Definitely Ollie."

"That was quick!"

"And you?"

His name was on the tip of my tongue but all I did was shrug.

19th ~ Pamsy's, Sussex

We were in Pamsy's room, trying on new clothes, when her dad called upstairs.

"Girls, you might want to come down and see this."

A United Airlines DC-10 crash-landed in Sioux City, Iowa. The news is slowly trickling out but it's evident from the horrific images that something catastrophic occurred. It was only back in December that Pan Am 103 exploded over Lockerbie, killing all 259 passengers, so seeing this has brought it all back again.

It's what we train for, in the hopes none of it will ever be put to the test. It's horrific for the loved ones of the passengers and crew who boarded that flight today, just like we have, hundreds of times, with the expectation we'll arrive safely.

From the smoke infused images, it's highly doubtful any of the 296 souls onboard, survived.

20th ~ At home

Mum rang last night after seeing the news of the crash, then she rang again this morning to see when I'd be home. Pamsy's mum said she understood exactly how mum felt.

When something of this magnitude occurs, it brings it home in a brutal way, and as crew, it's important to express our fears about such an event. Some of the passengers were found wandering in the cornfields, adjacent to where the plane crash-landed and the cockpit was so compressed, the rescuers didn't recognize it. Due to a special the airline was running, United Airlines flight 232 had 52 children onboard, four of whom were babies. It's being reported that ten children perished but miraculously, half the passengers survived. The swift actions of Captain Alfred Haynes and his crew are being touted as heroic.

Sebastian (Monarch cabin crew) sounded upset on the phone, so I invited him over. He just rang back to let me know Stephen is on his way, so they'll be here after Stephen's train gets in.

21st ~ At home

"Yeeeeessss?" I said, expecting Pamsy again.

"Did I catch you at a bad time?"

"Oh, hi Sean, sorry about that," I said, through a yawn I couldn't stifle.

"You sound knackered."

"I am, it was a late night."

"Where'd you go?"

"St. Albans, with my friends Stephen and Sebastian. Stephen wanted to go clubbing, but Sebastian wasn't having any of it."

"You make them sound like a couple," he said.

"They are."

"Wait." I imagined him holding up his hand. "They're *poofs*?"

"Gay is-"

"Same thing."

His indignant tone threw me into a tailspin. "Sean, it's considered derogatory to-"

"I don't understand why you went-"

"What don't you understand? They're my friends."

"But they're-"

"I don't appreciate your tone, Sean, or for that matter you-"

"I'm entitled to my opinion!"

"Your opinion is *shite!*" I said, before slamming the phone down.

Good riddance!

22nd ~ LHR – AUH
Hilton Hotel, Abu Dhabi, United Arab Emirates

I clocked him the second he set foot in the cabin and not ashamed to say I made a beeline for him. While he was getting situated in his seat, I flashed my best hostie smile, with an enthusiastic, "Welcome onboard."

"Thanks," he grinned. American. I knew it. Blond surfer boy hair fell slightly across his face and when he flicked it (moved might be more appropriate, flicked makes him sound like, ahhh.. stop and get on with it!). When he did whatever it was that he did to his hair, I imagined him sprinting towards the sea, with a surfboard tucked under his arm.

Kimberly was in the other aisle and when I turned and mouthed, "Wow," she fluttered her eyelashes comically. Turning my attention back to surfer guy, I asked if he'd like me to hang up his jacket (as is the norm in Club, not preferential treatment!).

"Sure," he said, glancing at my nametag. "Thanks, Karen." Best pronunciation of my name. Ever.

I tried to maintain an air of professionalism and avoid flirting with him (not easy!) but I did retrieve his name from the passenger manifest. During the meal service, I found out he's from Los Angeles and while I was setting up the duty- free trolley, he appeared in the galley.

"Hi," he smiled (is it just me or are good teeth really appealing?). "I hope I'm not disturbing you."

You are but not in the way you'd imagine!

"Not at all," I chirped, hoping my cheeks didn't look as flushed as they felt. "What can I do for you?"

Talk about a loaded question!

"Maybe some water?"
Would you like a lifelong commitment with that?
"Still or sparkling?"
Where should we live?
"Sparkling."
Like my engagement ring!
"Ice and lemon?"
Two kids or three?
"Sure, thanks, Karen."
Get used to saying that!

At the other side of the galley, Kimberly pretended to be busy, but her body language confirmed she was all ears. After I'd made a grand gesture of preparing the easiest drink ever, for my all-time favourite passenger, I expected him to go back to his seat, but instead we fell into an easy chat. He came across as a little shy which I found highly appealing.

Unlike yours truly, Mr. LA took the flight all the way to Delhi. Hopefully he'll get a nice surprise when he finds the note, I slipped into his jacket pocket.

23rd ~ Hilton Hotel, Abu Dhabi, United Arab Emirates

Stepping from the chilled lobby, into a sweltering 122 degrees this morning, Kimberly and I had the same reaction and promptly dashed back inside. In my room, Kimberly had me recall every interaction I had on the flight, with Mr. LA, which is the only reason I ate less than her.

24th ~ AUH – KUL
Kuala Lumpur, Malaysia

No idea what hotel we're in but after a while they all start to look the same. The flight was seven hours of hard slog, so I went straight to bed, waking with a start after a series of knocks on the door.

"I don't believe it!" I squealed, opening the door to Carl.

"Hello sis," he said, pecking my cheek. "Looks like I woke you up."

"How can you tell?" I joked, tousling my hair. "How long are you here for?"

"Leaving tonight, back to Abu Dhabi and the heat."

"I'm relieved to have a break from it, if only for a few days. Kimberly's here as well."

"I know, I saw her name on the list, but I came to see my big sis first."

"Thanks, baby bruv," I laughed. "Let's go and wake her up."

Over dinner in Chinatown, I gave Kimberly the run down on my trip to France. She had a few choice words for Ben, but I came to his defence by reminding her she was only hearing my side of the story. Her response was a whack to my arm.

"I wonder when Mr. LA will get in touch," she said wistfully.

"Do you think he will?" I said, catching her eye.

"I don't see why not. You got on like a house on fire."

"A chat in the galley hardly con-"

Interrupting me, she said, "I think he will."

I hope she's right.

25th ~ Flight from Kuala Lumpur to Penang
Penang, Malaysia

Writing from a deeply luxurious bed, in a place I only became aware of today!

After an hour with our crew at breakfast, Kimberly and I agreed that the prospect of spending several monotonous days by the pool talking about dieting isn't the reason we became cabin crew.

The travel agent recommended by the hotel, is an ex-Qantas hostie, and when we told her we wanted to escape our droll crew, she suggested Penang. The cost of the flight and hotel seemed more than fair but after she applied a hefty crew discount, it ended up being peanuts.

At the hotel, we found Elise, our CSD. Fortunately, she granted us permission to leave, which considering we'd already made the booking was helpful! After giving Elise the trip info, we quickly packed, caught a taxi to the airport, and boarded a Malaysian Airlines flight. Forty-five bumpy minutes later, we touched down on the island of Penang.

The huge room is beautifully appointed, and the view of the beach is postcard worthy. The bathroom is almost as big as the room and is clad entirely in white marble.

We were tired after dinner (nasi lemak to die for) but stopped in at the hotel disco. It was dead so we only stayed for a little while but from the sound of Kimberly snoring, it seems the Jungle Bird we each consumed was enough to knock her out. Then again, she only weighs about seven stone.

26th ~ Penang, Malaysia

We were up early and took a taxi to the Golden Sands resort, on Batu Ferringhi beach, where we rented bikes and had an enjoyable time cycling along the beach path. Somehow, we veered off the path and ended up in a heavily wooded area, where we came across an old woman, sitting outside what I can only describe as a house made of tree trunks and branches.

With hand gestures, we were able to ascertain that she has three young children and a husband, who is very large! She also had a monkey and when she opened the cage, the monkey took one look at Kimberly and leapt into her arms. Kimberly let out a scream, more from surprise I think than fear. While the monkey combed through Kimberly's hair, birds swarmed close by and when the woman whistled, two of them landed on each of her crinkly skinned wrists. From the crooked, makeshift doorway, two children eyed us suspiciously and seemed reluctant to come outside.

With the birds gone, and the monkey safely back in the cage, the woman linked her tiny fingers through ours and recited something that might have been some type of prayer, or blessing. She pressed a small piece of jade into each of our palms, gesturing that we always carry it with us.

We found our way back to the beach path and in a little craft shop, I found a silver ring I slipped on my finger as soon as I'd paid for it. Walking on the beach, we got stopped by several people asking if they could have their picture taken with us. We agreed the attraction is clearly the blonde hair neither of us was born with!

It was while we were getting ready to leave the beach that I realised my purse was missing. I thought I might have left it in the craft shop, so we cycled back. Fortunately, the man I bought the ring from spoke excellent English, but my purse was nowhere to be found.

This is th second time this year I've filed a theft report with the local police. With the language barrier, the word "ID" didn't come across well, so Kimberly took it upon herself to try and explain the importance of it.

"If we don't find it, she'll have to go back to Heathrow." Her manc accent was thicker than ever. "ID is like a passport, you know passport?"

The officers nodded but more in a gesture of bewilderment than understanding.

"As cabin crew," Kimberly continued, her voice getting louder with each word, "Our ID is dead important."

More baffled expressions.

"You know, air o plane?" She said, flapping her arms, at which point I could no longer bear it and asked her to please stop.

We returned the rental bikes and after we caught the bus back to the hotel, I rang Elise. While I was explaining what had happened, I burst into tears.

"I'll get on the blower, to London," she said calmly. "These things happen but I must say, this is a first for me, so I'll consider it a challenge."

"Will I be sent home?" I sniffed.

"I don't know…just keep your chin up and we'll hope for the best outcome."

I couldn't shake how foolish I felt and didn't feel like going out, so we ordered room service (most of which I scoffed) and just as we were about to call it a night, we hit the jackpot when Kimberly clicked on a channel with Tina Turner in concert. What an incredible entertainer she is (Tina, not Kimberly!). We jumped up on the beds and tried our best to mimic Tina's moves, but we most definitely don't have her legs. Or voice. During, "River Deep, Mountain High", Kimberly leapt off the bed (ugh, skinny girl antics!) and grabbed her ID. Up on the bed again, swinging the lanyard attached to it, she crooned into her fake microphone, "If I lost you, I would cry."

27th ~ Flight from Penang to Kuala Lumpur
Kuala Lumpur, Malaysia

The good news is that I'm staying on the trip, but Elise stressed my first stop after we land at LHR is the ID office.

We checked out of the hotel, surprised at how inexpensive all the room service was. Took the bus to the capital, George Town, and toured several temples, but the humidity was so heavy it detracted from the enjoyment. I could feel my body expanding by the second and my shorts became so snug I swear I'd have whipped them off, had I been wearing a longer top.

Kimberly can be fun one minute, then down in the doldrums the next. She whinged a lot today, and I'm sure I did as well, especially about the heat, but it seemed she wasn't happy with anything so on the flight back, I pretended to be asleep.

After getting reacquainted with my best friend, AC, I climbed into this huge bed, and wrote several letters, including one to Ben I know I won't send but I'll keep it as a reminder of how much I'm missing him tonight.

28th ~ KUL – AUH

Thankfully, we're halfway through this eight-hour flight. After a lengthy delay departing from KUL, pax were not happy campers but worse than that was Kimberly whining about how uncomfortable she felt in the heat. "At least you're skinny!" I wanted to scream, as the waistband on my skirt tightened its vice like grip.

The time changes are proving difficult on this trip (understatement) and I think I might be getting a cold. Feeling stuffy on the ground is bad enough but altitude only exacerbates it. The fact I've eaten mostly crap since leaving LHR probably isn't helping and might explain why I had to move my belt up another notch. I so wish we were heading home. And that I was thin.

29th ~ AUH – DEL
Hyatt Hotel, Delhi, India

Flight time from AUH was only three and half hours but the majority of the pax had boarded in LHR so as well as being lethargic, they were particularly unpleasant (or maybe that was me?). Too bad there weren't any LA guy lookalikes to make the flight more bearable.

Done my best to accommodate the grumpy pax, all the while avoiding Kimberly and her incessant moaning about pretty much everything. I know I'm not being terribly understanding, but she's really getting on my nerves.

The hotel is majestic, but the room feels dank. Regardless, I'm going to bed (not meeting the crew, can't be bothered) in the hopes I'll wake up in a better frame of mind.

30th ~ Hyatt Hotel, Delhi, India

Woke up crying from a dream about Ben and was still in bed, snivelling and feeling sorry for myself when Toby (Purser) rang to see if I wanted to go to the market. He stressed that the market experience was worth getting up for but in my wallowing state I wasn't convinced. However, it's my first time here so I thought I should at least make an effort to see something of the place before coming back to bed with my books, pens and paper (my lifelong friends).

After bumping into what felt like ten thousand people, I became agitated and made no attempt to hide my annoyance. In his Scouse accent that reminded me of Florence, Toby chided me for, "Havin' a cob on." Satisfying my tactile nature with vibrant coloured rugs and clothing, I began to feel better, scolding myself for being so uppity. *Chill out, you're in India*! Toby's witty banter continued to lift my spirits and his cheerfulness soon rubbed off on me.

Stopping for a rummage at one of the many tables piled high with clothing, the stall owner plucked a madras shirt, and held it out to Toby.

"For your wife?" He offered, in his lovely lilt.

Toby took the shirt and held it up for my inspection.

"G'wed," I joked, watching Toby as he tried not to laugh.

"How much?" He asked.

"I give you good price for wife."

"She's not for sale!" Toby chuckled.

"I am sorry, miss," the man smiled, clasping his hands. "I give you good price."

"We'll take it," came a voice from behind.

I spun around and couldn't believe my eyes.

"I saw you from all the way over there," he grinned, gesturing to the other end of the market, as I gave him a questioning look.

"Your hair," he explained, handing me the shirt the stall owner had rolled into a ball.

"Thank you," I sputtered, holding the shirt like a newborn.

At warp speed, we exchanged a bunch of words, questions, whatever, I don't know! My mind was working overtime...*Did he get the note? It's so hot here, he probably hasn't worn his jacket. Wow, he really is gorgeous. That hair! He just bought me a shirt. My favourite item of clothing ever! I wonder if he got my note. Who cares, Mr. LA is here. In India!*

Toby cleared his throat and I quickly introduced him to David.

"We met on the flight," Toby reminded him, as they shook hands.

"Where are you guys staying?" David asked.

"At the Hyatt," I said, much too fast.

Looking at me he smiled in response. "Cool, are you free later?"

"We're only here for the day," I said, my world collapsing around my dusty sandals. "What time is call, Toby?"

"Like two in the morning," he said, solemnly.

"That's too bad," David uttered.

I was so crestfallen I was stumped for words. Looking at my face like he was deciphering a map, David said, "Can you hang out? Like, now?"

Eh, let me think about that…YES! YES! YES!

"Sure," I said as coolly as I could muster, while inside, it felt like I was on a trampoline. Toby flashed a look I interpreted as *Will you be ok alone with him?* My silent answer was a quick, enthusiastic nod. I hoped he understood I'd be more than fine, alone with David, well when I say alone, that doesn't include the ten million population.

"Ta ra, girl," Toby sighed, as he kissed me on the cheek, whispering, "So f'ing unfair." He and David shook hands, and Toby left.

"How about a walking tour of the city?"

"You're that familiar with it?"

"I spend a lot of time here, it's incredible. Come on," he urged. "Lemme show you around."

Talking with ease on our way out of the market, I slipped my Wayfarers on and from behind the dark lenses I concluded that David is the perfect specimen. He's an inch or so shy of six feet, his body looks lithe, but his biceps suggest he's no stranger at the gym. His hair, ah, I've already written about that. His eyes, oh my! They're vivid blue, sparkly and kind. That probably sounds a bit *pass me the bucket*, but it's true. However, the most appealing thing about him is his manners and how gentle he seems. He lives, "real close to the ocean," in a place called Manhattan Beach, and he has a younger sister.

"She and my folks live in San Diego."

"Where exactly is that?"

"So cal."

I gave him a questioning look.

"Southern California."

"Is that where you're from?"

"I was born in San Diego, but I went to school at UCLA."

"School being university?"

"Yeah, the University of California, Los Angeles."

Ah, so much to learn! He works for an engineering company but had the day off. The market was a last-minute decision, after he remembered he needed a birthday present for his mum.

After exploring the city on foot (so glad I was wearing my verging on ugly but comfortable sandals) and popping in and out of various places for cool drinks and small plates of food (none of which I was familiar with, all of which I devoured!), it was close to midnight when we got back to the hotel. We ordered tea in the lobby, and with every fragrant sip, I sensed time tick tick ticking away.

David walked me to the lift and after he pressed the button, I took his outstretched hand. Slowly swaying our hands back and forth, I felt my breath gathering speed and thought my face might explode from the joy pulsating through every part of me. When the lift door dinged open, we ignored it and took a step closer to one another, and when it dinged shut, David stepped even closer.

With his palms resting on my bare shoulders, we kissed our way through one ding after another. I thought I might pass out from such sensual pleasure but as caught up as I was, I knew time was not on my side. "I have to go," I whispered, inhaling the scent of our perfect day.

"I know," he said, coming in for another kiss, as his hands slid to my lower back.

"This has been…" I breathed.

"*Serendipity.*"

"Thank you for showing me around," I uttered, suddenly feeling a little shy. "It was spectacular."

"It *is* spectacular," he said, kissing me again, as his hands dipped lower.

Another ding and this time when the door opened, I stepped into the lift, but we held hands until the door forced us to let go. Just as it was about to close, David's hand shot through, forcing it to open.

"Hey, Karen," he said with a jut of his perfect chin. "I forgot to say thanks."

"For what?"

"Your note," he mouthed, as the door slid shut and I began the floaty ascent way beyond my room on the tenth floor.

31st ~ DEL – AUH
Hilton Hotel, Abu Dhabi, United Arab Emirates

Less than an hour after getting back to my room, I sat with Kimberly on the crew bus, with Toby's head poking between us.

"Spill!"

"Later," I said.

"Fair enough, but just one thing," Toby said. "In a dozen years of service, I've *never* left anyone a note."

"That's your loss," I replied tartly, making Kimberly laugh.

"Mind you, to be honest," he added. "The punters rarely look like your guy."

My guy.

"You look happy," Kimberly said, smiling sweetly.

"I'm running on empty, but I feel on top of the world!"

"I'm sorry I've been such a moaning Minnie."

"When was that?" I joked. "Don't worry, I'm sure I've been no picnic either."

"I'm glad we got that sorted." In a whisper, she added, "Now tell *me* everything!"

On the Delhi routes (and several others) we work with crew based in that region. It helps with language/cultural differences and makes life easier for the passengers. On this leg of the trip, Poonam is the Indian national and tonight she took us to a restaurant where we sat on beaded cushions and ate with our hands. The food was out of this world and when I finally stopped eating, I could've given the belly dancers a run for their money.

At Safari, the hotel disco, Kimberly was full of beans and my head was still up in the clouds, the perfect pairing for dancing with abandon We left Poonam on the dance floor, and no sooner were we back at the banquette, when a young guy dressed in a thawb, appeared. Bowing his head, and without speaking, he passed each of us a red Cartier inscribed box. Bewildered, Kimberly and I looked at one another.

"Please open and accept," he uttered, motioning to the VIP area, but it was dark so I couldn't see anything. At the same time, Kimberly and I slowly opened the boxes. Cushioned on a bed of velvet, a pair of emerald and gold earrings sparkled, so much so that I actually gasped.

Storming over, Poonam yelled, "Send them back!" and slammed each box shut. After she tore the box out of my hand, she tossed it to the young man, and did the same with the other one. Kimberly opened her mouth in protest, but Poonam held her palm really close to Kimberly's cheek, and hissed, "I forbid!"

To say it felt awkward, watching as the young man scurried away, would be an understatement. Avoiding eye contact with Poonam, I downed the rest of my drink, and Kimberly did the same.

"Let's dance," Poonam announced, leaving no time for explanation.

The DJ was good and the three of us soon fell into a fun rhythm dancing together. It was a while before Kimberly said she needed a breather and excused herself. Poonam said she was going to the loo.

As soon as Kimberly and I sat down, the guy appeared again. Kimberly looked apprehensive, but not enough to refuse the box thrust towards her. I quickly scanned the area, but Poonam was nowhere in sight, so I took the other box and after a quick nod of acknowledgement, Kimberly and I clicked open the boxes. A gold bangle, encrusted with gemstones begged to be slipped on my wrist. I peered over to see what treasure Kimberly had. It was the same bangle. Out of the corner of my eye, I spotted Poonam.

"Shit!" I said, nodding to Kimberly. We slammed the boxes shut and quickly handed them to the guy, who wasted no time leaving.

All smiles, Poonam suggested we dance, but just as we were getting up, the guy appeared again. This time he held three boxes, all much larger than before. *Necklaces*? With a face like thunder, Poonam stood over him, spouting a slew of words I didn't need to understand. The guy bowed deeply and ran.

AUGUST

1st ~ **Hilton Hotel, Abu Dhabi, United Arab Emirates**

Over breakfast, before she left for Delhi, Poonam made it quite clear that we are not to accept anything from anyone, especially the guy in Safari. "It will only lead to trouble," she stated.

Spent the afternoon lounging at the beach club, or maybe I should say lolling because I was so tired, I couldn't even get through a few pages of the Sylvia Plath book of poems one of the pax left behind on the last leg (no room for my book bag on this trip).

I was about to drift off, when I heard Carl's voice. He'd just come from Delhi and couldn't sleep. Sipping frozen drinks that did zilch to cool us, Carl amused us with his tales of his latest trysts, and, as is the norm, it didn't take long before the subject of romance popped up.

"You expect me to believe you had tea with him in the lobby? At midnight?" He asked with his signature cheeky grin. "So innocent and so unlike you!"

I swatted his arm.

"Do you think you'll see him again?"

"He has my address," I said, crossing my fingers.

"What about you Kimberly?" Carl asked. "You gettin' any action on this trip?"

It was Kimberly's turn to swat his arm.

"You two are violent," Carl chuckled.

Studying her hands, Kimberly said, "I quite fancy Toby."

"Our purser?"

"Uh-huh." She looked bashful.

"I hate to burst your bubble, Kimberly," I said, tentatively, "but Toby showed me pictures of a guy from Copenhagen, he's hot and heavy with."

"I think you're mistaken," she huffed.

When I caught Carl's eye, he looked equally confused.

2nd ~ Hilton Hotel, Abu Dhabi, United Arab Emirates

Back to the beach club, where every degree of heat only seemed to add another inch to what was once my waist.

In the air-conditioned lobby, I came alive, and Carl and Kimberly commented on how much I seemed to be enjoying the sweet tea.

"I love this stuff," I gushed.

"When you like something, Karen, you really like it," Kimberly chuckled.

"Right girls," Carl said rubbing his hands together. "If we're out on the razz tonight, I'm off for a bit of shut eye. Give us a knock about eight, sis?"

"Will do," I said, reaching for another sugar cube.

It was dead in Hemingway's, so we went to Safari (not a box in sight!) but the music was crap, so we ended up at Carousel, which was jumping. Carl went to say hello to a mate of his on the dance floor, and Kimberly and I met Roland, BA's station manager, who was super nice. Toby showed up and asked me to introduce him to Roland, then they went to the bar together. Carl came back yelling, "I'm just letting you know my mate Terry just told me he fancies you."

"This might be my lucky night with Toby," Kimberly shrieked above the din.

I looked over at the bar, where Toby and Roland verged on canoodling.

"Ok," was all I said, as Kimberly made her way to what could only be disappointment.

When I saw Terry coming towards me, I looked away but when I looked again a minute later, his gaze was buried in the charms of well-endowed girl. Gesturing for Carl to have a look, he laughed, "Sorry sis, boobs win!"

"Check out Kimberly at the bar," I shouted.

Dancing his way to me, Carl shook his head at the sight of Kimberly gazing up at Toby, who was doing the same, only to Roland! Johnny Kemp came on and Carl and I wasted no time straining our vocal cords, "Just got paid, Friday night, party hopping, feeling fine."

3rd ~ Hilton Hotel, Abu Dhabi, United Arab Emirates

Back to the beach club (lengthy yawn) where my misery reached a new level and the humidity had me in such a bad mood, Carl suggested we go into town and exchange our dirham allowances to sterling.

"How'd you get on with Toby last night?" Carl asked Kimberly from the front seat of the luxurious taxi. A stream of pleasurable sounds escaped her pale pink lips. "He's soooo sweet, I really like him."

Carl made a face and to stop from laughing, I sucked on my cheek.

In Safari, it was a replay of last night with everyone chasing the attention of the wrong person. And just like last night, I danced with Carl for hours on end. When the DJ played, "Pump Up the Volume," a slew of people joined the dance floor, one of whom was Terry. He was all smiles and did his best to keep up with the mad dancing frenzy Carl and I love, but he soon lost interest.

"Maybe later?" Terry yelled but I pretended not to hear him.

"He's harmless," Carl said, after Terry slinked away.

When Richard Marx came on, I knew it was time to leave. I found Kimberly at the bar, talking to Toby, and when I say talking, I mean Toby was talking but not to Kimberly. He was talking to Sharif (from Carl's crew).

"I'm leaving," I announced.

"Me too," Kimberly said, throwing me for a loop.

With her arm linked through mine, we made our way around the perimeter of the dance floor, towards the exit, where we walked straight into Terry.

"You're not leaving, are ya?"

"I think the sun wore us out," Kimberly said, giving my arm a little squeeze.

"Come and have a slow dance with me." He held out his hand.

"Not tonight," I grimaced.

"Please," he pleaded, almost mockingly.

"Maybe another time," I said, shuffling away.

Once we were outside, Kimberly burst out laughing. "Your face was such a picture! You really can't hide anything can you?"

"I can't imagine anything worse than slow dancing to Richard Marx."

"I like that song," Kimberly pouted, reaching to press the button for the lift, before turning her back to me. With her arms wrapped around her body so it looked like someone was hugging her, she moaned, "Ohhhh, Terry." Running her hands up and down her willowy frame, she breathed, "This is my favourite song, I'm soooo happy you asked me to dance."

I was bent over from laughing when she started singing, "Wherever you go, whatever you do, I will be right here waiting for you." In the lift, she kept up the act, adding choice words that had me in stitches.

What a trip it's been, but it's time to go home.

4th ~ AUH – LHR
At home

Survived my longest trip to date and nine pax in the Club cabin meant oodles of crew rest.

Knowing mum would want a rundown of each and every day and destination, I started on day one.

"I met a really nice guy."

"Steward?"

I shook my head.

"Pilot?"

"Passenger. His name is David."

Before she had a chance to ask, I told her how I'd met him on the flight, then again in the market in Delhi. She was all ears and didn't interrupt as much as she usually does.

"Guess what else?"

"Och," she said, fanning her face. "I'm no sure I want to know!"

"Mum! Nothing like that! He told me he found the note."

"Whit if he shows up here?" she gasped.

"Not a chance."

"Och, ye never know, ye hear aboot stuff like this on the news." She sounded concerned.

"He won't," I said, making sure I had her full attention before I delivered the news that I knew she'd love.

5th ~ At home

No more playing the puppet with Ben. That's one of the many things on my mind after a very enjoyable night at Muswell's, with Flo and Morris, who are a treat to go out with. There's something comforting about being in the presence of a couple that have been together for, in their case, twenty years.

I hate to waste ink on him but after witnessing the ease with which Flo and her husband communicate my thoughts turned to Ben. He had so much control over me, which I stupidly allowed to continue, but never again. Having said that, I miss so much about him.

6th ~ At home

Mum was on a mission to thrash me (again) at table tennis and after what felt like hours, I feigned wrist pain, hoping she'd take the hint, but it only seemed to give her more reason to whack the tiny ball as if she had a personal vendetta against it.

Dad was in and out of the garden with cups of tea, none of which mum touched. Whenever I caught dad's eye, he'd shake his head and suppress a smile. The final straw came when he brought out a plate of cream cakes, fresh from the bakery across the street, where Lucy used to work. I was wracking my brain for another ailment excuse when the phone rang.

"Let dad answer it!" Mum shouted.

"It's probably for me," I said, dropping the paddle. "*Hallelujah*," I mouthed, dashing past dad.

"Karen, come back!"

"It might be LA calling," I shouted, darting through the back door.

Sadly, it wasn't.

7th ~ At home

I wonder if being in the place where you spent years with the person you loved, makes it more difficult (and longer) to get over them? Seems everywhere I turn holds a memory of Ben. I'm trying so hard to stay strong but there are moments when I doubt that I'll ever get over him.

After zero luck shopping for new jeans (is trying on three sizes normal?) I stopped outside our old pizza place and imagined what I'd think if I saw the two of us laughing as we munched our way through a pizza together. Just the thought of it brought tears to my eyes and I couldn't get to the car fast enough.

Just got home from an unexpected night out in Luton, with Sebastian and some of his friends. Sadly, he and Stephen have decided to call it a day because, according to Sebastian, "The distance is too much." And here I am, hoping to hear from someone who lives six thousand miles away.

8th ~ At home

"Karen! Wake up!"

I peeled my eyes open to find mum standing over me, frantically waving an envelope. "Look whit jist came in the post!"

"I can hear you mum," I tutted, but when I saw it was airmail, my interest piqued.

"It's fae David," mum beamed, as if she already knows him. I held out my hand and reluctantly, she passed the envelope. I was tempted to rip it open, but I wanted to savour the moment. In private.

The second mum took Tini out for his afternoon walk, I dashed upstairs and retrieved the envelope from under my pillow. I brushed my fingers over the flimsy envelope with the American stamp and after using the silver letter opener nana gave me, I marvelled at the sight of three pages of David's words....*as I got closer to you in the market, I kept thinking, there's no way it's her and when I heard your voice, I still couldn't believe I'd found you.*

9th ~ Kimberly, Lorna, Meryl's, Richmond upon Thames

"He's a total dreamboat," Kimberly sighed at the mention of David's name.

"Aye but he's American," Lorna said in a huffy tone.

"What's wrong with that?" Meryl asked.

"Let's face it," Lorna continued. "The yanks are full of hot air."

"Wow, Lorna, you've met every American?" I tutted. "Now, that's impressive!" Scowling, she stuck out her tongue.

"What else did he say in the letter?" Kimberly asked.

"That he loved our time together in Delhi and that he's looking forward to showing me around LA."

"How exciting," Meryl smiled. "When are you going?"

"It's not a TriStar route, so-"

"You should just buy a ticket and go," Kimberly suggested.

"Trust me, I'd love to, but I've already used up all my leave."

Lorna stood up. "Och listen to the three of you. He needs to come here and see you."

Kimberly waved her hand in Lorna's direction. "I think LA will be a lot more exciting than London, besides, we'll be licenced to fly on the jumbo soon, then you can request a trip to LA."

"As soon as we're on the seven four seven the four of us should request the same trip, that'd be brilliant," Meryl burred.

"Plenty of fish in the sea," Lorna said with a heavy eye roll.

"Yeah, but compared to David they're all mingers," piped Kimberly.

With a dreamy look in her eyes, Meryl said, "Is he really that good looking?"

"Gorgeous, gorgeous, gorgeous," sang Kimberly.

"Are you sure it's no you that fancies him?" Lorna teased.

"Karen saw him first. And he chatted her up in the galley. For ages. Of course she gave it right back," she winked. "And for the rest of the flight she was buzzin'."

Meryl released a contented sigh. "He sounds amazing, Karen, I'm so glad he's been in touch."

"I guess my brazen move with the note paid off," I laughed.

Lorna plopped down on the couch next to Meryl. "Aye, well they're all fantastic in the beginning then before you know it, it all goes to pot."

At the same time, the three of us spun to face Lorna.

"Then again," she smirked, hands in the air. "There's always an exception."

10th ~ Kimberly, Lorna, Meryl's, Richmond upon Thames

Made it through today's block of standby without getting called out and who knows if tomorrow will be the same, or if I'll be going to bed on a different continent.

Carl and Daniel (from training) popped round to the flat and after standby was over, we went to the pub with Meryl and Kimberly (Lorna left first thing, didn't think to ask where she was flying to!). It was a perfect Pimm's afternoon with sunshine, strawberries and cream. "Just like Wimbledon, only cheaper," Meryl said.

We left the pub slightly worse for wear (but happy!) and Carl suggested we go clubbing. At the flat, we downed a few more drinks while we got into our glad rags, then took a taxi to Cinderella's in Kingston, where we'd gone to celebrate, after getting our Wings. Kimberly was in one of her moods and I felt myself getting annoyed with her but I'm vowing to be a supportive friend. Still, if she could just keep it to a minimum.

While Carl and I were dancing, a girl the spitting image of the lead singer of The Bangles (the one Ben used to drool over) stepped on my toes trying to get closer to Carl. He shrugged an apology and flashed his, *Sorry, sis*! smile so I left them to it and a few songs later, they were in each other's clutches.

11th ~ Kimberly, Lorna, Meryl's, Richmond upon Thames

Ten minutes before standby ended, I got called out, throwing Kimberly into a sulk, declaring, "I detest standby."

"I don't think anyone actually likes it, but it's part and parcel."

"At least you know where you're going."

"Maybe you'll get called out for Harare, and you can surprise Meryl."

"I don't want to go to Harare," huffed the petulant child within.

"You have four hours left, then freedom will once again reign!"

"I hate having to stay in."

"Well, it's not like you can take the phone outside," I said, my well of encouragement finally dry.

Various versions of that conversation continued and after a couple of hours my patience was gone.

"I might just go home. Check in isn't 'til tomorrow night."

Kimberly's face fell and I reminded myself of the promise I'd made to be more understanding.

"I'd rather not be alone." She looked close to tears.

"I don't *have to* go home," I said. "Let's have a look through the BA timetable and see how many flights go to LA." (Like I haven't already done that!).

Kimberly gave me a questioning look.

"So that I can fantasise about going to see David."

"That's a bad idea."

The little voice in my head urged me to Be nice but I still paused before I spoke. "Just the other day you said I should just buy and ticket and show up."

"I don't know why I said that. I don't think you should see him again; he lives too far away. Besides, I prefer Jon. I think you should go out with him again."

Arghhhhhhhhhhhhhhhh!!!

12th ~ LGW – AGP – LGW
Hilton Hotel, Gatwick Airport

Because we're flying again tomorrow (went to Malaga today!) accommodation is provided and after I got settled in my room, I ventured down to the lobby to ring home.

"Och, is that you Karen?" Considering I'm an only child, mum's frequently used expression amuses me no end. "The phone hasnae stopped all day, I feel like a receptionist."

"Who rang?"

"Stephen was first to phone this morning, he's a scream sure he is. Then Pamsy. I told her we miss her, and she should come up. Then nana phoned, she's no been feeling too well, I think the heat's wearing her oot."

"Poor nana, I'll get her something nice in Cyprus. Was that the last call of your workday?" I joked.

"Far from it. Frankie was next, she sounds like a lovely wee soul, very genuine. And that's me just off the phone with LA."

Thinking I'd misheard, I said, "What?"

"I thought I'd save the best fur last. He's got a lovely voice, och I could've listened to him all day."

"*David rang?*"

"Aye, he wanted to talk to ye before he left for the weekend."

"Where was-"

With a mixture of mum's regular Glaswegian and an exaggerated American accent, she said, "I'm heading to my folks' place in San Diego, for the weekend."

"Did he leave their phone number?"

"Uff, I knew there was something I forgot to ask."

"That's it, you're fired!"

215

In an attempt to get off the phone, I fibbed and said I was running out of coins. I felt a mixture of excitement knowing David had been in touch but disappointed I'd missed him. I was so lost in thought that I jumped when I heard, "Evening, Miss M."

"Annabel!"

"How are you, poppet?" She clipped, placing her hands on my shoulders.

"Really well," I said, through Annabel's three air kisses. "What are you doing here?"

"I stopped by to say hello to a friend." The way she said it told me the friend was male.

"Anyone I know?"

"Possibly," she grinned, tossing her chestnut locks to one side "But we can chat about it more, later. Are you coming or going?"

"Staying. I just checked in a short while ago, it's not worth me going all the way home only to come back again first thing."

"Let me guess," she said, waving the antique emerald ring she always wears. "Cyprus?"

I nodded.

"Fab route, incredible fresh fish." She paused. "Come to London?"

"I'd love to, when?"

"Now! We must stop at my flat first, I need to change, and I've arranged to meet some friends later, in Bell-grey-v-ah."

I couldn't help but smile. "Are you sure?"

"Absolutely! You'll love them, do come."

Staring down at my stonewashed jeans and espadrilles, I said I should change.

"No, you mustn't," she said, grabbing my hand. "You look simply divine."

13th ~ LGW – LCA

Presently on crew rest but not for long as flight time is only four and a half hours. Same crew as yesterday's quick hop to Spain and they seem nice so I'm looking forward to exploring Cyprus.

To quote Annabel, last night was, "An absolute hoot." While we were on our way to London, I asked who she'd been with, at the hotel.

"Just a friend," she said, acting distracted by the traffic.

"I don't believe you."

"Miss M, has anyone ever told you you're much too astute for your own good?"

"Daily," I smirked. "Who were you with?"

"You must promise not to tell anyone."

"I shan't say a word," I said mimicking her accent, as she changed lanes and sped up.

"I was enjoying a rather active afternoon with a chap I recently met."

"Cabin crew?"

"Why do you need to know?"

"I don't but given he was at that particular hotel, I imagine he's either cabin or flight crew."

"You ought to be a detective," she grinned.

"So, does this crew member have a name?"

She shook her head.

"You won't even tell me his name? Please don't tell me he's married."

"Oh gosh no, that would be ghastly. Fine! His first initial is T."

"Thomas?"

"No, but I'm rather partial to the name."

"Timothy?"

"Goodness, no! Daddy would have a stroke if I so dared as to kiss a Catholic boy."

"Teddy?"

She cracked up laughing. "He's a chap, not a dog."

"Wait, I know! It's toe-knee," I said in my best cockney accent.

"Tony? Ugh! I couldn't possibly be intimate with anyone bearing such a pedestrian name."

"Of course you couldn't."

"I shan't tell you his name," she smirked, finger raised. "However, I will share a story with you. On a recent trip that T claimed was becoming rather tedious, he asked one of the newer crew members if she'd like to go to the market. He didn't actually say this, but I got the impression he rather fancied her and was using the market as a ploy to garner some interest."

"Crafty!"

"Indeed, so this new girl-"

"What was her name?"

"He failed to say, but she'd previously confided in him that she'd slipped a note, with her address no less, into the jacket pocket of a Club passenger." Checking her lipstick in the mirror, she uttered, "Thankfully, he wasn't in Economy, can you imagine?"

"What a hussy!" I said, trying not to let my face give anything away.

"I must say, I rather admire her gumption, and T did add that the passenger in question was extremely yummy, but wait, the best is yet to come."

"Oh, there's more?"

"Oh yes, much. While they were haggling, in the market-"

"Where?" I couldn't help myself.

"Delhi? I think it was in Delhi, anyway T and the new girl-"

"You mean the hussy."

"Ya, T and the hussy were haggling, and you'll never guess what happened?"

"They got something for free?"

Annabel's expression was the definition of disdainful. "The chap she, *hussy,* had left the note for appeared in the market! T said their reunion was like something out of those old, romantic films." While Annabel clutched at her heart, mine was racing at the memory of that moment and I must've shaken my head because she blurted, "You don't believe me?"

"Stuff like that never happens."

"There's absolutely no reason for T to fabricate such a thing."

"Sorry Annabel but I think Toby got a bit carried away."

She shot me a look. "Did you say *Toby*?"

I met her look of surprise with my widest smile.

14th ~ Larnaca, Cyprus

218

After arriving at half five this morning, I arranged to meet up with some of the girls at the beach club, but I slept through the alarm and didn't stir until late afternoon.

Holiday vibes galore during dinner, with fresh caught fish, chilled white wine, balmy air and a view of Finikoudes beach.

Given the amount of brandy sours in my bloodstream I probably shouldn't start a letter to David, but I can decide tomorrow whether to send it, or not.

15th ~ LCA – LGW
At home

Easy flight home this morning, crew transport back to LHR, then trouble in the staff car park, when my car kept sputtering. It eventually started but I should probably get it checked. That's the last thing I need after a night flight.

Ben's letter (heart flutter at the sight of it) gave the impression he's lonely, so I hope he's ok. I try so hard to shut down my feelings for him, but I can't imagine ever not caring about him. I'm consciously not using the L word, but it might be more appropriate.

Better than Ben's letter was the postcard from David that arrived in the afternoon post. He was in Tokyo but should be home now. I'm tempted to ring him but with such a huge time difference, it's difficult to catch him, plus I'm sure he'll be jetlagged, so I'll hold off on ringing but I'm drifting off to sleep with his words…*I hope we can meet up sooner or later, somewhere in the world.*

Me too, David, me too.

16th ~ At home

When we moved to Milton Keynes, I hated it. I missed my best friend Linda far too much and wanted nothing more than to return to the place where I was born, the place where nana lived close enough that I could visit anytime.

The first time that mum and I saw this house was the day we moved in. After living in flats for most of her life, mum was ecstatic to have, "A back and front door," the latter leading to a generous sized garden. Mum expected my level of excitement to match hers, but I hated the new surroundings and at least once an hour, I'd ask when we'd be moving back to Scotland.

The following Monday, I cycled in the direction of the new school I knew nothing about. Speeding up to get through the underpass, jeered at by the early morning student smokers, I was tempted to go home but I knew mum would only send me back. With trembling fingers, I fumbled with the combination lock, and asked the punk girl next to me where the main office was. The school I'd left a few days before had a strict uniform code, where undoing the top button of the uniform blouse was considered rebellious, so seeing a student in full punk regalia was shocking, to say the least.

The first teacher I encountered had long black hair, streaked with silver, and the swoosh of her ankle length skirt collided with the rattling strings of beads she wore. "*Do call me Marion*," escorted me to her classroom and I felt my cheeks fire up as she introduced me to a smattering of spotty faces. I remember wondering where everyone was, only to soon discover the class size was half that of what I was used to. Melting inside the Arran jumper nana knitted, I caught the eye of a pretty, dark-haired girl seated in the middle of the room. Smiling, she gestured to the empty seat next to her. I waited for Marion to tell me to sit but after a few minutes it was obvious that wasn't going to happen, so I awkwardly made my way to the vacant seat.

"Alright?" the girl asked, in an accent I'd only heard on *Eastenders*.

Over lunch in the cafeteria, Sarah told me she was, "toe tally in luv," with her boyfriend and suggested I, "find a decent bloke," to go out with as soon as possible. When I discovered Sarah lived two streets away, I remember feeling relieved that I'd have someone to ride to school with.

A few weeks later, Lucy was the new girl, and I watched as the colour rose in her pale cheeks, when Marion introduced her. I smiled at her and gestured to the empty seat beside me.

Tonight, at the pub, the three of us reminisced about those awkward, gangly teen years that felt like they would never end.

17th ~ At home

"Phone," Lucy croaked from the bed on the other side of the room.

"My mum'll get it."

"Karen! Get the phone!"

"Guess not, "Lucy laughed, retreating under the duvet.

Groggily, I made my way downstairs, the scent of lemon pledge filling my nostrils. I was in no rush to converse with anyone, so I took my time getting settled in the phone chair, all the while watching mum, polish the ornate dining table dad insisted would fit in the small space (it doesn't.)

"Hello?"

At the sound of, "Hey babe," my heart deceived me.

"Ben…it's you…." I stuttered. "Is everything ok?"

"Yeah, I just wanted to hear your, in this case, raspy voice."

"I just woke up."

"Sounds sexy," he purred, making me wish I could climb through the phone.

"How are you?"

"To be honest I'm exhausted and can't wait to leave."

"And then you'll be back?"

"Yeah, I'll be home within the next month, hopefully sooner."

Ben. In close proximity.

"I know you'll be busy and that, but I'd love, I mean like, I'd like to see you, Karen."

"I'll be here," I said, much too fast. So much for playing it cool.

I wonder if First Love (yes, it deserves capitals!) is this potent for everyone. I know it's special and I've heard it talked about in an almost sacred way, so there must be something to it. I feel like I'm on cloud nine just from talking to him and I could kick myself for allowing his voice to knock me into such a tizzy, but I don't seem to have any control over it.

18th ~ At home

All night, I lingered by the phone, willing it to ring, willing it to be Ben. I've loved him since I was sixteen but has the time come to make a go it with someone new? Someone who doesn't live close but has my attention.

19th ~ LGW – JFK
Omni Park Central Hotel, New York

Back in my favourite city, with Kimberly, aka Matilda, but I'll get to that.

Flight time to this wonderous place was just over seven hours, most of which I engaged in conversation with as many pax as possible. Plans for the evening were made on the bumpy ride into Manhattan, all whilst trying not to spill glass after glass of brown milk. When it was obvious that most of the crew wanted to go to the Irish bar close to the hotel, Kimberly piped up that we had, "Tickets to see a show." She sounded so convincing I believed we were going to the theatre, but after I got to my room, she rang and confessed she'd only said it to get out of meeting up with the crew.

Quick change before we giggled our way into a yellow cab and made our way to MK's, which, being Saturday, was mobbed. We started out in the downstairs bar and in the unlikely event we got separated, we arranged to meet by the stuffed Doberman's framing the door (obviously not real dogs!). Within minutes of entering the bar filled with French antiques, we got chatted up by two Americans, one of whom piqued my interest with his strong no guesses where from accent, but I'd made a pact with Kimberly to make tonight about dancing and having fun, not mingling with the opposite sex. So, we claimed to speak very little English, and it worked wonders because a few minutes into our stilted conversation, they lost interest.

In the basement, Matilda adopted an attitude that somehow gained us entry to the members only club, and when, Lil Louis, "French Kiss" played, the place really came alive. From there, we moved through each floor, all the way up to the top, known as the bedroom floor.

20th ~ Omni Park Central Hotel, New York

If you were to spend your entire life in New York, I doubt you'd ever run out of new experiences, which is one of the many reasons it appeals to me.

At the hotel, I literally walked into Joe from Air Europe days. As fubsy as he looks, he still managed to pick me up and spin me in circles.

"A cannae believe it!" he bellowed in his broad Glaswegian accent.

"Put me down, you're making me dizzy!"

Stopping with the ease of someone half his weight, he said, "Ye here fur the night?"

"We are," I nodded, holding out my arms to steady myself.

"Whit's the plan, then?" He said after I'd introduced him to Kimberly.

"We're meeting a friend of mine who lives here."

"Friend or *friend*?"

"The former, unfortunately," Kimberly chimed.

When I rang Christopher to let him know Joe would be joining us for dinner, he picked up on the second ring.

"Hi Christo-" I began, quickly stopping when I realised it was the answering machine. After leaving a long-winded message about Joe joining us (didn't think it'd be cool to show up with an extra person) I collapsed on the bed and opened the latest by Mary Higgins Clark. Set in New York, it's called, *While My Pretty One Sleeps*.

When the phone rang a few minutes later, I grabbed it. Expecting it to be Christopher, I said, "Ola mi amigo."

"Karen?"

"David!"

"Hi, did I catch you at a bad time?"

"Not at all, this is a lovely surprise, where are you?"

"Home, in LA. I called you at home, your mom told me where you are."

"She's good like that," I laughed. Being New York, we stay in a handful of hotels, and never know which one, until we arrive, so I asked how he knew where to find me.

"I'm good like that," he chuckled, but didn't elaborate. "So, how's the big apple?"

"It's the total dogs you know what."

I wasn't sure he'd get the reference, but if he didn't, he never let on.

"I've never visited."

"Are you kidding? Then again, it's the same distance from here to LA as it is from London, and I can't imagine it's terrible there."

"LA is cool."

Like you!

"I'll have to take your word for it," I said in my flirtiest tone but flirting on the phone isn't exactly my strong suit (nor is flirting in person!).

Still giddy from my chat with David, I met Kimberly and Joe in the lobby, and when Joe's ginger barnet came barrelling in my direction, I shrieked, "Don't pick me up!"

"Nae chance," he grinned. "I think ye broke ma back earlier."

"Cheeky bizim," I said, swiping his meaty arm.

We met Christopher at Café Dante in Greenwich Village and sat outside, watching the world go by. Christopher was his usual attentive, gracious self and after a couple of rounds Joe leaned against me. "It's a bloody shame," he slurred, "he's oan your team and no mine."

When it came time to give up the table (there's no way the cues from the impatient waitress could be misconstrued as anything other than, *Get outta here!*) Christopher had a suggestion.

In the cab, when Kimberly told Joe and Christopher how much fun we'd had as Matilda and Abby, they said they wanted in on the act. Joe became Andreas, whose German accent sounded on point (at least to me it did!).

"I ain't so good with the accent thing," Christopher said.

"Ye could be a New Yorker," Joe teased.

"How about being French?" Kimberly said excitedly.

"I don't think I can pull it off."

"Course ye can, Pierre," Joe said. "Jist shrug yer big shoulders and keep yer mooth shut!"

The queue to get into Nell's was ridiculous but when Christopher's friend Jessica spotted him getting out of the cab, she beckoned for us to go to the door. While they exchanged pleasantries, I scanned the line of hopeful's, wishing I'd worn something more suited to clubbing.

The rich fabrics and leather banquettes were inviting, and I made a mental note to tell Annabel about Nell's.

"You good here?" Christopher said, over the din.

"Nice choice," I gushed. "Well done you!"

"I figured you'd like it," he said, looking jubilant.

Kimberly, Joe and I managed to stay in character, but our ami, Pierre soon became Christopher the New Yorker, who mentioned more than once how nuts we are, but that it was one of the best nights he's ever had.

When Joe finally found the decency to stop flirting with Christopher (not a quick process) he sidled up next to me.

"Are ye sure yer jist pals?"

I nodded .

"Then yer a dunderheid," he chortled. "Look at him. He's pure perfect."

When Christopher invited us to his apartment for a nightcap, Joe's gleeful demeanour soon changed after I politely declined, and for the first time ever, I got cursed in a combination of German and Glaswegian!

21st ~ JFK – LGW

With the top of the skyscrapers piercing the clouds, we left behind the city that seeps into every pore. For the remainder of crew rest, I'll be polishing off the sticky toffee pudding the First Class Purser sent down the back for us lowly folk.

Kimberly said this has been her best trip yet, which was lovely to hear. I know she often finds it difficult to gel with certain people (don't we all!) and is much happier in small groups. Having said that, when it comes to dealing with passengers, she's outstanding, so perhaps I don't know what I'm talking about!

Christopher insisted on picking up the tab for the entire evening (can't imagine the bill at Nell's was inexpensive) so I rang to thank him.

"I won't keep you, I'm sure you're busy."

"You're good, I'll be working late tonight."

"You seem to work late quite a lot."

"Music biz," he sighed. "Goes with the territory. Hey, I've been meaning to ask you something."

"No, I don't want to appear on MTV as singing sensation Abby."

He laughed. "Would you consider going to LA with me?"

"*LA?*"

"Los Angeles."

"Sorry, I know what you mean I just wasn't ehm…"

"MTV's video music awards, September sixth. I've been invited to-"

"Wow, good for you!" I said, grabbing my fakeofax, wondering how I could sneak in a trip to LA during days off.

"Arsenio Hall is the host."

"Oh, I like him, I've seen his show a few times."

"He's a cool guy."

"Yeah, he is," I said, exhausting the matter.

After a slight pause, Christopher said, "Do you think it's something you might be interested in?"

"Hang on a sec," I said, running my finger over the September calendar.

"We'd have separate rooms if you-"

"Shit! I have a class that week."

"For what?" He sounded despondent.

"To get licenced to fly on the seven four seven."

"That's cool."

"No, what's *cool* is that you've been invited to the awards."

"I'm guessing you can't change it?"

"Not really, I mean I could pull a sickie, but I've been on the list to get on the course for ages."

"Better routes?"

"Without it, I'll never get to Australia, or the Far East."

Or LA. Ah, the irony!

22nd ~ At home

Plopped on the bottom stair, I was halfway through the second page of Ben's double-sided slanted scribble, when I heard the key in the lock. Through the frosted glass I saw mum's silhouette, so I quickly got up and stuffed the letter inside my uniform handbag.

I made a move to open the door, but mum was already inside.

"Hullo hen," she said, turning her cheek for a kiss. "Is that ye jist in?"

"I've been home for about half an hour," I said, picking up the rest of the post.

In between whistling, "New York, New York," mum gushed, "I cannae wait to hear aboot it!"

I was chomping at the bit to read the rest of Ben's letter, but mum was anxious to hear about her favourite place and of course, my chat with David.

"He's got a lovely calming voice sure he does."

"You're only saying that because he's American."

"Yer no far off the mark there," she chuckled.

"How long did you speak to him before you told him where I was?"

"No too long, I could tell he was eager to get hold of ye."

"It was a lovely surprise, but I have no idea how he knew what hotel to find me in."

"I told him." Mum's nonchalant tone prompted my quizzical look.

"The last time Frankie phoned, it came up that I used to work in New York, and she mentioned the hotels BA puts you up in."

"Mum, *I* don't even have that information!"

"Aye well ye should've asked Frankie."

23rd ~ At home

Between the downpours and continuing coverage of the horrific Marchioness disaster, I spent much of the dreary day on the phone.

Pamsy – "Sounds like this David geezer really made an impression on you."

Carl – "What are you like with the Yanks? This one had better not be all mouth and no trousers!"

Sam – "I just flew with a gorge Purser called Toby. Is it true you tucked a note inside a punter's *trouser* pocket?"

Nana – "Yer mammy told me aboot the American boy ye met oan the plane. I wonder if his family has Scottish roots?"

Florence – "Karen, luv, come round. I have wine. And I want to hear about this fella from Los Anjilees."

Lolly – "Thanks for your note, mate. Now spill the beans on the bloke from Hollywood."

Sarah – "I wish your American boyfriend was here so you could bring him over. We could make hamburgers. Is it true they all like hamburgers?"

24th ~ At home

Ben rang first thing and I'd go as far as to say the chat was one of our best. Not only because it was so lovely to hear his voice again, but we had a good laugh about some of the stuff that's happened since we last saw each other.

Ben claims he hasn't been with anyone else. I don't believe him but if we're talking about the possibility of getting back together (oh yes, it was mentioned more than once!) we need to put the past behind us. We know each other so well and regardless of where I am or who I'm with, I feel he's always somewhere in my head. And heart.

Still on a high, I jumped on my bike and pedalled like mad to the city centre. Before hitting the shops, I stopped at the fountain in

Queen's Court to catch my breath. With the sun spilling its warmth over my face, I shut my eyes and began to replay my chat with Ben, grinning about some of the more suggestive language that had spilled from his oh so beautiful mouth.

"Karen?"

"Oh, hello Lee," I said, my eyes squinting against the sun. "I haven't seen you for yonks."

"Not since your commuting days."

"Don't remind me," I groaned. "No work today?"

"I took the week off, needed a break. Do you have time to grab a coffee? Oh wait, you're allergic to coffee."

"Good memory," I laughed.

Strolling through Middleton Hall, I noticed a few girls checking Lee out. In casual jeans and a fitted shirt, he looked different to the guy in the dowdy trench coat. The thick rimmed glasses (favoured by oap's) had been replaced with a designer pair that framed his face so much better.

While I tucked into Mille-feuille (because two layers of puff pastry isn't nearly enough!) in Café Rouge, Lee filled me in on what he's been up to and when only the crumbs remained, he smiled and said, "Your turn."

As is typical of me, I ended up sharing too much, and when I mentioned Ben's call, Lee rolled his eyes (first time for everything!). "I thought that would've fizzled out by now."

"It did. We split up back in June when I visited him on the continent."

"And now you might be getting back together?"

"I wouldn't say that."

"Then what would you say?" His sharp tone took me by surprise.

"We're planning on seeing each other when he comes back. As friends."

"How do you see that playing out?" He gestured to my mouth.

"Thanks," I said, wiping a trace of custard. "I don't know how it'll go."

"You must have some idea. Actually," he continued, sitting up straight. "Let me rephrase that."

"Shit Lee, are you sure you're not a lawyer?"

He cracked a tiny smile. "What would you like to see happening with you and Ben upon his return?"

"I'd like to spend time with him and see where it goes."

"*Again,*" he stressed, with a forced smile that left me feeling like a fool.

25th ~ At home

I wasn't expecting to come home this early on a Friday night, but Sarah and Simon quarrelled like there was no tomorrow and the entire evening turned into a lengthy gripe about household chores and who should do what and when and how often. Exhausting!

David's letter (today's treat!) describes where he lives in such a way that it makes me want to throw caution to the wind, get on a plane and go see for myself. Had I been able to go to LA with Christopher it'd have been the perfect excuse, but I can't imagine just showing up with the sole purpose of seeing David.

I'm really enjoying his phone calls and love receiving his letters but if he were to show up, how would I feel? If Ben were to appear at the door, I know I'd want him, like I always have, but David is a different kettle of fish. Having said that, if Delhi is any indication of how things might progress, we could be onto something, dare I say, *wonderful*?

I was so caught up from hearing Ben's voice that I dove back into the deep end and went along with some of the things he said about the possibility of us getting back together. Now I've had time to think (which should always be a prerequisite) part of me feels like getting revenge for the way he treated me, particularly in France. If I were to act vile towards him, would it get this niggling feeling out of my system? Or is the turmoil I experience with Ben just the nature of our relationship?

26th ~ Flight from Heathrow to Larnaca

Larnaca, Cyprus

As the crew retrieved their suitcases, I thought mine might have mistakenly been loaded in the hold alongside passenger luggage, but alas, it never appeared.

Fortunately, we're only here for the night before operating the flight back to LHR, that is of course if my case shows up, otherwise I'll be deadheading as I don't have my uniform.

Flight made a quick stop in Rome, so I at least got a good whiff of Italia!

27th ~ Flight from Larnaca to Heathrow
At home

As soon as my eyes flickered open, there it was, the flashing red message light. Expecting it to be news about my wayward Samsonite, I clicked to listen, only to find out we'd be deadheading home.

Opening the balcony doors to the sun streaming in from a feather-streaked sky, felt like waking up on holiday. On the balcony next door, sat my affable Purser, Johanna.

"Who goes there?" She laughed, putting down her book.

"It's Karen, is anyone about?"

"You're safe," she said, as I gingerly stepped out onto the balcony, wrapped in a bed sheet. "*Armani*?" she joked. "I take it your case hasn't appeared. Do you need anything?"

"You wouldn't happen to have a spare toothbrush, would you?"

Johanna was on the phone for a while, but I couldn't make out what she was saying, so I thought she might be ringing housekeeping for extra supplies (something it never occurred to me to do!).

"You can keep that," Johanna said, passing a First Class toiletry bag over the waist high wall.

"Acquired during a recent upgrade on a staff travel ticket, to visit my sister in Oz," she winked, before going back inside to answer the forceful knock at the door.

Lost in the view, I jumped at the chorus of, "Surprise!" There, on Johanna's balcony, stood four of my crew, all draped in bed linens!

Cracking up laughing, I took Jayshree's outstretched hand and climbed over the wall.

"We didn't want you to feel left out," Johanna grinned.

"And *I* didn't want to be outdone," Bruce said tartly, as he reached deep into the nether regions of his designer toga and produced two bottles of wine.

28th ~ At home

I made the mistake of sharing some stuff with mum about my recent chat with Ben. For a few hours afterwards, she carried on as normal and over dinner, with dad, she made no mention of anything I'd shared, but after dad went to bed, she motioned to the tv and said, "Shut that thing off."

After what felt like being read the riot act, mum softened. "I see ye light up after trips, when ye tell me aboot all the smashing people ye meet, living it up in far-flung places. All the things ye should be doing at yer age. Making lifelong friends, like Frankie, Carl, the toffee-nosed lassie, whit's her name again?"

"Annabel."

"Aye, Annabel. I think ye'd be better off leaving *you know who* behind and go in the direction I think ye want to go in."

"You mean David?"

"I think ye should at least give him a wee chance."

"You haven't even met him!"

"I've a good sense of who he is fae talking to him on the phone."

"Yeah, an American with a nice voice," I tutted, like a stroppy teenager. Mum didn't respond but her expression told me everything. "Sorry, mum, that was uncalled for."

Clearly unfazed, she said, "Ye've got the whole world at yer feet, hen."

"I know," I nodded, feeling utterly conflicted.

Squeezing my arm, mum said, "I jist want ma lassie to be happy.

In that, we can agree.

29th ~ At home

In bed with my headphones on, listening to Teddy Pendergrass crooning, "Can we be lovers?" I keep rewinding the cassette because I love this song like there's no tomorrow. *You're the missing part, that can heal my lonely nights, you're the missing part, that makes my day so bright.* Ah, sing it to me, Teddy.

Torrential rain the entire drive to LHR in rush hour traffic, only to be told the Paris I was scheduled to operate had been cancelled. After getting stuck behind an endless stream of lorries spraying all sorts on the windshield, I decided I need a zippier car.

After a nice dinner with mum and dad, I rode my bike to Susan and Stan's. Even without Ben there, I get such a feeling of comfort being in his house.

While I was putting my bike in the shed, mum came dashing through the gate.

"Guess whit? David's comin' tae London!"

"Is he now?" I grinned, giving my bike a good heave into place.

"He phoned aboot an hour ago and he's flying into Heathrow, this Friday."

Shit!

30th ~ LHR – CDG – LHR
At home

Today I went to Paris and saw nothing of it! Came home to another letter from Ben, the tedious tone of which came across as boring and put me in a foul mood, but when I re-read it tonight, his words made me feel sad and miss him more than ever. Now I wish I hadn't opened it.

I really am pathetic.

31st ~ At home

"Blimey," Pamsy quipped, after I told her about David's upcoming visit. "I wonder how long your mum kept him on the phone!"

"She didn't say but I can't imagine it was a quick chat."

"Bless, she must be so excited. Dare I ask what you and Mr. LA will be doing this weekend?"

"A lot of sightseeing, I expect."

"That's not what I meant! Do you think *it* will happen?"

"What? Going to *London*? Most definitely!"

"Oh, I see what you're doing," she chuckled. "So, *London*, huh? More than once, maybe?"

"Phew, I hope so," I said, trying not to laugh.

SEPTEMBER

1st ~ At home

According to mum, David's flight from LAX was due to arrive this afternoon, but it's almost midnight and I haven't heard a peep from him. With my imagination roaming wildly, I've gone through every scenario from him missing the flight, to having a change of heart. The worst feeling is when you don't know what's happening.

2nd ~ At home

In mum's excitement, she muddled up the date of David's arrival!

"Now that we've established you won't be here, what are your plans for the weekend?" I asked, when we finally got to chat around six tonight (ten am in his world).

"I'm going to San Diego."

I assumed he was going to visit his parents but didn't want to sound pushy by asking, so instead I asked how far it was.

"In weekend traffic, probably close to three hours."

"About the same time that it takes me to drive to Heathrow." "I love driving in the UK," he gushed. "I'm renting a car so we can go anywhere you want."

"Sounds great."

"And when you come out to LA, we'll take a ride on the PCH."

Future plans!

"Is there anything in particular you'd like to see while you're here?"

"Just London," he stated. "I love London. I've only visited a few times but each time I leave wanting more. It's so cool you live so close."

"This weekend San Diego, next weekend London!"

In more ways than one!

"Crazy, huh? I don't travel nearly as much as you, but I think it makes you appreciate home more, don't you think?"

"Sometimes," I uttered, recalling some recent lonely weekends.

"I don't know how you flight attendants do it. Those trips back and forth to Delhi and Tokyo are kickin' my ass."

At the mention of Delhi, my mind wandered to our first kiss, back in July.

"Karen? You there?"

Ahhh, say my name again. And again and again and again.

"Yep, I'm here, but I should probably let you go, so you can get on the road."

"Yeah, my folks are expecting me for lunch and my mom will get upset if I'm late."

Ah, a family visit.

"Have a lovely time and I'll see you next week."

When I weigh at least a stone less and my legs are silky smooth after applying an entire bottle of Nair!

"Too cool, I'll call you as soon as I get to the hotel. Think about what you might wanna do in London, ok?"

Like I don't already know!

3rd ~ At home

Carl was nursing "a bastard of a hangover," after turning twenty-one yesterday, but we still managed to chat for ages. He's throwing a proper party next month, so that's one event I don't want to miss.

Lots of downtime today meant time to think. My wish is that things will go so well with David that I'll lose all memory of B…*Sorry, who*?

236

On the phone tonight with nana, she said she loves receiving the cards and letters I send. "I read them time and time again," she said. "So much so that I've memorised most of them."

I know the feeling, nana.

4th ~ Kimberly, Lorna, Meryl's, Richmond upon Thames

Day in the classroom with Kimberly and Sam, who kept us thoroughly entertained.

"After we start flying on the Queen of the skies, the world will literally be our oyster," Sam said, excitedly. Come to think of it, there isn't much Sam says without sounding like he's about to hyperventilate.

"What do you mean?" Kimberly asked.

"Men, darling! I mean men! More destinations equal more men."

"Ohhh," she stuttered in a way that made us crack up.

From across the table, Sam pointed at me. "You're not saying much over there, missy."

"Karen already has a boyfriend in LA. And there's a guy in New York called Christopher who likes her, but she doesn't think they have chemistry," Kimberly rattled.

"No chem, no go," Sam stated. "But you have it with the one from LA?"

"I'm hoping to find out this weekend," I grinned lasciviously.

5th ~ Kimberly, Lorna, Meryl's, Richmond upon Thames

Kimberly is a diehard *Emmerdale Farm* fan, so while we were studying last night (with wine!) we watched, and still managed top marks today.

We learnt that the first Boeing 747 passenger flight was in 1970, on a Pan Am flight from New York to London. In Seattle, Washington, Joe Stutter led the engineering team that created what I believe is the most beautiful aircraft ever. Onboard, we got familiar with the layout and the First, Club and Economy cabins, but my favourite feature is the spiral staircase that leads to the Upper Deck. When the 747 was first introduced, it was a lounge but nowadays it seats passengers.

After class, Kimberly, Sam and I went to Henley to see Xavier's new flat. As nice as it is, parking proved a major issue so the idea of a house in the French countryside is still appealing.

6th ~ Kimberly, Lorna, Meryl's, Richmond upon Thames

With foil containers of Chinese takeout spread across the floor, Kimberly and I sat on cushions, with the telly on in the background.

"Thanks for driving to Crankebank every day," she said. "I'm glad we ended up on the same Jumbo course."

"Thanks for letting me stay here. The three of you did well to find a place so close to the airport."

"You know you're always welcome. It's rare for the three of us to be here at the same time."

"We do have a most unusual job," I said, topping up her wine.

"True," she nodded. "Not many people can say they spent the day on an empty aircraft, trying to locate the safety equipment."

"Shit!" I said, waving the empty wine bottle in the air. "I just remembered Christopher is in LA tonight."

"You mean David?"

"No, Christopher. He's at the MTV Video Music Awards."

"You should be there!" She squealed. "I heard The Cure are playing. Can you imagine?"

"Where'd you hear that?"

"There was something in the paper about it being their first appearance on American tv."

"I wish we could watch it," I sighed. "I can't wait to go to LA."

"Nor can I," she said, getting up. "For different reasons of course." Using the wine bottle as a microphone, in a tv announcer voice, she yelled, "For one night only, Los Angeles, yes that's right folks, the land of the angels." Making the sound of a drum roll, wagging her finger in my direction, she continued, "LA is coming to youuuuuuuuu."

I jumped up and we danced into the kitchen, for yet another bottle of wine.

7th ~ Kimberly, Lorna, Meryl's, Richmond upon Thames

Jon treated Kimberly and me to dinner at a quaint old pub in Windsor. Unfortunately, Kimberly was in a sulky mood and complained nonstop about absolutely everything. When she went to the loo, Jon commented that she was being a bit of a nightmare.

"I don't think she can help it," I said, coming to her defence, but when he dropped us off with the excuse that he was going rowing (which he recently took up) he looked relieved.

We'd only been back in the flat a short time, when David rang (special thanks to mum for giving him the phone number!).

"I'm still packing but I wanted to catch you before you go to bed."

Bed!

"I hope you have a good flight," I said.

"Red eyes aren't my favourite, but I had a late night so hopefully I'll sleep."

Desperate to know the cause of the late night, I chirped, "I hope it was a fun one."

"I stayed up way too late watching the MTV music video awards."

"Oh, how was it?"

"Awesome, do you like The Cure?"

"Love 'em!"

"They performed and oh man, I need to buy every piece of their music this weekend."

"Tower Records here we come," I laughed. "Was Madonna there?"

"Yeah, she opened with "Like a Prayer," and presented an award to George Michael."

"He won? Brilliant, I love him."

"He's awesome. Madonna was obnoxious, not as bad as Andrew Dice Clay though, that dude has zero talent."

"Who else was there?"

He laughed. "I guess you're a big music fan, huh? Bon Jovi performed. Cher..Paula Abdul-"

"What a great dancer!"

"She kinda is, yeah, oh and Neil Young won for best video."

"For what?" I asked, as he cracked up laughing.

"I just got the significance of the song title."

"Sorry, I'm not too familiar with his music, what's the song called?"

Still laughing, he said, "This note's for you."

8th ~ Penta Hotel, Heathrow Airport

I've long been a sucker for floppy haired guys, and even while David sleeps, his hair looks like he spent ages styling it. It falls across his face in such a way that all I want to do is brush it away and kiss his delectable perfectly shaped lips.

On the drive here, I could hardly believe I was coming to see David. In the parking lot, I sat in my car for ages trying to gather my thoughts and calm down. Walking into the lobby, my stomach was doing somersaults, but when I spotted David, I remembered why I'd left the note.

"Hey you," he greeted me, with a kiss on the lips. "You're wearing your Delhi shirt, looks awesome. Wanna grab a drink here first and figure out what we're doing?"

"You're the guest, we'll do whatever you fancy."

"I'd love to go to London."

"Me too," I grinned.

We zoomed off in, "The totally uncool Orion rental car," and managed to find a parking spot close to Covent Garden. It was David's first time there and being the start of the weekend, everywhere was packed with that energetic Friday night atmosphere I love, with people spilling out from the pubs onto the street.

"I'd enjoy Trafalgar Square more without the pigeon droppings," I laughed as we navigated our way through the crowd.

"Let's go sit up there," David said, pointing to one of the massive bronze lions surrounding Nelson's Column.

"The Landseer Lions," I said. "According to legend, if Big Ben chimes thirteen times, they'll come to life, but how do you propose we get up there?"

Gripping David's shoulder, I stepped into his clasped hands, and in one fell swoop, he propelled me up towards the lion's mane. Once I got situated, I held out my hand to help him up. With our bodies wedged close together, it didn't take long for his lips to find mine.

When I opened my eyes, the lights of London looked twinklier than ever, and with my head resting against David's shoulder, we watched the world unfold below us. As much as I was enjoying the moment, I was eager to see what else London had in store!

"Do you remember where you parked?"

"Yeah, why?" he said.

"Let's take a taxi back to the car, it'll be faster than walking."

"Sounds like a plan," David grinned, sliding down the base of the sculpture. Ahhhh….London.

9th ~ Penta Hotel, Heathrow Airport

David has a dimple in the middle of his chin that the tip of my index finger fits perfectly into.

"You're the first person ever to have noticed that."

"It's rather fetching."

"Fetching," he uttered, as I lowered my lips to his.

A few hours later, sifting through my stuff, strewn across the spare bed, I realised I didn't have my uniform jacket.

"Shit! I need it for my trip tomorrow."

"We can go pick it up," David said, in an easy tone. "And then, if you want, we'll go to London again."

He had a good chuckle after I filled him in on the double entendre.

"This is sooo unfair," Meryl huffed, following me around the bedroom, while I looked for my jacket.

"What is?"

"This whole thing," she said, waving her slender arms. "You need to sit down and tell me everything."

"There's no time, Meryl. This is our last day together."

"*Ouft!*" she exclaimed in her Scottish brogue.

"Ah, there's my jacket, on the chair where I left it," I said, kissing her on the cheek. "I promise I'll ring you after my trip."

First stop was at Chopard, where David picked up his new watch that was designed as part of the *Mille Miglia* series (a vintage car race that started in Italy, something I only found out about today!). When the yuppie girl behind the counter finally stopped flirting with David (extra points to him for appearing oblivious, extra points to her because I couldn't blame her for trying) long enough to package up the watch, he turned to me. "See anything you like?"

Prompted by an unkind glare (is there a nice glare?) from yup yup at the other end of the counter, I sidled up to him and breathed, "Yes, absolutely."

"What?" He asked, all innocence.

"You," I whispered in his ear.

Next stop was Harrods where we (I) made a beeline upstairs, to the toy department, gushing, "I can't believe you've never been in Harrods!"

"Guess I was waiting for you to show me around," David said, from a few steps behind.

"This is one place I know my way around," I said heading for the corner, where the teddy bears live. When I picked up the white Steiff, David grinned and uttered the three words I already knew. "You need him."

For the remainder of the day, we meandered through the city, ending up on a park bench in Hyde Park, just as the sun was about to set.

"You know," David said, looking a little pensive. "Spending time with you in Delhi was awesome, but London..wow…London has been off the charts."

I felt everything churning inside, as David's fingers made circles on my thigh.

"Do you agree?"

I nodded, then kissed him. Hard.

Standing up, with his hand outstretched, David said, "There's one last place we need to go."

I got up and cocked my head in question.

"The Hard Rock Café."

"No way," I said. "Much too touristy, we can't go there."

"My sister specifically asked for a sweatshirt."

"In that case," I smiled. "Follow me.

10th ~ LGW – BDA
Somewhere over the Atlantic

Presently winging our way to Bermuda, which is usually a good thing. Just not today. Not even with extra biscuits and extended crew rest.

I lost count of the number of times I hit the snooze button and because of that, it was a mad rush to get ready. Sitting on the edge of the bed, with David stroking my back while I slipped my shoes on, I was sorely tempted to pull a sickie, but I knew if I did, I'd lose my upcoming fourteen-day trip and I need the money to put towards a new car. Plus, I'd run the risk of missing Carl's 21st and that's not an option. I did however take my sweet time pondering all of the above, while David kissed various parts of me goodbye. When I breathed, "I really have to go," I swear a little piece of my heart broke off and fell into bed beside him.

When I came out of the loo, David was at the foot of the bed.

"What are you doing?"

"I'll walk you to the car," he said, buckling his belt.

"I'd rather you didn't."

He stopped and gave me a questioning look.

"I can't kiss you in uniform and to be honest, leaving feels torturous enough."

"I know," he nodded. "But are you sure?"

My turn to nod.

"Then come here."

11th – Hamilton Princess, Bermuda

Scribbly writing tells the story of a girl in Bermuda who drank too much Goslings rum with her friend Kimberly, stumbled back to her room and began reflecting on life and la la la la la la la la la ....LOVE!

I love my job, but will it ever allow me to have a romantic relationship that lasts longer than a weekend? I'll use David, as an example. Total wow guy, gorgeous, witty, intelligent, a little shy, yet still confident. Driven. Adventurous, and if I wasn't so sleepy, I'd continue, but what did I fail to mention? Oh yes, he lives six thousand miles away! How on earth could we ever make it work?

I've never been to LA...I might hate it...I don't think so...I think I'll absolutely love it...David! Sunshine! Surfers! What's not to love about that? Ah, love love, love, love, love...complicated, seemingly unattainable love.

I will pay for this tomorrow. Heavily.

12th ~ BDA – TPA – BDA

Over breakfast at Macmillan's, Kimberly slid pancakes from one side of the plate to the other, while I tucked into eggs benedict. Still hungry, it took everything I had not to ask her if I could pinch a pancake. There's a reason Kimberly wears belts with everything.

Nobody wanted to go to the pool, so I grabbed my book bag, which, after a recent sort out is a lot lighter than it was. Just past the little archway that leads to the patio area, I found a quiet spot and got lost in Hemingway's, *Farewell to Arms*. What a great, albeit tragic story, I almost cried over Catherine Barkley's tragic demise.

Tampa shuttle was a piece of cake, but I forgot to take my fakeofax, so I didn't get a chance to ring Miriam or Liza.

No crew interest in going out tonight, so I wasted no time changing out of uniform, showering, then....bed! Wrote a particularly long letter to David that I'll pop in with his birthday card. I wonder where he'll celebrate his birthday (not allowing my mind to wander to who he might spend it with).

Just started a new book by Margaret Atwood called, *Cat's Eye*, that I'm loving so much I might stay up and finish. Regardless, my liver is writing a thank you card for giving it the night off.

13th ~ Hamilton Princess, Bermuda

Finished the book (so good!) at five this morning and a few hours later, I was on the ferry with Kimberly. On the beach at the Southampton Princess, she said she wasn't, "in a people mood," so she took to the water, while I caught up with a few familiar faces, which is always enjoyable.

Back at the hotel, I got the best surprise when David rang (I may have dropped the name of the hotel during one of our pillow talks!).

"You really need to get out here," he said, more than once.

Like I need any encouragement!

"The weather's perfect and I'm looking at the ocean."

"Isn't the weather always perfect in LA?"

"I guess," he laughed. "So, when are you coming?"

"I don't qualify for staff travel concessions until I've been with the company for a year, so the end of January."

"That's way too long."

"Unless of course I get rostered a trip to LA, which is highly possible, now that I'm licenced to fly on the glamour jet."

He laughed. "Let me take down where you're going next."

"I'm only rostered for the next three weeks, but the new one should be there when I get home."

I heard paper rustling, possibly a Filofax?

"Darn! I'll be on my way to Tokyo when you get home."

"Eh, I think they have phones in Tokyo."

"I was thinking more along the lines of the time difference."

"It's a pity you went home first. You might've been better off just flying from Heathrow, to Tokyo."

"Man, why didn't I think of that?"

Because you were so consumed with me you couldn't think straight?

245

"We need to figure this out," he said, sounding serious. "I don't know how or when or where, but we'll figure out it."

Yes, we will!

14th ~ BDA - LGW

In the briefing room, Ainsley looked, to quote nana, "Like butter wouldn't melt in her mouth," so I was more than surprised tonight, when she started sharing details about the torrid love affair that she's having with a married Captain she met five months ago (on her third trip!). He has three kids, one of whom is our age.

"He's a perfect gent," she gushed. "And I've already picked out a house for us, in Sussex."

"Su sicks," I said, in a not so hushed tone that got Ainsley's attention.

"What? You don't think he'll leave his wife?"

Without missing a beat, Kimberly chirped, "Probably not."

Once Kimberly gets going there's no stopping her. Brutally honest. Not always a welcome trait.

Looking at me, Ainsley asked, "What do you think?"

"I, I don't know, "I sputtered. "You're obviously serious about him but-"

"You'll get hurt," Kimberly interjected.

"I won't," Ainsley declared. "We're in love."

15th ~ At home

Came home to find mum in the kitchen, with the talk radio station blaring.

"Mum!"

"Oh, bejesus!" She screamed, spinning to meet me. "Ye gave me a fright!"

"Sorry," I yelled. "Do you mind if I turn this down?"

"Turn it off, all they've been on aboot is the ambulance driver's strike. Ye look good wi some colour on yer face," she said, as I pecked her cheek.

"We spent a lot of time on the beach, weather was gorgeous."

"I'll make ye a wee cup of tea, d'ye want toast?"

"Yes, please."

"I got the strawberry jam ye like, the French stuff."

"Ah, thanks, mum. I'll get changed, then I'll tell you about the trip."

"And?"

"And what?"

"And whit happened *before* ye went to Bermuda."

I cocked my head in question.

"Did ye no jist see David?"

"I did, sorry, I'm a bit tired, yes I did, oh, so much to tell you!"

"I'll make extra toast!"

"We might need sausages and eggs as well," I said with a chuckle. "For the juicy bits!"

"Away wi ye," she said, smacking my arm.

Upstairs in my bedroom, I could hear mum singing above the sound of rattling dishes. I quickly got out of uniform and tossed the striped skirt and blouse (there's a reason we call it the deckchair) in the hamper. Sighed in satisfaction after all traces of make-up were gone (love that feeling) then brushed my teeth.

When I came downstairs, the postman had been. First thing I grabbed was the envelope with the BA logo. Sensing it was the new roster, I carefully peeled it open.

"Shit!"

"Don't swear! Whit is it?"

"Look," I said, pointing to the letters.

"Lax?" Mum asked, pronouncing the letters like she would in laxative.

"No mum, it's L A X."

"Whit does it mean?"

Jumping in the air like a cheerleader, I waved the page. "L A X," I screeched. "It's the three- letter code for Los Angeles."

Pumping her fist in the air, mum hollered, "Yasssssssss!"

"Finally!" I screamed. "I'm going to LA!"

16th ~ Carl's, Surrey

It's almost three in the morning and the stragglers from Carl's birthday party just left. While we were dancing in the living room, Lorna grabbed my arm. "Come with me, I've got something to tell you." The kitchen door groaned open, and Lorna peeked in to make sure we'd be alone. "I've met someone."

I was confused. "You mean Alistair?" Her long-time boyfriend who flew down from Scotland to spend the weekend with her.

"No, no, no, someone else."

"Who?" I asked, as the door creaked open. Kimberly crept over to us, by the sink.

"Are you telling Karen about him?" she whispered.

Lorna nodded and in barely a hush, she said, "He's a pilot. With KLM."

I leaned closer to her. "Where'd you meet him?"

"In Nairobi." Her eyes darted from me to Kimberly, to the door. "He's smashing, you'll love him."

"I can't wait to meet him," Kimberly said, forgetting to whisper.

"Shhhhhh," Lorna scolded.

The kitchen door squeaked and when Lorna saw it was Alistair, she turned her back to the door. "Well, I'm glad we were able to make it tonight." She turned to face Alistair. "Hiya honey, you enjoying yourself?"

"Oh aye, brilliant night," he smiled. "I'm jist grabbing another beer, whit's shakin' here?"

"Just a bit of galley gossip," I chirped.

"Be out in a wee minute, honey," Lorna cooed.

"You're a bad girl," I teased.

Clinking her glass to mine, she said, "Takes one to know one."

Kimberly and Carl's brother, Connor, flirted for hours before they ended up kissing. I missed the whole thing, but Lorna said, "It looked like they were digging for gold."

When "Ride on Time," came on, Carl and I were first up to dance.

"We've danced to this a lot together, sis," he yelled, making me laugh. "What's so funny about that?"

"The fact you call me sis means you don't fancy me, which is perfect, because-"

"You don't fancy me either!"

"Exactly! Happy birthday, bruv!"

17th ~ At home

Connor's suitcase took pride of place in the passenger seat of his TR7, which left Kimberly no option, other than to squeeze into the back seat, but as comical as that was, it was Carl's breathless impersonation of Brooke Shields that cracked me up, "Nobody comes between me and my....*Samonsite*!"

"There's post in the kitchen," mum said as I poked my head in to say hello after what felt like a never-ending drive.

"Did ye enjoy the party?" dad asked.

"It was great fun, so glad I was able to make it."

"Aye it's no easy flying roon the world, is it?" he teased.

"Well, *you know*," I sighed exaggeratedly.

"Don't forget to get yer post."

Focusing on mum, I said, "I take it from your enthusiasm, there's something from David?"

"Caught again, Liz," dad chuckled. "By the way, I'm going to Mercedes and Harry's later for dinner, mum cannae make it, she has a meeting at the church."

"I'll go with you, dad, I'm in the mood for some nice nosh."

"Whitever Harry makes, it'll be delishio," mum gushed. "Janice and Terry'll be there as well."

"Great, I haven't seen them for ages. Ok, I'm off to check the post, put you out of your misery, mum."

Mum followed me into the hall.

"Did anyone ring?"

"Aye Pamsy. And Sebastian. He wanted ye to go to a party with him, in London."

"Oooh, lovely, when?"

"Last night."

The postcard from David pictured the lions in Trafalgar Square. *Wish we were there again. I love going to London with you xxx*

18th ~ At home

Still basking from our delicious chat, I smiled when the phone rang again.

Ah, he can't stay away from me!

In my most seductive voice, I breathed, "Hello again."

"Oohhhh, get you," Pamsy chuckled.

"Shit, it's you!"

"Sorry to burst your bubble. Who were you expecting?"

I paused before I said, "Ben."

"Ben?" she yelled. "Why are you still talking to him?"

"I don't-"

"What did he want?"

"Nothing, just letting me know he's coming home in a few weeks."

"Arghhhh," she shrieked. "What about David?"

"I don't know what to make of any of that."

"In the letter you sent from Bermuda, you said you had the most fantastic time with him, what happened?"

"Nothing really, just that he's in Tokyo with no way of me contacting him. He just travels soooo much."

"I hate to state the obvious mate, but-"

"Yes, but it's our job."

"And travelling is part of his job."

"It's different." I hated how whiny I sounded but couldn't seem to help it.

"How so?"

"Ugh," I groaned. "I don't know, I'm soooo confused. David lives so far away. I just don't know how we could ever-"

"Whoa! Hold your horses. It's such early days. You've hardly spent any time together, yet you're already in doom and gloom mode because you're trying to look too far ahead."

"Six thousand-"

"Stop!" she yelled, enough to get my complete attention.

"I always forget how bossy you are," I laughed.

"Assertive, mate. The word you're looking for is assertive."

"Then you're incredibly assertive."

"And so are you. Don't forget that. Just relax and see how everything plays out. Ok?"

"Ok."

"And now the assertive side of me is going to suggest you ring me when you get back from your trip, when?"

"In two weeks."

19th ~ LHR – AUH

I've been up since four, so this extended crew rest is much appreciated. Made possible by the efficient nature of our Purser, who's a bit of a banana clip girl, but lovely all the same. It makes a huge difference when you work with someone who still embraces the nature of the job and looks out, not only for the crew, but also the pax.

In TriStar House, I bumped into Graeme.

"Hello stranger," he grinned, pecking each cheek long enough to allow me a citrusy whiff of Bijan, which always reminds me of Bermuda. "You look well."

"As do you, where you off to?"

"Honkers."

"Nice, I can't wait to go there."

"Spectacular, you'll love it, but not as much as Bermuda," he laughed. "By the way, thanks for ringing."

I expected to feel the warmth in my cheeks, but it didn't happen.

"Thanks for the humourous notes you've been leaving in my mail slot."

"Oh, you saw them, then."

"Yes, and I apologise for not responding."

"Are you seeing someone?"

"Kind of," I uttered.

"Mysterious as always," he said narrowing his eyes. "I like that about you."

"It's a long story."

Scratching his chin comically, he uttered, "Hmmm, that tells me absolutely nothing."

"Perhaps that was my intention," I cooed, in more than a flirty tone.

Who am I?

"In that case, mission accomplished. You still have my number?" He glanced at his watch and before I could answer, he blurted, "Gotta go!"

"Give my love to Hong Kong and tell her I'll be there as soon as I can."

Gathering up his cabin bag, he said, "I forgot to ask, where you off to?"

"Fourteen-day Abu Dhabi, Delhi, KL."

"I hate long trips," he groaned, with another peck to my cheek. "Unless of course-"

"Off with you!" I said, as he turned and mouthed, "*Ring me!*"

20th ~ Hilton Hotel, Abu Dhabi, United Arab Emirates

With half the crew under the age of 25, this trip holds tremendous potential for some shenanigans!

The more senior crew are usually the ones to host room parties (better rooms) so I quickly showered and changed, but as swift as I was, most of the crew were already milling about our CSD, Mr. Fenwick's top floor, executive style room. Several glasses of champagne in, someone suggested, "Popping downstairs to the Safari club." There were so many of us, we had to squeeze into three lifts, which for some reason seemed like the funniest thing ever.

Wasting no time, a bunch of us made our way onto the dance floor and "Pump Up the Jam," came on, I found myself dancing with a guy called Marc, here on business, from Cape Town. He was a terrific dancer and when he asked what I'm doing here, I told him I'm also here on business, which isn't entirely untruthful!

I sensed I'd gone over my bubbles limit when, many dances later, we were dancing a lot closer. With such a good- looking guy (especially one doused in Obsession for Men) it'd be easy to predict what'd happen next, but instead of falling into territory I'm no longer a stranger to, I excused myself.

On my way to the loo (slightly cursing myself for being sensible) the gaudy purple and gold carpet seemed to take on a life of its own. Pushing open the ridiculously heavy door, I chuckled at the sight of a girl bent at the waist, her hair flying in every direction, from the air rushing out from underneath the hand dryer. When I tapped her on the shoulder, she shot up, narrowly missing whacking her head on the edge of the dryer. Bouncing up and down, she squealed question after question, none of which I answered, not even to ask Frankie how her hair got wet.

21st ~ AUH - KUL

Time to rest my twinkle toes, overdose on Earl Grey and see how many chocolate biscuits I can devour during this hour of crew rest.

Leisurely day at the beach club with Frankie, who is now travelling in the opposite direction, while we wing our way to Malaysia. Last night was epic and I got to meet the guy Frankie calls The Viking, who more than fit the bill

While we were taxiing out to the runway, a foul stench wafted its way to the mid-section of the aircraft, where Mavis and I were strapped in for take-off.

"What's that smell?" She asked, crinkling up her freckled nose.

With my hand over my mouth (lipreaders are everywhere!) I was about to answer, when Mr. Fenwick's soothing tone came over the PA. "Ladies and gentlemen, this is your Cabin Service Director. Some of you may have noticed a rather, uhm, unpleasant odour in the cabin. We will be returning to the gate momentarily, where the ground crew will work to remedy the situation, as quickly as possible."

"I knew this would be a shitty trip," Mavis joked.

All hell broke loose after Mr. Fenwick's announcement and the fetor got so bad, several passengers threw up, which is always delightful, especially when they're seated in your cabin.

22nd ~ Kuala Lumpur, Malaysia

On the crew bus, I sat with a cool girl called Millie, who joined our crew in Abu Dhabi. As shattered as we were, we still managed to gab all the way to the hotel, laughing over what Mr. Fenwick called, "Shitgate." Seems the awful stench occurred after the First Class sinks and toilets began backing up with, to quote the Captain, "Expensive excrement!"

After such a hellish flight, there was no mention of meeting up at five, like we usually do, but I did arrange to meet up with Millie and Mavis at eight to go to the night markets. When I finally woke up, I found an envelope that'd been pushed under the door. Inside, were several drinks vouchers to redeem at the hotel bar. On a torn sheet of hotel stationery, was a note from the First Officer. *Hello Karen, not sure what your evening plans are but I'll be in the hotel bar between ten and midnight. Hope you'll come and join me for a drink. Mike.*

When I looked at the clock, I couldn't believe it was half eleven, which meant I'd slept the entire day. After showering, I felt wide-awake and considered popping down to the hotel bar, but the drink chits seemed more than tacky and the only time I'd talked to Mike was during a flight deck visit with a long-retired pilot and his granddaughter. I decided to stay in my room, where, for the past few hours I've written tons of letters, including two for David because one isn't nearly enough to cover all that's been happening. It's strange knowing it's lunchtime in his world…yesterday.

I've run out of stationery, so all that remains is to order chocolate mousse from room service.

23rd ~ Kuala Lumpur, Malaysia

Around four this morning, I was beyond bored, so I scribbled a note on the back of the little brown envelope our allowances come in and made my way to Millie's room. Just as I was crouching down to slip the note under the door, it flew open, startling me so much I let out a scream.

"Get in here, before we get in trouble!"

"You can't sleep either?"

She shook her head. "I'm sorry I didn't meet you and Mavis. I forget to set the alarm and didn't wake up 'til eleven."

"Same here. *Shit,* I hope Mavis isn't upset with us."

"Oh, I didn't even think about that, we should stick a note under her door to apologise."

"You're in your nightie," I said.

"Nobody will see me at this hour."

An hour later, while Millie and I were gorging on hokkien fried noodles, toast, and carrot cake (totally bizarre combo) there was a light knock at the door. Bending to peer through the peephole, Millie said, "Mavis," and opened the door.

"I'm so glad you left that note, hi Karen," Mavis said, pushing hair off her face. "I've been tossing and turning for hours. I was in such a deep sleep I didn't hear the alarm go off."

"That flight really took it out of us."

"In seven years of flying I've never experienced such a putrid smell."

"Aw, I was only fifteen when you started flying, Millie."

"And I was only fourteen," Mavis added.

"Hush your mouth," Millie joked.

Perched on the edge of the bed, Mavis said, "I didn't wake up 'til after eleven."

"We clearly have the same circadian rhythm," I said.

"I don't know what that is," Mavis yawned, reaching for a slice of carrot cake. "But we're definitely on the same wave-length." She brushed crumbs off her lap and suddenly looked serious. "Listen, you two. I have to tell you something, but you mustn't say a word to anyone else on the crew."

Millie gestured, *go ahead,* as I reached for another forkful of noodles.

"When I woke up there was a note under my door from Mike the FO."

I squirmed against the low backed chair.

"What did he want?" asked Millie.

"It was weird, he said he'd be in the hotel bar between eight and ten, and that he'd like me to have a drink with him."

"That's a bit creepy," Millie said, swiping the last of the carrot cake I'd been eyeing.

"That's what I thought, but wait, it gets worse. Inside the envelope were several vouchers for free drinks at the hotel bar."

With her hand over her mouth, Millie mumbled, "Are you kidding?"

"Isn't that tacky?" Mavis said, shaking her head.

"Beyond tacky," I added, hoping my face wouldn't give me away.

24th ~ Kuala Lumpur, Malaysia

Mobbed and humid is a bad combination but the market was worth it, all until I'd had enough of weaving in and out of clusters of shoppers. Millie said she was, "Done in from the heat," and Mavis said if we didn't leave right there and then she'd melt before our very eyes, so with that we caught a taxi back to the hotel.

I rang home from the lobby (bye bye allowances!) and mum was getting ready to go out but found the time to let me know, "A letter wi a lovely Japanese stamp," had arrived. I was tempted to ask her to open it but after an excess of *London* experiences with David (it had to be from him!) I wasn't sure what would be inside so, much to mum's dismay, I told her I'll open it when I get home.

After a nap in the arctic chilled room (heavenly) I met Mavis and Millie in the lobby at seven. The flyer for the Tin Mine at the Hilton, touted it as, "The Studio 54 of Malaysia." The fact that Studio 54 closed almost ten years ago didn't bode well for the evening. I love the stories about the famed New York nightspot, but the best must surely be the time Bianca Jagger rode a white stallion through the club, on her 30th birthday.

The Tin Mine was full of tourists, ex-pats and other airline crew and even with the DJ playing some of my favourites, I just wasn't feeling it. By the time midnight rolled around I felt groggy and tired but not from alcohol as I'd only had soft drinks. I told the girls I was wiped out and after they waved me off in a taxi, they tottered back inside.

I feel a marathon writing session coming on and if only to keep my creative juices flowing, I might order chocolate mousse. So glad I remembered to pack my Walkman, because the onslaught of a night of words wouldn't be complete without a quick bop around the room to the dulcet tones of Luther singing, "Never too Much."

25th ~ KUL - AUH

The early hours brought a not so gentle knock at the door, and through the peephole I watched miniature versions of Millie and Mavis, swaying in unison. Opening the door, I joked, "Sorry, this is a lush free zone."

"O v ish lee not," Mavis slurred.

With matching expressions of surprise, they eyed the bed, strewn with reams of pages I'd written.

"Can I read some of them?" Millie asked, almost toppling on top of my pile of dreams.

"Absolutely not!" I said, blocking her.

"Ooooh, testy," she quipped. "Must be about us."

It was after five when I finally got rid of them, then we met at nine for breakfast. The temperature was nearing triple digits, so we spent most of the day hiding under poolside umbrellas, before retreating to our rooms for some rest before pick-up.

26th ~ AUH - DEL

And now to India, after an eventful twenty-four hours in AUH.

"Sorry you didn't make it to the bar in KL," Mike, the FO said as we made our way to Safari.

"Speaking of, I ought to return your drink vouchers."

"Whatever for?" His smug tone matched his expression.

"Just in case you want to pass them along to someone else." I waited until he was looking at me, before I said, "Like, Mavis."

Without a word, he stepped up his gait to catch up with the CSD.

27th ~ Hyatt Hotel, Delhi, India

Shortly after checking in after yet another gruelling flight, Millie and I caught a taxi to the spot where the coach was due to depart. Convinced we were being ripped off, Millie bickered with the taxi driver, causing him to narrowly miss hitting several vehicles along the way. I didn't want to miss the coach so with just three words I got him to agree to half of what he'd originally quoted.

"Honestly, Millie," I tutted, when we were finally out of the taxi. "All you had to say was British Airways crew. Works every time!"

As we piled into the rusty old van, with gaping holes doubling as windows, Millie grunted loud enough for the other tourists to hear. "This is it?"

"Yes, miss," the driver nodded, as he checked our tickets.

"How long is the journey?" she snipped.

"Travel time for Agra three hours, miss, maybe more."

"We'll never last that long without air conditioning," she barked.

"I drive fast," he lilted with a lovely smile.

Half an hour into the drive and half a stone less from perspiration loss (there's an upside to everything!) the van screeched to a halt.

"What the!" Millie snarled.

"Miss and misters, please in seats stay," the driver announced but Millie was already on her feet. "There's a cow in the middle of the bloody road!"

There was much clicking of cameras and general chatter, all uttered in an array of languages.

"Can you shoo it away?" Millie asked the driver.

"No, no, miss. Cow is the source of progress and prosperity."

"*Progress and prosperity*," I uttered, so as not to forget.

"The words of Mahatma Gandhi," explained the driver.

The sacred cow made no attempt to move off the road. A handful of children surrounded the van, their hands outstretched, as Millie and I dug deep into our bags for fruit pastilles and polo mints.

"I wish we had better sweets, these are crap."

"Or something to draw with," pondered Millie.

"I've got some hotel stationery and a few pens.

"Course you do," she clucked.

A sea of young, curious faces soon joined the other children.

"We don't have enough paper or pens for everyone," I said.

Waving her hand dismissively, Millie shouted, "Who wants a picture?"

Sitting cross legged on the ground, Millie quickly sketched a picture of a plane. She held it up and passed it to a little boy standing over her. She tore a sheet of paper in half and handed it, along with a pen to a barefoot girl who looked about four or five. It took everything I had not to react to the sight of her tiny, deformed feet as she smiled shyly and crouched on the ground beside me.

Millie tore the paper into small pieces she handed out to each child, while the other tourists rummaged in bags and pockets for anything to write with. Sketching picture after picture, Millie remained on the ground, until the cow lazily got up.

When we were back in the van, children reached their hands through the openings. We squeezed their small fingers and matched their sweet smiles as the driver waited for the cow to move fully out of harm's way.

Taj Mahal means Crown of Palaces. The structure was built to house the tomb of Mumtaz Mahal, the third wife of emperor Shah Jahan, who was heartbroken after his wife died giving birth to their fourteenth child. It took 20,000 workers and assistance from 1,000 elephants twenty-two years to complete. It's made mostly of white marble, laced with intricate pieces of gemstones that sparkle magically in the light, but what I learnt today far exceeded anything related to the Taj Mahal.

28th ~ Hyatt Hotel, Delhi, India

259

I'm finding the time differences quite draining, so it was lovely to lounge this morning before meeting Millie. We caught a tuk-tuk to the market where David and I had our chance meeting.

"How does it feel being here again?" She asked, as we wound our way through the crowd.

"Feels nice," I said, stopping to pick up a white cotton shirt.

"That thing is filthy!"

"I don't care, I love it enough to buy it."

"It'll make everything in your suitcase smell awful."

"*Shitgate* already seen to that!"

"I hope the shirt David gave you wasn't as grubby as that one."

"Stop getting shirty with me," I joked, as Millie rolled her eyes.

"And for your information it was clean as a." When I dared to whistle, she glared at me.

"Sorry, being here reminds me so much of him and makes me excited to see him again soon."

"He's going to London again, so soon?"

"No, my next trip is to LA." Just saying the words caused my insides to jump for joy.

"You never told me that!"

"I thought I'd mentioned it."

"No, you did not," she said in an accusing tone.

"Sorry," I uttered, unsure what I was apologising for.

We didn't speak for a while, which felt awkward, but I was determined not to be the one to break the silence, like I usually do.

"Let's go for a champi."

"What's that?" I asked, expecting her to say it was some sort of drink.

"A head massage."

"Ok."

"Just *ok*?" She scowled. "That's your response?"

Perhaps if I hadn't felt like I was about to keel over from lack of sleep and the back of my top wasn't soaked in sweat, I'd have been a little more amiable, but I'd reached the end of my tether.

"What *exactly* is your problem, Millie?"

"Pipe down, I was only kidding." Linking her arm through mine, she said, "You're going to think you've died and gone to heaven after you experience champi."

No, Millie, heaven is next week, when I'm in LA. With David.

29th ~ DEL - AUH
Hilton Hotel, Abu Dhabi, United Arab Emirates

Call time was at half two this morning, an unearthly hour when it goes against everything to get up, shower, slap on some make-up and get into uniform.

We arrived to a message from crewing in London advising us of an extra sector to the trip (to Delhi) which will extend the trip by several days.

Over dinner, we discussed the difficulties of this unscheduled change. It's in times like this my heart goes out to crew, with children. I can't imagine trying to juggle family life from the other side of the world at the best of times, but something like this really throws a spanner in the works.

The roster change means I won't be going to LA, which is why I'm crying.

30th ~ On the tarmac, Abu Dhabi, United Arab Emirates

Shortly after we took off from AUH, while Millie and I were still strapped in our jumpseats, she turned to me with an expression that said, *That doesn't sound right.*

"Ladies and gentlemen, this is your Captain speaking. I do apologise for any inconvenience, but we will shortly be returning to the stand where we'll-"

Nudging me, Millie said, "Do you know what's happening?"

"I would if you hadn't interrupted the Captain's PA."

"It's the undercarriage," she whispered. "I've had this happen before."

"What was the outcome?"

The phone rang and Millie answered, while I smiled reassuringly at the middle-aged woman in the seat facing us, whose worry beads were in peril of being worn away.

"That was Fenny," Millie mouthed. "It's the undercarriage, it won't go up. He's about to make an announcement so buckle up, this lot are not going to be happy campers."

Two hours later, still on the ground, hoping to appease the passengers, we carried out the drinks and meal service, which only put us in the line of fire.

28E – "I should never have booked with you useless lot. I've problems with my veins, I need to get off and stretch my legs. When are we leaving? I demand to speak to someone in charge. Now!"

Terribly sorry to hear that, sir. I wouldn't mind stretching my legs either, if only to escape you and your disgruntled fogies. And for your information, the person in charge is rather preoccupied, attempting to take care of this shit show.

34A – "I say, young lady. My husband (no sign of husband!) mistakenly packed my heart tablets in with the luggage. Is there any possible way (fake smile) you or one of those (she pointed to the army of ground crew) people *down there* could fetch them?"

Certainly madam, let me just slip through the imaginary hatch that leads to the hold…navy suitcase you said, with beige piping? Not a problem…anything else while I'm at it? Perhaps a scarf, to go with that garish blouse you overpaid for?

36C – Desperately trying to impress the Yasmin Le Bon lookalike next to him, as he helps her pronounce, "Kathmandu."

She's way out of your league dumpy boy. Go back to reading your guidebook.

Bounding into the galley, Mr. Fenwick said it best, "Basically, the bugger won't budge!"

And it still hasn't, so here we are, stuck on the aircraft, five hours after we were due to depart. Pax were offloaded a couple of hours ago, but we just found out they're boarding again soon. Oh, what joy that will bring!

OCTOBER

1st ~ Hilton Hotel, Abu Dhabi, United Arab Emirates

The flight fiasco ended at sunrise, after a slew of engineers concluded the undercarriage was inoperable. Once again, the pax were offloaded, none too happy with the fact they'd be spending an undetermined amount of time in the UAE. I felt sorry for the ground crew, faced with the mammoth task of locating last minute hotel rooms for hundreds of disgruntled travellers.

The entire crew showed up in Mr. Fenwick's room for what he promised would be, "An excellent game of charades, accompanied by generous nightcaps." The fact that it was morning never entered the equation as we wearily bundled into his room, where, during charades, he informed us we're going home tomorrow!

After the raucous applause died down, Mr. Fenwick plopped on the floor between me and Millie.

"You seem a little quiet," he said.

"She's upset about the roster change," quipped Millie. "She lost a trip to LA."

"What's so great about smell A?" he asked, adjusting his corpulent frame.

"She has a guy there."

Gesturing to our empty glasses, Mr. Fenwick said, "Be a love Millie and grab us a top up, cheers!"

"If I must," she tutted, getting up. Staring down at me, she huffed, "What do you want?"

"Same again, please."

"I'm not a mind reader!"

"White wine, please."

"What about you, Fenny?"

"*Mr. Fenwick* to you," he said, half mockingly. "I'd love another g and t with a huge wedge. Thanks, love."

His attitude was so upbeat you'd never have guessed he'd been up all night, handling one problem after another.

"That'll keep her busy for a while," he grinned. "There's not a lick of gin in this joint, I'm on the vodka. Now spill, girl, and go heavy on the juicy LA lover boy bits."

2nd ~ AUH - LHR
At home

After walking eight plus hours in the air, I was desperate to head home but Millie suggested we check our mail slots before catching the bus to the car park.

As well as several notes, there was a small package wrapped in patterned tissue paper. I looked to see if Millie was close, but she was at the far end of the room, talking to her Fleet Manager, so I read the accompanying note.

As you've yet to experience the wonder of Hong Kong, I thought you'd like this.

Give me a ring!

Hope you had a good trip. Give me a jingle and tell me about it.

I'm sure you're tired from the night flight, so drive safe. And maybe after you recover, you'll get on the ole dog and bone.

FYI (hint hint!) I'm on leave 'til the 12th, when I go to LAX.

Give me a bell!

Talk soon (Hopefully!)

G xxx

"Ooohhhh, that's gorgeous." Millie said, startling me from behind.

"Shit, you scared me!"

"Mind your p's and q's!" Came a voice from inside one of the offices.

"Where'd that come from?" Millie asked.

265

"Hong Kong."

"I meant *who* not where."

"A friend," I said, trying to act blasé.

Brushing her fingers over the scarf, she shrugged. "Real silk. Nice friend. Who is he?"

"Nobody you know," I said cockily.

"I might! Don't forget I've been around a lot longer than you have."

"He's not your type."

"Stop being so crotchety."

"Sorry," I said. "I'm just really knackered, aren't you?"

"Dead on my feet, let's go."

Closer to home I got stuck in rush hour traffic and finally rolled in after six.

"Is that you, Karen?" Mum called from the kitchen.

"Yep," I replied, maneuvering my Samsonite through the front door that seems to get smaller after every trip.

"Hullo hen," dad said halfway down the stairs "Jist leave that, I'll get it."

"Thanks, dad. Phew, it's good to finally be home."

"Yer jist in time for dinner."

"Smells amazing," I said, kicking off my shoes.

"Mum went all out; I think she missed you. Och, we both did."

"Hi mum," I smiled, opening the kitchen door.

"Hullo hen," she said, squeezing me tight. "Perfect timing." With her hands on my shoulders, she held me at arm's length. "That's a crackin' scarf, I like that colour on ye. Did it come fae India?"

I shook my head.

"Right ladies and gentlemen," mum continued. "Take yer seats, and Karen you should probably take the scarf off, ye don't need anything spilled on it, especially since I'll be asking tae borrow it."

After the trip rundown, with mum and dad oohing and ahhing over the little bits and bobs I bought in various markets, we rang nana to wish her happy birthday. Mum talked first and relayed pretty much everything I'd just shared.

"That was some trip," nana said, after I'd finally pried the phone out of mum's hands. "I cannae believe ye went all the way to the Taj Mahal, and I only made it up tae the shops in Springburn."

"I hear Glasgow's lovely this time of year," I laughed. "I bought you a birthday present in Malaysia, so I'm sorry it's late but I'll post it tomorrow."

"Yer a good lassie. And thank you for the sentimental card. I must admit, yer words brought a wee tear tae my eye."

"I'm glad you like it."

"Oh aye, it's taken pride of place on the mantlepiece."

"Happy birthday, nana. And here's to many more."

3rd ~ At home

Feeling unsettled after a dream about palm trees with giant fronds, I bolted upright and wasn't surprised to see it was only 3:18 am. Knowing there was no way I'd get back to sleep, I slipped downstairs and when I clicked on the kitchen light, my eye was drawn to the far end of the kitchen counter, where an airmail letter sat atop the small pile of post. My first reaction was to tear it open and read it on the spot, but I knew if I did, it'd only leave me feeling disappointed that I hadn't taken the time to savour every word.

In the cupboard I found a packet of Custard Creams, with only a few missing. While I made tea, I munched on one and scanned the rest of the post, pleased to see a postcard from Christopher, with a picture of a koala bear (is there anything cuter?). He'd mentioned ages ago that he was going to Australia and New Zealand, so I'm glad he made it.

Made tea in the pot and set the table as though expecting company. *Good morning, David. You must be exhausted from all our trips to London. May I offer you a cuppa?* Read the rest of the post, poured the tea, added milk, then painstakingly opened the flimsy envelope. Inside were six pages (one sided) I pored over, stopping halfway to enjoy a few sips of tea and several biscuits (sometimes when I say several, I mean four or five!). Every page transported me to the intriguing metropolis and made me long to be in Tokyo (or anywhere!) with David.

267

4th ~ At home

Long haul cabin crew lifestyle suits me to a T, but every sector of that last trip encountered some sort of hiccup that extended the duty days well beyond the point of exhaustion, not to mention the lingering jet lag.

Walking through Bradwell village with mum, the nip in the air and autumn colours makes me look forward to chillier days wearing my favourite scarves and footwear, but for mum this is the time of year when she slows down, mentally and physically. I know the signs to watch for but witnessing even a glimmer of change in mum's demeanour scares me, because I know how far she can travel into what she calls, "the dark tunnel." I say this every year, but hopefully this one will be different.

At the bottom of the bag I use in New York, I came across the cd Christopher gave me last time I was there. I don't often listen to the Cocteau Twins, but *Blue Bell Knoll* is brilliant. I'm slightly amused that it took an American to put the famed Scottish band in my hands.

Another letter from David, first thing, with more Tokyo stories, only to be followed by a letter from Ben in the afternoon post, that I've yet to open because I didn't want his words to knock me into a tizzy, prior to talking to David.

I waited until ten tonight before ringing David. Some nasally sounding girl answered his office line and said he was, "At a lunch meeting with a client." She didn't ask if I wanted to leave a message. Half an hour later, I rang again, this time prepared for whatever clogged nose would try and fob me off with, but David answered. I waited for him to reel off his name and work title.

"Hi, it's Karen."

"Hey, what's up?" I loved how genuinely surprised he sounded.

"Not too much, how was your lunch meeting?"

"My lunch meeting?"

"The girl with the, eh, your secretary said you were at a lunch meeting, with a client."

A slight laugh. "I swung out to a new hole in the wall that has awesome burritos. Remind me to take you there."

"Actually," I sighed, "that's the reason I'm calling."

"Please don't say something has changed."

"I'm sorry, I can't make it, is that better?" I said trying to lighten the disappointment coursing through me.

"Oh man, I had some cool stuff planned for us."

Us.

"I'm on standby, so hopefully somebody will ring in sick."

"Not that we'd want anyone to get so sick they'd miss a trip to LA, right?"

I loved his mischievous tone.

"No, nothing too serious, perhaps just a slight case of bubonic plague."

His laugh. I hope it fills my ears for a long time to come.

5th ~ At home

It was bucketing down this morning, so I stayed in bed reading *Smash Hits*, with Wet Wet Wet on the cover. I'm not a big fan but mum loves Marti Pellow. Inside is a Tears for Fears poster I might leave in Frankie's mail slot for fun.

"Isn't that always the way?" Mum said in what I call her Lady Elizabeth voice, as I descended the stairs.

"Who's that?"

Mum shooed me away, so I went into the kitchen and watched through the glass wall as she talked with her hands and laughed a lot. Halfway through my second bite of marmite slathered toast, mum tapped on the glass. "For you," she mouthed, pointing to the phone.

"You have got to be kidding," I muttered going into the hall.

"Well, I must say, Annabel, it's been lovely talking to you again, and don't forget," my mother, the esteemed Lady herself continued, "You must grace us with your presence soon."

I flashed mum "a look" as she handed me the phone.

"Morning, Annabel."

"Gosh, what a delightful, witty woman."

"Yes, she uh, she's something else," I said after making sure mum was out of earshot.

269

"So," Annabel said, pronouncing it as *sew*. "I recently flew with a fervent admirer of yours. He was so charming, I rather fancied him myself."

"Whom are you speaking of?" I said, sounding equally as plummy.

"In fact," she continued. "Had he not talked incessantly about you, I may possibly have-"

"Annabel, just tell me who you're talking about!"

She giggled. "Have a guess."

Remembering how intense Annabel can be when she gets into something, I said, "No guessing, just tell me, actually I think I know, was it Graeme?"

"Yes! Glorious, gregarious, Graeme. Oh, and gorgeous. Gosh, I feel quite giddy at the mere mention of his name. You didn't, by any chance get a glimpse of his bod, did you?"

"Eh, parts of it," I stuttered.

"Delectable, at least from what I was able to discern by the pool in fragrant harbour."

"Wait, you flew with him to-"

"Ya, isn't Hong Kong shopping ah may zing?"

She didn't give me a chance to answer.

"Graeme found the most exquisite silk scarf. He has rather refined taste, you know. And you flat out refuse to ring him? True or false?"

"True," I said, joining her in a deep, belly laugh.

6th ~ At home

It's been almost four months since I last saw Ben. In some ways, I feel better than I did back then but there are other times (tonight) when it seems I'm back at square one, and the ache from missing him feels raw. I was hoping that with time and distance, the pain would diminish but it seems I was mistaken.

Since we split up, I haven't exactly been sitting at home feeling sorry for myself and meeting David has certainly been a shining light. Ah, David, the guy in possession of so many traits I find incredibly

270

appealing. I keep thinking if he and Ben were to show up together, who would I want? Deep inside, I'm quite sure I know the answer. I'm also quite sure it's the wrong one but I can't help how I feel.

I'd arranged to meet mum at The Point to go to the pictures, but she never showed up, so I rang home. She eventually answered, but I think she's starting to crash again. I hope I'm wrong, but I've lived with her long enough to detect the signs, plus this is the time of year when her depression rears its incredibly ugly head.

7th ~ At home

David asked me to get in touch, if I got called out, so I rang him at home but no answer. It's midnight here, so I don't suppose I'll be hearing from him. I wonder where he is on Saturday afternoon.

Rang the girls' flats and Carl's brother Connor answered! He and Carl sound so alike, that I thought it was him until it struck me how impatient he sounded, unlike Carl who's very laid back.

"What's he doing there?" I asked Lorna. "Are he and Kimberly, as the Americans say, *an item*?"

"Nah, I don't think so, he's not her type."

"I agree, but love is strange."

"Aye, that's something you're an expert on, doll. Speaking of love, I'm off to the land of the clogs tomorrow."

"I guess things are going well with Mr. KLM?"

"D'ye know, it's absolutely smashing," she said, sounding a lot like mum. "He's so easy-ozy, nothing seems to bother him."

"Unlike you," I teased.

"Aye well look who's talking."

"Learned from the best."

"That's a good one," she laughed. "Listen, don't worry about working on the Jumbo, it's a fab aircraft, and so much nicer than the TriStar."

"Good to know, thanks."

"You've nothing to worry about, well at least not in that department."

"What do you mean?"

"We need to get you sorted out with somebody and I don't mean big bad you know who."

"I didn't even mention him!"

"Aye but I know that's what you were thinking."

"Oh, so you're a mind reader now?"

"Uff, doll, I doubt even a clairvoyant could keep track of your love life."

8th ~ LHR – MIA
Hotel Inter-Continental, Miami, Florida

My first operational flight on the beautiful Boeing 747 is over and the first noticeable difference was the number of crew in the briefing room. Surprisingly, I got to pick a working position, so I chose Bar 3, which was much better than being stuck down the back with the smokers.

I love this hotel room with the oversized window overlooking Biscayne Bay. Stretching the phone cord, I was able to watch the boats and jet skiers, while I caught up with Liza in Orlando. The big news is that Gabriel and Maria are getting married. Yes, love is indeed strange, but I hope they'll be very happy together. Gabriel is such a lovely guy. I never think about him without smiling.

Shortly after checking in, we walked to the bar next door, and sat outside. Stefan (the Club Purser who grew extra hands inflight, ugh!) insisted I order Sex on the Beach. When I ordered a Cuba Libre, he shifted his attention to the gobby girl next to him.

To welcome me to the Jumbo fleet, Shelia the CSD announced the cocktails were on her, which was incredibly generous. And well received!

9th ~ MIA – LHR
35,000 feet over the Atlantic

Monday in Miami began at four am, when I woke up feeling famished. Crew never meet for breakfast before nine, so I rang room service, and ten minutes later, a feast was wheeled into the room (you know you've ordered well when it arrives on wheels instead of a tray!).

I got to the Bayside shopping area before the shops were open, so I wrote a few postcards, then depleted every cent of my allowances, mostly on Esprit clothes that I'll have to shed mega pounds to fit into.

Message light on the phone was flashing and after I found about the three-hour delay, I went shopping again!

By the time I'd removed all the labels from my new purchases and folded everything neatly in my Samsonite, it was time for call. There's no shortage of attractive men in the Club cabin, so staying awake tonight won't be a problem.

10th ~ At home

After dinner, I asked mum is she fancied going to the pictures.
"Are ye no tired?" Dad asked, looking genuinely concerned.
"I think I went past it a few hours ago, now I'm just bored."
Looking at mum, he said, "Oh to be young again, eh, Lizzie?"
"I quite fancy seeing that new film wi that French actress."
"Which one?"
"I cannae remember her name, she's got black hair."
"Not Catherine Deneuve, then."
"Naw, no her, this yin's much younger, och she's lovely."
"That's not much help, mum."
"Uff, I wish I could remember her name."
"Or the name of the film," dad suggested with a heavy eye roll.
"It's aboot a wedding," mum said. "Her ma was Ingrid Bergman."
"Whose Mother?" I asked.
"The French actress."
"Ingrid Bergman was Swedish," dad stated.
"Maybe so but her lassie is French," mum declared.
"Dad, do you know who mum's talking about?"
"Nay idea, but I'm talking aboot Ingrid Bergman. D'ye remember her in *Casablanca*?"
"Oh aye, she was a cracker, sure she was?"

"No a bad looking lassie," dad shrugged comically.

Pointing at dad, mum said, "Here's looking at you kid!"

"We'll always have Paris," he crooned.

Utterly bewildered, I went to find out what was playing.

"*Cousins*," mum yelled from the kitchen as I dialled the number to The Point.

"Is that the name of the film?"

"Aye, and the actress's name sounds something like leela slosa eeny. Uff, I'm sure it'll come tae me."

I continued dialling, if only to find out what time we'd be watching the Italian actress, Isabella Rossellini.

11th ~ At home

Halfway home from dropping mum off at Janice's, my car started losing power, eventually sputtering to a halt. It was on a quiet stretch of road but in the dark it felt scary. Fortunately, I got it to start again but I still felt a little shaken when I came in.

"Just me," I said, hanging my coat on the brass hook under the stairs. I knew if I mentioned anything about the car, dad would just worry. He has no experience with cars, possibly the only thing he knows nothing about.

"What are you watching?" I asked, going into the living room. "Oh, is that Michael Douglas?"

"Aye, is he the one mum likes?"

"She may have mentioned how handsome he is, on more than one occasion," I laughed.

"Danny DeVito's in it as well."

"You don't have to worry about him," I joked. "Who else is in this?"

"Kathleen Turner."

"Oh, that voice." I was about to add something about her hair and how gorgeous she is, but I doubted dad would appreciate any of that, so I said I'd watch it with him.

12th ~Stephen's, Brighton

I'd arranged to come to Brighton tonight but after I got off the phone with Ben, I was so out of sorts that I almost rang Stephen to say I couldn't make it. All I wanted to do was hide away, with a mountain of paper and a pile of chocolate, but I didn't have the heart to let Stephen down.

Parking in Brighton is a nightmare, and I was in no mood for faffing about, so I parked at Gatwick, then jumped on the train. On reflection, the train was probably a bad idea as it gave me time to think about Ben. During our lengthy chat, he said he really wants us to make a go of it again, which is what he said last time we talked. Had I heard those words a couple of months ago, I'd have jumped at the chance of a future with him, but now they leave me feeling confused. Yes, I really do want to see him, but no, I don't want to go down that destructive path again where our relationship consumes me and he has the power to…I don't know, make me feel like I'm crumbling. I know that's past behaviour, but it still manages to creep its way into my thoughts.

When the train pulled in, I took a deep breath, hoping it'd help lift my mood. Stephen was waiting on the platform and waved when he spotted me.

"Hello gorgeous," he beamed, bending to hug me.

"You're looking well."

"Glamour never takes a day off." Resting his hand in the crook of my arm, he took a step back and looked at my feet.

"What are you doing?"

"Seeing what shoes you're in. It's such a nice night, I thought we'd walk to mine."

"Good idea, I could really do with some fresh air."

"Clear out the 'ole cobwebs and that?"

"Is it that obvious?" I asked.

"It wasn't, until I saw those ugly clodhoppers you're wearing."

I swiped his arm and tried to keep a straight face.

"Let me guess, problems with the male species?"

"Pretty much," I sighed.

"Tell me about it," he said theatrically, linking his arm through mine. "Nothing a few bevvies at the Frock and Jacket won't cure."

13th ~Stephen's, Brighton

"Whoever you are, go away," Stephen moaned when I pounded on his bedroom door.

"Get up!" I barked, striding into his room where, with a flourish, I drew open the curtains.

"Toooooo bright!" he cried.

"And you, my dear, are a sight!" I sang. "How are you feeling?"

"Somebody at the Beacon Royal must've slipped me a dirty ice cube."

"Obviously. I mean it couldn't possibly have anything to do with the amount of tequila you drowned in. Get up, chuck some clothes on and we'll go for a brisk walk."

"I hate you!" he shouted as I ran out of his bedroom to avoid being hit by a pillow.

The brisk walk was more akin to a saunter, before we stopped at one of the benches facing the pebbly beach. Laughing about last night's antics, I heard, "McGarr!"

I spun my head and there, in his car, was Jon.

"What are you doing this far from home?" I yelled, making my way towards him.

"I've been at a conference at The Grand, we finished early."

"This is mental. I'm with my friend Stephen." I pointed to the bench, where Stephen waved as though he was on a parade float. "Come and join us."

"Are you sure?"

"Of course, but good luck finding somewhere to park."

"Well, well, well," Stephen smirked when I re-claimed my spot on the bench. "I guess it's adios to the cobwebs."

"Jon's just a friend."

"Ah, that old chestnut."

Sandwiched between Stephen and Jon, with my head moving as though I was umpiring a tennis match, I listened as they talked effortlessly, before Stephen claimed he was feeling worse for wear and needed to go home.

Jon and I chatted our way down the Palace Pier. It was his first time there but as a fan of The Who, he's always wanted to see where the mod film, *Quadrophenia*, was filmed. After giving in, to the greasy but appealing smell of chips, we slathered them in vinegar and watched the world go by, from the deck chairs.

"What's up McGarr? You don't seem yourself."

"It's a long story."

"This is a big bag of chips," Jon laughed. "And we can always get more."

I don't know what compelled me to tell Jon about my mixed feelings about seeing Ben again but once I started, I couldn't seem to stop.

"I think you're worrying far too much," he said with ease. "Just wait and see how you feel when you see him again. That's when you'll know."

"Do you think so?"

"I know so."

The wind was starting to whip up and Jon seemed in no hurry to leave so I asked if he wanted to come to Stephen's.

"He won't mind?"

"Not if we show up with a few bottles of plonk."

A bunch of Stephen's eclectic friends came over tonight and I asked Jon if he wanted to come out with us. He looked unsure so I called over to Stephen, who along with his old mate Todd, was smoking out the window.

"Stephen!"

"Yes darling?"

"Jon's thinking about coming out with us."

"If that's alright-" Jon began.

"You're in the mix now, honey," Todd said, blowing smoke rings out the window.

"That's right," Stephen added. "You can't leave, even if you want to."

By the time we spilled onto the teeming street, I felt pretty tipsy and the smell of the sea air only seemed to make me giddier. Walking a few paces behind the others as we made our way along the seafront, Jon and I talked nonstop. At The Zap, there was a queue to get in, but Todd was already at the door, waving us in.

Acid house music vibrated through me, as Jon and I made our way onto the dance floor, where Stephen slurred, "You two really suit each other."

"Do you know she used to be my girlfriend?" Jon shouted over the thumping bass.

"I know it all!" Stephen declared, with a slight sway. "There are no secrets between me and Kazalofski."

Jon looked at me, confused.

"One of my many nicknames," I explained, as Stephen led us deeper into the throng.

14th ~ At home

I have no idea what time we stumbled back to Stephen's, but he insisted on playing the new Gloria Estefan cd, so the two of us danced to, "Oye Mi Canto," which, according to Stephen, means "Hear my voice." An apt title for the way he belted, "Take me, only for what I am," as Jon looked on in amusement.

This morning I kept my movements in the kitchen to a minimum, so as not to disturb Jon, only a few feet away.

"I'm awake, McGarr. Liquid. Please. Anything. Soon," he pleaded.

"I'm never drinking again," Jon lied as I sat at the other end of the futon cupping a mug of tea. With the ruched sheet resting below his navel, I had to keep averting my eyes upwards of his naked torso. Finishing my tea in record time, I got up and made my way to Stephen's room.

"I'm never drinking again," came Stephen's muffled lies from under the duvet. With his head poking out like a turtle, he whispered, "Did you shag him?"

"No! I slept in the spare room. Jon's out on the futon."

"He's got it bad for you."

"He does not, we already did all of that, now we're just friends."

"We're just friends," he said mimicking me.

Finding what I hoped was his leg under the duvet, I gave it a hearty smack. "I'll leave you to wake up," I said tartly. "And do something with that face of yours."

15th ~ LGW – LOS
Hotel Intercontinental, Lagos, Nigeria

First time on the continent of Africa, namely Lagos, Nigeria. Seems incredible that seven hours in the air can transport us to such a vastly different landscape.

Seeing Lorna in the briefing room was a welcome sight. She got called out ten minutes before standby ended and thought Kimberly was joking when she said it was crewing on the phone.

Four hours after the ETD, we finally took off. The delay was due to a generator that needed replaced, nothing too serious!

After a quick glass of wine in the CSD's room, I got up to leave.

"Come to my room, doll," Lorna said. "We'll order room service."

"Thanks, but I'm not really in the mood."

"Wait a wee minute," she said, reaching for my arm. "What's bugging you?"

"Nothing," I shrugged. "I'm just tired.

"You're coming with me." She tugged on my sleeve and marched me to her room.

I wasn't hungry (is the world ending?) but Lorna insisted on ordering an assortment of goodies.

"So," she said, glaring at me. "Is it bad boy again?"

"No, it's my mum."

"Is she alright?"

"I don't know." No sooner were the words out when I burst into tears. "My mum suffers badly from depression. When I got home last night, she was really down."

"I take it this isn't the first time?"

I shook my head. "She's been afflicted with it most of her life."

"Does she get help?"

"Sometimes," I sniffed.

"How long do the episodes last?"

"Weeks, months, it's hard to tell. I just know she's on her way there."

"Poor soul," Lorna soothed.

"I'm always hopeful it won't come back but-"

"I know, doll, I know. It's an awful thing for anybody to go through. You know I was a nurse before this," she gestured to the sparsely furnished, dated hotel room. "This life of glamour and glitz took over."

I couldn't help but smile. "That's why you got the highest scores when we covered AvMed during training."

"But did you know I specialised in psychiatry?"

I shook my head.

"Well now you do, so grab a wee cake and tell Auntie Lorna everything."

16th ~ Hotel Intercontinental, Lagos, Nigeria

Getting comfy on the sun lounger, I thanked Lorna for listening to my woes last night.

"Anytime, doll. I hope a wee bit of insight helped."

"You explained a lot I wasn't aware of, and it helps knowing what's happening when my mum starts crashing."

"I used to have some great books, but I've moved so many times I don't know where they ended up."

Discussing the changes in our lives since joining BA, Lorna said, "I think it's a bit of a double-edged sword. We hardly spend any time at home, and when we do it's rarely during the weekend when everyone is free. And it's knackering. All of that combined makes it hard to meet anyone, at least at home."

"Too true."

"And then," she continued. "You might meet somebody you like on a trip, but the chances of seeing them again are slim to nil."

"But not in your case with the Dutch boy."

"He's no boy, he's a man!" she bellowed, pretending to shake all over.

"Oh, Lorna," I laughed.

"I think the best thing is just to make the most of whatever's happening, wherever you may be and just go for it. Right?"

I nodded. "I think I'm doing that, or at least trying."

"Good! So does this mean everything is done and dusted where bad boy is concerned?"

With a heavy sigh, I said I didn't think so. Lorna shot up out of the sun lounger. "You're not still in touch, are you?"

Not daring to look at her, I said, "I'm about to tell you something but you must promise to keep calm."

Looming over me, she waited for my eyes to meet hers. "If it's something to do with him, I'm making no promises, but I'll try."

"He arrives back in the UK tomorrow."

"Ochfurbeepsake!" she screamed.

"I didn't know you were already fluent in Dutch."

Grinning, she sat across from me. "I could throttle you!"

"Please don't. I didn't come to Nigeria to die."

"Listen," she said, bowing her head close to mine. "I'm just going to say one more thing."

"Just one?" I teased.

"Love. Shouldn't. Be. Complicated."

I opened my mouth to speak but she hushed me with her finger. "When it's right, doll, everything falls into place."

17th ~ LOS – LGW

One would think, that after one had trouble zipping up one's uniform skirt, that perhaps, just perhaps, one might, four hours later, refrain from eating the biscuits one eyeballed in the First Class galley. However, judging by the crumbs on one's plate, it would appear one has yet to learn how to curb one's cravings for all things sweet, particularly as one flies in a tin can, at 35,000 feet.

18th ~ At home

I've gone from being on cloud nine, to shedding more tears than I know what to do with.

As soon as I got home this morning, I made a mad dash for the phone, trembling as I dialled the six numbers forever imprinted on my brain. It rang four times, long enough for my stomach to rise and twist, all the while knowing Ben was only a few miles away.

"Hi Susan, it's Karen."

"Hello love, how are you?"

"Fine, thanks. Is Ben home?"

"Not at the moment, no."

"But he made it home?"

"He did, love, yes."

"Do you know where he is?"

"He's ehm, in Birmingham."

"Oh…what's he doing there?"

"I'm not sure love, but he said he'll be back tomorrow so maybe you can talk to him then."

Susan's tone told me something was off, and I could feel the heavy lump forming in my throat, so I quickly hung up. My mind raced to all sorts of scenario's, none of them good, so I went upstairs and knocked on mum and dad's bedroom door, before going in.

"Mum? Are you awake?"

Mum was in bed, her back to me, so I climbed on the bed and sat behind her. "I just wanted to let you know I'm back." I rubbed her shoulder. She didn't answer but I could tell from her breathing she was awake. "Do you want anything? Are you hungry?"

Nothing.

"Alright, I'll let you get some rest, but I'll keep the door open, so if you want anything, just shout."

I changed out of uniform and took Tini for a much-needed walk. The slate sky looked low enough to touch and the sight of falling leaves left me feeling sad. By this afternoon, I could no longer bear not knowing what Ben was up to, so I rang him again but there was no answer. I rang again tonight and had the most awkward chat I've ever had with Susan.

In my last chat with Ben, he said he couldn't wait to get home and that he hoped we could work everything out so we could be together, this time for good, so why the hell isn't he here? More importantly, what is he doing in Birmingham?

19th ~ At home

Her name is Mandy. They met in France. She was so smitten with him that she forgot to go home.

Looking utterly dishevelled, Ben finally showed up this afternoon, claiming he'd just come off the train from Birmingham.

"There's so much I have to tell you." He said, from across the kitchen table. On reflection, I shouldn't have given him the time of day, but I sat there, listening to him tell me about the girl he went to see. She came home last week, with the expectation they'd continue their relationship, but after our last conversation, Ben realised he wants to be with me, so he went to finish it with her.

While he was spewing, I watched him closely and for the first time, it occurred to me what an actor he is. It was almost as if he was reading from a script. I wanted to tear out his eyes and kiss him, all at the same time.

From out of nowhere, mum came crashing through the kitchen door. She was in her nightie and from the glazed look in her eyes, I suspected she'd taken one too many tablets. With one look at Ben, she hissed. "You better leave. Right now!"

Ben looked at me, but I couldn't find any words.

"I'm sorry," he uttered, getting up.

"Get out!" mum screamed.

"He's leaving, mum, it's ok."

I followed Ben out to the hall and the sound of something crashing against the glass wall was enough for me to quickly usher him out.

"I love you," he said, as I began to close the door. "This can't be the end of us."

20th ~ At home

I didn't sleep a wink last night and from the sounds of it, neither did dad. Several times throughout the night, I heard his movements, up and down the stairs, and at one point I think he went out to the garden. I know it was dad, because mum is much heavier on her feet, plus she rarely gets out of bed now. The pattern is always the same, which means mum is only going to get worse.

Before dad left for work, he knocked on my bedroom door, then poked his head in and asked me to keep an eye on mum.

I made tea and toast and left it on mum's bedside table, then I took Tini out but no sooner had I reached the shops, when the sky darkened, and it began to pour.

Back in the house, feeling agitated, I paced up and down, with a gnawing feeling that I had to talk to Ben. Upstairs, I checked on mum. The tea was stone cold, and she was asleep.

Absolutely drenched, I knocked on Ben's door. I knew his mum and dad were at work, so I wasn't concerned about seeing them, but my breathing felt all wrong, like half of me was running while the other half stood still. There was no answer, so I rang the bell, and knocked again.

Looking bleary eyed, Ben opened the door, wearing only a pair of shorts. "You're soaked," he said, stepping aside to allow me into the tiny foyer. I slipped out of my coat, shook the rain from it, and hung it on one of the hooks, like I've done hundreds of times before. Ben closed the door and as I followed him into the kitchen, I felt an overwhelming desire to reach out and caress his broad shoulders.

I stood by the washing machine and after Ben filled the kettle, he turned to face me. With his bare feet slightly apart, and his arms crossed just enough to accentuate his biceps, we stared at each other. For a long time. When he opened his arms to me, I fell into the all too familiar feeling and scent of him.

21st ~ LGW – MBJ
Holiday Inn, Montego Bay, Jamaica

Big surprise this morning, when David rang, from Manchester! Apparently, he left the name of the hotel with mum last week, while I was away. Mum assured him she'd pass the message along but sadly that never happened.

While I was talking to David (our worst chat ever, felt totally stilted, all my doing) Ben showed up. I gestured for him to wait in the kitchen and through the glass wall, I fixated on the back of his neck, wanting nothing more than to kiss it.

"Sorry, David, I have to go," I stuttered.

"Ok, eh, I'll be back in LA when you get home from Jamaica, give me a call?"

"Sure," I said, flatly.

"Who was that?" Ben asked when I went into the kitchen.

"None of your business."

"Fair enough. Listen, I rented a car for a few days so I can drop you off at the airport if you want."

"I have a car," I snipped.

"I just thought it'd be a good way for us to talk."

Being in the car allowed us to talk at length and from what Ben said, I don't think he knows what or who he wants. He claims he loves me and wants us to be together but listening to him bounce from one idea to the next, gives me the impression he's uncertain. About everything. He didn't offer to pick me up when I return, and I certainly wasn't going to ask him to. I put on a brave face when we said goodbye, but in TriStar House, I hid in the loo until the tears subsided.

"You look awful," were Frankie's first words in the briefing room.

"I'm not feeling well," I fibbed. "And the thought of hundreds of needy passengers is making me feel worse."

"Poor baby," she cooed, sympathetically. "But what's the real story?"

One I'm really tired of.

22nd ~ Flight from Montego Bay to Gatwick

"Gosh, isn't this a treat," Frankie gushed as we took our seats in the Club World cabin.

"Next time I complain about crew life, be sure to smack me," I said, opening Anita Shreve's *Eden Close*. Gesturing for me to come closer, Frankie whispered, "Are we allowed to have a drink?"

"I don't see why not, we're not in uniform. Although *technically*, we're still working."

"Let's go with the first thing you said."

A few chapters in, I conked out, and woke up just as we were starting the descent.

"Ben might be waiting to surprise you," Frankie gushed, in her ever-hopeful tone.

I highly doubt it.

23rd ~ At home

Not even an hour after getting home, I made an excuse about going out and from the phone box across the road, I rang Ben.

If only to clear my head, I walked to his, but when Susan answered the door, I could tell something was amiss. Had I known what was in store with Ben, I wouldn't have bounded up the stairs to his room.

From his spot at the head of the bed, Ben proceeded to tell me that after he dropped me off, he turned around and went to Birmingham, where he spent a few days with Mandy, during which they decided to get back together. There was much more said, but I can't go there right now.

Wasn't it just a few days ago that he poured his heart out and pleaded for me to be with him again? *Forever*. That's the word he used when he said he wanted us to be together. That I'm the only one he's ever *truly loved*. The one who *understands* him like no one else.

By the time I got home, I was soaked through. My car keys weren't on the hook by the door, so I went into the kitchen to see if I'd left them there. Reaching to grab them from the breakfast bar, I jumped when dad said, "Whit're ye doin'?"

From the far end of the table, dad looked like he had the weight of the world on his shoulders.

"I'm eh…I'm just going for a drive," I sputtered, barely able to hold it together.

"Yer no goin' oot in this weather," he said in a tone I knew not to question, so I dropped the keys and came upstairs to my room. I wish I could talk to mum.

24th ~ At home

I know nothing will ever be the same between us but more than that, I can't imagine a life without Ben in it. Maybe not in a huge, all-encompassing way, but somewhere.

Perhaps the only way to get over him is to move. Far, far away.

25th ~ At home

In the dream, I was on the observation deck of the Empire State, with Ben. It was night and a carpet of city lights sparkled below us, while cabs formed a solid yellow line, still evident from that great height. While I was snapping pictures, I felt a hand on my back, pushing me. I lost my footing and began to fall but my descent was in slow motion. Strands of hair (long in the dream) covered my face and I kept pushing it away, my eyes fixed on Ben, secure in his spot. I opened my mouth, but the scream was silent. Ben started cackling, and that's when the sound of the phone woke me.

"Hello?"

"Hullo, hen."

"Nana," I whimpered like a child. "I'm so glad it's you."

"I was jist phoning to see how yer mammy is."

"She hasn't been out of bed since I got home a few days ago."

"Mibbe I should come doon. If I catch the early train, I can be there the morra night." She paused. "D'ye think I should?"

"To be honest, nana, I don't think it'd make any difference. You know mum stops responding-"

"Aye, sadly I do, as do you and yer poor daddy."

"It's so awful," I said, my voice cracking.

"I know it is, hen. D'ye think she'd be open to going into hospital?"

"Nothing helps!" I cried. "Sorry, I'm just so upset. Ugh, I wish I wasn't such a cry baby."

"Yer no a wean, yer a young lassie wi a big heart."

"A big broken heart," I sobbed.

"Och, don't tell me you know who's been playing up again. Whit does your daddy have to say aboot that?"

"I haven't said a word. Dad has his hands full just trying to take care of mum."

"Ach, it's a terrible thing sure it is. It's lashing here and the weatherman said it's no gonny let up, so I'll be staying put. Why don't ye go and make yerself a nice cuppa tea and mibbe a wee bit of buttery toast, then phone me back."

"You make it sound so appealing."

"We'll put our heads the gither and hopefully between the two of us, we'll come up wi something that'll make life a wee bit easier, eh?"

"Thank you, nana."

26th ~ At home

Rang in sick for the Hong Kong trip.

27th ~ At home

A lengthy letter from David. Six thousand miles might as well be another planet.

28th ~ At home

Ben rang first thing and asked if we could meet. He offered to come over but there was no way mum, or dad for that matter, would want him here.

288

When I spotted him standing under the maple tree by the phone box, my heart wobbled but it was his smile that just about finished me off. "Hey you," he said, quietly. "Wanna walk?"

We headed for the bike path, an all too familiar place for us. At the spot where we almost kissed for the first time on a wintery night many moons ago, I felt tears spring to my eyes. Fortunately, Ben was forging ahead and never noticed. The more we walked, the easier it felt to talk, and by the time we reached the city centre, we were laughing.

"Are you hungry?"

"When am I not hungry?"

"Common bond," he grinned.

After gorging on heaps of pasta, Ben asked if I was ready to go home. Dad was with mum, so I didn't feel the need to rush back.

"It's just that *Dead Poets Society* is playing at The Point."

"I figured, being a Saturday, you'd have plans tonight," I said, in a flippant tone.

With Mandy.

"Nope, I'm game if you are."

After the film (excellent) we grabbed a quick drink and when we stepped outside, it was already dark. And chilly. When I finished wrapping my oversized scarf around my head and neck, Ben laughed and said he couldn't see me.

We ended up walking home and as we neared my house, Ben said, "Maybe we can do the friend thing after all, eh?"

I smiled, inside and out, hating every inch of myself for being so weak.

29th ~ At home

It was the smell of bacon, wafting up the stairs that roused me out of bed.

"Hiya dad," I chirped, grabbing a slice of toast from the toast rack, noticing that the table was set. For three. "Smells amazing," I said, slathering the toast in butter.

"I hope yer hungry."

"Can't you tell," I said, waving the toast.

289

"Go and see if mum wants to come doon. She needs to eat."

I knew there was no way mum would get out of bed, but from the way dad said it and the way he'd set the table, it was obvious he was craving some sort of normalcy.

After taking the stairs two at a time, I lightly knocked on the bedroom door. When there was no reply, I slowly opened it. Mum was in bed, her back to me. Gently, I put my hand on her clammy shoulder. "Mum, are you awake? Dad's cooking up a storm down there, do you think you can get up?" The movement was slight but enough that I noticed her moving away from me. I got up and opened the blind. Sun filtered in through the slats. "It's a really nice day, chilly, but the sky is so blue, can you see?" Knowing how disappointed dad would be, I asked mum again if she was awake. When she didn't answer, I said, "I'll make you a bacon butty and bring it up."

By the time my slipper hit the bottom stair, I felt ten pounds heavier.

30th ~ At home

Rang in fit for work, so I'm on standby. Hopefully I'll get called out, if only to escape.

31st ~ Excelsior Hotel, Heathrow Airport

On my way here, I stopped in to see if any of the girls were at the flat and was surprised to find them all home.

Thanks to Lorna's crash course on mental health during our time in Lagos, I suspect Kimberly also suffers from depression, but she's able to function, something mum is incapable of right now.

Here on QRS (quick response standby) and while I was fumbling with the keycard, two girls and a guy stumbled out of the lift and made their way down the corridor, to the room next door. From the sight of their matching French maid costumes, I'm guessing it's a Halloween party.

NOVEMBER

1st~ **At home**

The commotion next door only worsened as the night wore on, so I gave up trying to sleep and went down to the lobby.

"Sis!" Carl exclaimed, bolting out of the bench by the door. " "What are you doing here?"

"Probably the same as you," I said, returning his squeeze.

"How much longer?"

"I finish at noon," I sighed. "Tomorrow."

"Same here."

"So, we're both stuck here," I groaned.

"All is not lost. We can't leave the hotel, but we can go to the bar."

"Us, at a bar, drinking non-alcoholic beverages?"

"First time for everything," he laughed.

"And probably the last."

"Exactly, but before we overdose on sugary drinks I'm going up to my room to grab some pictures to show you, from my last trip."

"It had better not be LA!"

"Nah, I wouldn't do that to you. Banjul."

"Good trip?"

"You can decide after you see the photos."

2nd ~ At home

I tried coaxing mum out of bed, but she wasn't having any of it and by the afternoon I was bored out of my skull, so I drove to the shopping centre and when I came out of John Lewis, there he was, up ahead, walking hand in hand, with man dee.

She has dirty blonde hair, she's thin (ugh!) and was wearing a peach jacket I wouldn't be seen dead in. Even from a distance, I sensed Ben's smug attitude, and when he turned to her and stole a kiss, I despised him in a way I never thought possible.

I sobbed in the car for ages and came home to find mum in the kitchen. Her faraway expression suggested excess and I was so upset, I lost my temper and yelled that it was time she went to hospital. We ended up in a screaming match and were still at it when dad got home. He looked frayed as mum, bawling her eyes out, told him I'd threatened to send her to hospital. Avoiding my gaze, dad reassured mum that won't happen, which seemed to calm her. A little.

I want my mum back. And my boyfriend. The one who used to love only me.

3rd ~ At home

It was good to get out tonight and I'm glad I didn't drive, otherwise my car would still be in Stony Stratford, but as usual I'm getting ahead of myself.

Lovely surprise this morning, with Millie on the phone.

"Where have you been hiding? I've been ringing you for days, why don't you have an answering machine?"

"I live with the Flintstones."

She laughed. "Mine are a bit like that, never mind, I enjoy having a natter with your mum, who talks for ages before she says, 'Och, Mill eh, Karen's no here.'"

"You sound just like her," I said, a wave of sadness washing over me. "Actually, my mum's not up for much at the moment."

"Sorry to hear that, is she poorly?"

""Hmm, a little," I uttered, not wanting to get into anything more.

"Tell her I send my love and look forward to actually meeting her."

Anxious to change to the subject, I said, "So, how's the weekend looking for you?"

"I imagine you wish it was yours and not mine."

"Sorry, you lost me there."

"I just got called out for a trip, tomorrow. To LA."

Sarah invited me out with them and, "A few of Simon's mates." Whenever she uses that expression, it roughly translates to; You're a sad and lonely girl about to spend Friday night alone. You don't have a boyfriend, which, in the eyes of a friend in a committed relationship is akin to death. So, with that in mind, come and meet some naff blokes, one of whom you might take a shine to, or at least have a laugh with. Or, you can say you're staying in, to wash your hair.

The blokes were not naff. They were a decent, witty bunch, out enjoying a few drinks at the end of the work week. Ryan was very sweet, and we talked at length about travel.

"You have a bit of an unfair advantage," he joked, before asking for my number.

4th ~ At home

I finally got up the courage to step on the scale. I'm four ounces away from nine stone (125 pounds of pure butter, oh and maybe some sugar!). I'm convinced sadness adds pounds but it's hard trying to stay upbeat, when it feels like everything is falling apart.

Mum surfaced this afternoon and I sat at the kitchen table, feigning interest in *The People's Friend* nana gets me a subscription to every year, but out of the corner of my eye, I watched mum moving about as if it was her first time here.

Dad came home, laden with all sorts of goodies I can't eat. He asked if I had plans for the evening, which I didn't, until Sebastian (Stephen made it clear he has no issue with me remaining friends with his ex) invited me to a Guy Fawkes party, at his friend Trey's.

I was expecting a small gathering, but the party was outside, complete with raging bonfire. Trey's boyfriend Mason is cabin crew with Monarch, but he desperately wants to join BA, so he had a lot of questions about the interview process and seemed surprised by how involved it is.

Just before midnight, we tucked into baked potatoes slathered in beans and coleslaw (my last meal, sob, sob) and somebody set off fireworks.

"Moments like this make me miss Stephen," Sebastian sighed wistfully.

"Aw, sorry you're feeling that way."

"Don't worry," he chuckled, "it'll soon pass. Don't you think he'd love this?"

I looked at the crowd, some of whom were dancing close to the bonfire, their arms reaching in the air while shooting flames lit up the sky. At the end of the winding stone path, a well-stocked makeshift bar shone under fairy lights.

"Right up his alley," I smiled.

"So?"

I tilted my head in question.

"Who do you miss in moments like this?"

"Nobody," I lied.

5th ~ LHR - CDG - LHR
Excelsior Hotel, Heathrow

While I was cleaning up the kitchen, I came across a pile of post, stuffed in the corner of the breakfast bar. "Oh, mum," I uttered as I flicked through what appeared to be mostly junk, all except for the envelope with the British Airways emblem.

"Yes! Yes! Yes!" I exclaimed when I spotted LHR – NRT. It was much too early to ring David, so I quickly penned a letter, then walked Tini over to the post box.

I hope David will be equally excited when he finds out we'll be in Japan at the same time.

6th ~ LHR - CDG - LHR
Excelsior Hotel, Heathrow

Dianne Wiest was on today's outbound flight, as were De La Soul ("The Magic Number," is my current ear worm!). Ms. Wiest was utterly charming, and when I told her mum and I have watched, *Hannah and her Sisters* a bunch of times, she squeezed my hand and said, "Thank you, sweet girl," in that silvery soft voice of hers. "You know," she continued. "Playing Holly was very special."

"My mum always cries during Holly's final scene."

"Then I guess I did a good job."

"Hence, the Oscar," I said, with my widest hostie smile, wishing we were on a longer sector.

Got back to the hotel around seven and in the lobby, I recognised another distinctive voice I've come to love.

"No! You *mustn't* send me back to that wretched, dreary room!"

"Annabel," I said, coming up behind her.

"By Jove, Miss M!" she exclaimed, spinning to meet me. "You gave me a bloody fright!"

"Sorry," I said, returning her Chanel number 5 scented hug. "Are you causing trouble?"

"Not at all," she clipped, her nose in the air. "What are you doing here?"

"Day two of Paris dailies. You?"

"Same actually, I came up early to avoid rush hour."

"Do you have any plans?"

"I do now," she grinned.

7th ~ LHR - CDG - LHR
Excelsior Hotel, Heathrow

Daniel just left, Lorna disappeared hours ago, and Meryl is in my bed, but as usual I'm getting ahead of myself.

Last night's chance meeting with Annabel ended in the early hours, after I stumbled back to my room and zonked out until two this afternoon! It was another easy duty day but not nearly as interesting as yesterday.

I couldn't wait to climb into bed and read until I fell asleep (wild is my middle name!) however, that all changed after I met Lorna in the lobby.

"Och, look what the cat dragged in!"

"Thanks, Lorna, just what I need to hear. Hiya, Daniel," I said, kissing his cheek.

"Remind me to avoid Paris if that's what it does to you," Lorna teased.

"How do you know where I've been? And what are you two doing   here?"

"We met your posh pal, Annabel, this morning," Daniel explained.

"Oh, so you're all on the same crew?"

Lorna nodded. "That Annabel's a scream, I thought she was putting it on but-"

"It's real," I said as Lorna looked over my shoulder. I turned, expecting Annabel. "Meryl, what a surprise."

"Hello you lot. Let me guess, Paris?"

Daniel nodded. "It's like a reunion."

When I yawned, Lorna stuck her finger in my face. "None of that, doll."

"Pub it is," Daniel said rubbing his hands together. "How long do you need to get changed, Karen?"

"About ten minutes."

"Hurry up!" Lorna shouted. "We don't have all bloody night!"

8th ~ LHR - CDG - LHR
Excelsior Hotel, Heathrow

In the early hours of this morning, Lorna appeared at my door.

"Where have you been?" I whispered, so as not to wake Meryl.

"Downstairs at the bar," she slurred in a huffy, not so quiet tone.

"Shhhhh," I said, nodding towards Meryl.

"What the hell is Meryl doing in your bed?"

I started to say, "Keep your voice down," but Lorna's expression was so comical, I cracked up laughing.

Shooting out of bed, Meryl made a mad dash for the loo.

"Ugh," Lorna said, her face contorting at the sound of Meryl vomiting.

"Poor thing," I said. "She's really going to regret this."

"Is that why she's in your bed? Because she got drunk? She seemed fine at the pub, I didn't think she drank that much."

"Nor did I but shortly after we got back, she was absolutely legless."

"A feeling we know all too well," Lorna said, swaying exaggeratedly.

"Stop changing the subject, where have you been?"

"I told you, I was at the bar. I bumped into an old pal."

"Who?"

"It's a long story, can we get room service? I could eat a horse."

"It's three in the morning."

"Who are you? The food Police?"

After Lorna managed to coax Meryl away from the porcelain throne, I held my breath as she scurried past me.

"There you go, doll," Lorna said, tucking Meryl into *my* bed.

"I guess I'll be sleeping on the couch."

"Actually, I was going to ask if I could stay here." For the first time ever, Lorna looked embarrassed.

"Why can't you go to your room?"

"Uff, it's a long story."

After we'd polished off the stale sandwiches, I lay at the opposite end of the bed to Meryl, trying hard to ignore the pong, coming from the bathroom. No sooner had I switched off the light, when the phone rang.

"It's Daniel, I think my ID might be in your room. Pick up is in ten minutes, I can't go to Paris without it."

"Hang on a sec, I'll have a scout around."

I turned on the light and scanned the room. Lorna was sprawled out on the couch, asleep. Meryl was already snoring. Sliding my arm under the bed as far as I could reach, I pierced the lanyard with my nail and dragged the ID towards me. Crawling on the floor, back to the phone, the absurdity of the night hit me, and I tried not to laugh.

In the doorway, Daniel said, "What's that terrible smell?"

"I'm too tired to explain."

He poked his head in. "Is that Lorna on the couch?"

Shut up and go to Paris!

When the sun came up (can't imagine why it escaped me to close the curtains!) the sight of Meryl's hair plastered across her face reminded me of Frankie, in Christopher's apartment. Lorna demanded breakfast from room service, and after I finally got rid of the pair of them, I took a shower, got into uniform, and went to work.

Fresh from Paris, the room smelled fresh, and the fresh linens and towels were exactly what I needed. A few hours later, the alarm shrilled, and I wasted no time getting dressed, before heading down to the lobby.

"McGarr," Jon grinned. "How the devil are you?"

"Slightly knackered," I said, enjoying a lovely whiff of Paco Rabanne, as he kissed my cheek.

"You don't look it, you look great."

"Thank you for lying, I need that right now."

"It's true, you always look great, McGarr."

"As do you," I said, stepping back for a better look at the dapper tailored jacket he'd paired with jeans.

"Nice get up."

"Thanks for noticing," he smiled.

In and out of various wine bars, in Henley-on-Thames, Jon asked a slew of questions about Ben, concluding with, "Sorry, McGarr, but he sounds like a prize prick."

"Don't hold back," I laughed. "Tell me what you really think."

9th ~ LHR - CDG - LHR
Excelsior Hotel, Heathrow

Call came four hours after Jon dropped me off and I'd have given anything to stay in bed, but once again *La Ville Lumiere* was calling.

Back at the hotel, it was a quick change before Sam was due to arrive. After half an hour had passed, I began to wonder if I'd muddled up the time, but then came a knock on the door.

I cracked the door open, expecting Sam to bound through it, in his usual manner.

"What's the matter?" I said, at the sight of his tear-streaked cheeks. He waved his hand dismissively and I led him to the chair by the window. I clicked the kettle on, then remembered the wine Jon brought.

I opened the bottle and poured us each a glass. Sam chugged the wine back in one go, and I did the same, before topping up our glasses.

"I can't face anyone tonight," Sam sniffed, wiping a fresh tear.

"That's ok. I'll ring Lolly in a minute and let her know we can't make it."

"Gavin," he uttered, softly.

"Sorry," I said, soothingly. "Who's Gavin?"

"He was a friend. From home. Close," he croaked.

"Did something happen to him?" I said, feeling a sense of dread.

"AIDS," he nodded.

"I'm so sorry," I said, tears suddenly springing to my eyes, at the thought of so many beautiful friends who remain terrrorised by those four letters.

10th ~ LHR - CDG - LHR
At home

Mum was asleep when I got home, so I took Tini for a quick walk, then drove to the city centre.

Wandering aimlessly, I thought about last night and how devastated Sam is, by the loss of his friend. We stayed up most of the night talking, and much of what Sam said reminded me of many a conversation I've shared with Stephen.

I thought about popping in to see Susan at work, but I knew I'd only end up asking about Ben and as much as I'm yearning to know how he is, hearing his name would only upset me, so I surprised myself and came home.

I'd planned on talking to dad about what we can do to help mum, but the fall of the Berlin Wall had his attention. Watching droves of people walk freely through the gates to the excited cheers from residents on the Western side, was so uplifting.

"Dad, did he just say the wall is twenty-eight miles long?"

"Aye, did ye no know that?"

"I had no idea it was that long. Imagine seeing that monstrosity every day of your life, and how it would affect you."

"This is something I never thought I'd see in my lifetime," dad said, turning away, but not before I saw him wipe away a tear.

11th ~ At home

"Hey, Karen, it's David."

Ahhh, say it again. Pleeeeeeezzzzzz!

"You're up early," I chirped.

"Old habits die hard."

"Ah, the beauty of a routine filled life."

"Something you don't get to enjoy much of. I have a real hard time dealing with time zones when I travel."

"I do too, I don't think I'll ever get used to it."

"I'm surprised you picked up, I figured I'd be talking to your mom first."

Glancing at the stairs, I felt a pang of sadness.

"Karen?"

"Sorry, my mum hasn't been feeling well recently."

"That's too bad, does she have like flu or something?"

"Something like that," I uttered, not quite knowing what else to say.

"Please send her my best and I hope she feels better soon."

"I will, thanks," I said, suddenly welling up.

"So, I talked to a buddy of mine here at work, he's pretty familiar with Tokyo and I guess there's a train that goes from Tokyo to Narita."

"Oh, that sounds promising."

Laughing, he said, "I love your expressions. I also had another idea."

"Go on, then."

He laughed again. "How about I get a room at your hotel? I could stay for two nights before I fly back to LAX."

Visions of pleasurable *London* experiences swirled in my head, so much so that I felt my cheeks flush when I said, "That sounds like a great idea."

"You sure?"

"Absolutely. Let's do it!"

12th ~ Excelsior Hotel, Heathrow

Dad waved me off this morning, and all I could think about was how difficult it must be for him, holding everything together, especially when mum is retreating more and more. I cried all the way to the motorway, then after a stern chat with myself, I allowed my thoughts to drift to the lovely chat I'd had with David, focusing on how fantastic it'll be to experience Japan together.

Here at the hotel, I made my way to Lorna's room. She just got back from Holland, where it seems everything is going swimmingly with Mr. KLM. At the pub this afternoon (Sunday roast and the pub, a match made in heaven!) Daniel thanked Lorna for letting him stay in her room.

"You know missy here is staying as well? You'll be on the couch, Daniel."

"Anything's better than dealing with rush hour traffic for an early check-in."

I asked where he was going.

"JFK, how about you?"

"Four-day Muscat."

"That's a nice wee trip," Lorna said. "The crew hotel's right on the beach, and the allowances are good but not as good as Narita."

"With overtime and box payments," Daniel interjected. "I think Narita and Hong Kong are the best paying trips."

"So, I'll be minted after Narita," Lorna said.

Yes! We're going to Japan together.

13th ~ LHR - MCT
Hotel Inter-Continental, Muscat, Oman

After a late night with Daniel and Lorna, seven hours in the air seemed to drag, especially since Shalimar Sonja's mood swings proved difficult to keep up with. As a Purser, I'd have hoped Sonja would have the sense to know that drowning in perfume (as lovely as it is) isn't professional, nor is barking orders at us juniors.

We arrived in the dark, so I have no idea what lies beyond these walls. However, the bed is so outrageously comfortable that I might just forget to get up.

14th ~ Hotel Inter-Continental, Muscat, Oman

Went to the lobby at nine but nobody showed up (surely, they're not all on a saving trip?). I popped out to the beach, but it was deserted so I came back to the room and ordered room service. Contemplated ringing some of my crew to see if anyone wanted to meet, but then I opened *The Joy Luck Club*, by Amy Tan and got carried away. Ended up finishing the book, then ordered more room service. A lonely trip is a bad time to stop eating.

Started writing and it's now 2:47am. I never know what will come out when the ink starts flowing, but tonight's pages pondered if I'll ever be in love again. I've read so much about how common it is to carry a torch for your first love, sometimes decades after the relationship ended.

I don't want to be that person, but occasionally, I think that maybe, just maybe, I've already experienced the best and that any love interest from this point on, will pale in comparison.

I hope that's not the case, but when I meet someone like Sonja, who's clearly bitter about the past, it makes me see how important it is to make the right choices. The question of course is, which choice is the right one?

15th ~ MCT - RUH – LHR

I didn't see any of my crew 'til pick up and on the crew bus there was no mention of what anyone did, so I think we were all hermits. I would hate that to be the norm but sometimes it's nice to relax in the comfort of an opulent hotel room, reading, writing and eating chocolate mousse.

Thanks to an upswing in Sonja's mood (zero trace of perfume, perhaps somebody said something) I'm on crew rest for two hours. At pick up, Sonja was full of beans and when we stopped in Riyadh to pick up passengers, she was overly sweet to everyone that joined the flight but an hour into it, she barked orders in the galley and had Sasha in tears.

16th ~ At home

The heat on the crew bus was on the blink and the chill made me want to wee, so at TriStar House, I made a mad dash for the loo, then popped upstairs to check my mail slot.

He was standing next to the filing cabinet, his back to me.

"Hiya Graeme!" I shrieked.

"Fu-" He began, spinning to face me, as somebody yelled, "No swearing in uniform!"

"Sorry I didn't mean to scare you." I tried to stifle the yawn, but it came out in full force.

"Thanks for that, good for my ego," he teased. "I just left something in your mail slot."

"What is it," I asked, flicking through the folders to the letter M.

"An invitation, to my thirtieth."

"I didn't realise you were that much ol-"

Flicking a piece of lint off my jacket, he said, "Don't say it! Say I look good for my age."

"You look good for your age."

"That wasn't exactly sincere."

"Sorry," I yawned. "Best I can do at the moment."

"It'll be a brilliant knees-up; I really hope you can make it. Oh, and my number is on the invitation, so you can ring me!"

"Will do."

"Have a nice sleep."

"Thanks, by the way where are you off to?" Pretending to sniff the air, he joked, "Do I look that fresh?"

"You do, of course that'll change after the big three o."

"Ow!" he said, swatting my arm playfully. "I'm off to la la land."

"Give me strength!"

"Sorry, what?"

"Nothing, ehm, I'll let you know about this," I waved the embossed card.

With a peck to my cheek, he said, "Gotta go, Tinseltown is calling!"

"When's your party?"

"A week from Sunday. November the twenty-sixth."

The day I fly to Japan, to meet David.

17th ~ At home

When mum is well, home is a lovely place to be, but when she's down, it feels like all the joy gets sucked out and all the sadness pours in.

18th ~ Kimberly, Lorna, Meryl's, Richmond upon Thames

I feel mum's absence the most when I sit at the kitchen table. She's usually pottering about, cleaning something that's already clean, cooking or generally being her inquisitive self. When I saw dad glance at mum's empty chair, I broached the subject of mum going to hospital.

"It's time, isn't it?" he said, wearily.

"I think so."

"I just dread mum's reaction and hate upsetting her."

"Mum needs treatment, dad. She's only getting worse."

"Aye, yer right. Whit are ye doin' today?"

"I thought I'd go to Waitrose and grab a few bits, we're low on everything."

"D'ye have somewhere ye can go? To stay I mean."

I gave him a questioning look.

305

"It might be better if yer no here when I talk to mum. And afterwards as well, I think it'd be best if yer no here. Fur any of it."

"Do you think her reaction will be that bad?"

"Insisting it's time to be admitted to the psychiatric unit?"

The mere mention of the dreaded place turned my stomach. "Pamsy's away this week but I can ring Lorna, I'm sure she won't mind, besides I leave on a trip tomorrow, so it'd only be for one night. And then I can come home, after the trip?"

"Aye, of course. I jist don't want ye in the middle of-"

"I understand but are you sure you don't want me to stay and help?"

"I'm sure, aye. I'll give ye a few bob, so ye can treat the lassies to a wee night oot."

19th ~ LHR - ORD
The Westin Hotel, Chicago, Illinois

First time in the windy city and I like it. With towering buildings and American flags fluttering in the wind, there's no mistaking where we are. American hotels have the best showers but this one is especially nice, even more so after a nine-hour flight, most of which was spent on my feet.

Met up with most of the crew in the lobby, where we split, half to the hotel bar, the other half ventured out. The second the wind smacked my face I gasped and was tempted to run back inside but I really wanted to see the city at night. Christian, who I worked with down the back, is quite possibly the best looking human, ever! To qualify how good looking he is, he was approached not once, but three times, by various people asking which modelling agency he's signed with! From the way he handled them, I got the impression it's a regular occurrence.

I rang home from TriStar House this morning, but dad didn't pick up. I want to call again, but it's dawn at home, so I'll have to wait.

I rang David and got that warm, fuzzy feeling I get from the sound of his voice. Too bad it was only on his answering machine.

20th ~ ORD – LHR

I've been desperate for this crew rest, so I can write about what happened earlier. However, I'm going to start at the very beginning (apparently a very good place to start!). Argh, now I can't get Julie Andrews out of my head. Seriously, I need to calm down and get on with it, so in that vein…Stirred several hours before crew breakfast, so I used every scrap of hotel stationery to pen a story about a girl circling the globe. Write what you know, isn't that what they say? I also wrote two letters; one for David, the other for nana, who will no doubt appreciate the linen stationery.

Finally, it came time to meet up and braving the elements, we made our way to a diner Christian recommended. Breakfast, the likes of which can only be found in the States (stuffed French toast!) was ample and delicious. Quick peek at Lake Michigan (brrrr) then back to my room in time to watch *Sally Jesse Raphael*.

Pick up was at five pm and off we went, back to O'Hare. Because of the wind chill, we literally ran from the crew bus to the terminal. No running in uniform! *Unless you're in Chicago, in which case, leg it*!

While the Captain was getting the gate number from the station manager, I glanced around the terminal, not quite believing my eyes when I saw him. I thought the frigid temps might have gone to my brain, but there was no denying the hair belonged only to him.

Moving at quite a clip, in a trench coat that looked nothing like the ratty ones I remember from commuting days, we held each other's gaze, and a few steps from me, he uttered my name. Grinning like a Chesire cat, I exclaimed, "Fancy meeting you here!"

"I guess it'd be dumb to ask what you're doing here?"

"Right back atcha, David," I laughed.

"This is crazy, this isn't my terminal, I'm on my way to the lounge."

"Are you in transit?"

Slight shake of the head, enough to shift his hair in the most appealing way. "I've been here for two days, I'm heading home."

"I wish I'd known you were here," I sighed wistfully, looking at him in question.

"I guess you didn't get my letter?"

I made a sad face.

"*Oh, man*," he groaned. "There's gotta be a better way."

At that point I desperately wanted to:

Kiss David (No Public Displays of Affection Whilst in Uniform!).

Go to LA with him (Cabin Crew Must Complete the Trip or Be Sacked!) I just made that up, but the first one is true.

"Looks like we're on the move. It was nice to meet you, David," Christian said, shaking David's hand. "See you in a minute, Karen."

"You just made my year," David whispered. "And you totally rock that uniform."

All in a tither, with my cheeks feeling like they were on fire, I quickly checked to make sure none of my crew were lagging, before I kissed him on the lips. And again.

"Have a good flight home, sweetie," he smiled. "See you in Japan."

21st ~ At home

On the drive home, I replayed David's words and gestures and sorry, Christian, but David surpasses you in the looks department.

I was shocked, but happy to find mum in the kitchen.

"Hello mum," I said, kissing her clammy cheek. "How are you?"

"No too bad, hen."

"You look better." Her hair was matted, and she seemed unsteady on her feet but at least she was out of bed. "Have a seat, I'll make the tea."

Looking distant, mum asked where I'd been.

"Chicago," I said brightly.

"Chicago? I never knew ye were in America."

"Dad didn't tell you?"

"Dad's no very happy wi me." She burst into tears.

"Oh, mum, it's going to be ok." My instinct was to comfort her, but I sensed she needed space, so I held back.

"Dad's adamant that it's time for me to go…ye know where."

"And you don't want to?"

Shaking her head furiously, she said, "I never want to go there again."

"We just want you to get better, mum. I know it's really hard when you feel like this."

"I'm trying my best," she croaked.

"You're up," I said in my most cheerful tone. "That's a start, isn't it?"

"D'ye think so?"

"Definitely!"

"Dad said," she stopped and blew her nose. "Dad said it's like living wi a zombie."

"He only said that because he's upset. He didn't mean it."

"Aye, I know," she nodded.

"It's hard on him."

Facing me with tear-filled eyes, she sniffed, "And you, as well, hen."

22nd ~ At home

Just got off the phone with Annabel, always an experience.

"Have you heard the news, about the near miss?"

"Not a peep."

"Where have you been?" She didn't allow me to answer. "You don't know about the seven four that came so close to the Penta hotel on landing that it set off the car alarms?"

"Shit, when did that happen?"

"Yesterday."

"What airline?"

"The world's favourite, of course. I wouldn't be interested had it not been one of ours."

"What happened?"

"It was super foggy-"

"Yeah, we circled for ninety minutes before we got clearance to land."

"Apparently, the Captain was alone in the cockpit."

"Why?"

"Allow me to finish! Gosh, you can be terribly impatient."

"Sorry," I said, unable to stop grinning. "Go on."

"The FO and the Engineer were both incapacitated."

"From what?"

"Diarrhea," she stated, with, I imagine, her signature shudder. "Isn't that just the ghastliest word?"

"It is but I wouldn't consider having diarr, I mean an upset stomach as being incapacitated."

Slowly, she said, "It can be considered as such, when one is stuck on the lav, or as it was in this case, two."

"Ok, point taken."

"Prior to being in Bahrain, the crew were in Mauritius, where most of them somehow ended up with gastroenteritis."

"Poor things, there's nothing worse than flying with a dicky tummy."

"Due to the dense fog, the Captain mistook the hotel lights for the ruddy runway and almost came down on the roof of the hotel. Talk about guts for garters!"

"You were on the flight?"

"No, but I was at the Penta when it happened, after which all hell broke loose. Several witnesses were terribly upset."

"What were you doing at the Penta?"

"That's not important-"

"You really are a dark horse, Annabel."

"Perhaps," she chuckled. "Everyone is safe, shaken of course but thankfully, the Captain realised his mistake in time. It could have been positively catastrophic."

"How frightening, I'm sure there'll be a major investigation."

"Indeed," she stated. "After which, heads will surely roll."

23rd ~ At home

With no desire to get stuck on the motorway when my old banger sputters its last breath, I bit the bullet and popped down the VW dealership in Bletchley. It didn't take long for the helpful sales guy to convince me I needed a shiny red Golf! I'll pick it up when I get back from Japan.

Driving home, I felt excited and wanted to share my good news, but dad was at work and mum was asleep, so I rang Jon.

"I would've gone with you."

"No need, I got a good deal."

"What did you end up paying?"

"Eh, I don't actually know the exact figure, but I can afford the monthly payments."

"I guess the most important question is do you love it?"

"Yes!"

"Then that's all that matters. I can come up if you fancy going out to celebrate."

"Sorry, I'm going to a friend's house."

"Oh, ok." He sounded disappointed, so I felt the need to explain.

"We met many moons ago, when I worked in a boring office."

"McGarr," he laughed, "I doubt anywhere you've ever worked was boring."

24th ~ Sebastian's, Bedfordshire

Domestic day at home, catching up with what seemed like piles of laundry, especially bedding. Dad got home just after five, asked if I had any plans.

"I'm going to Sebastian's."

"Let me guess, party?"

I laughed. "You're good at this."

It was so nice to see him smile.

"Sebastian's throwing a surprise birthday party for his friend Adam. His thirtieth, I think."

"Ye need younger pals!" dad joked. "So ye definitely won't be home the night?"

I shook my head.

"That's good, I don't want ye on the roads in the early hours. They're saying the temperature's about to plummet."

"I'm not surprised, it was bitter today."

"How has mum been? Did ye get a chance to talk to her?"

"I did. She was dying for fish and chips, so I ran over to the chippy. We ate them in the garden."

He looked surprised but encouraged.

"I know, good news, huh? I think mum might almost be out of the woods, this episode seems to be passing, at least I think it is. And sorry, but I have to get going, I promised Sebastian that I'd help him set up."

"Ok, hen, enjoy yerself and drive safe."

"Thanks dad," I said, kissing stubbly cheek. "I'll just run up and say bye to mum."

25th ~ Kimberly, Lorna, Meryl's, Richmond upon Thames

In less than five hours, the alarm on my handy dandy travel clock will make a piercing sound. With my eyes still shut, I'll reach for it on the floor, and after I locate the tiny switch that cancels the alarm, I'll wish I'd called it a night much earlier than this.

I'll shower, get into uniform, drink tea, eat toast (hopefully there's bread!) with jam (hopefully there's jam!) then drive, with Lorna, to the staff car park. Knowing Lorna as I do, she'll yap the entire way, even after I drop heavy hints about still waking up.

From the car park, we'll take the shuttle bus to TriStar House and after we drop off our suitcases, we'll head to the briefing room. Lorna's staff number is one digit ahead of mine, so she'll get to choose a working position before I do. It's almost a given that the two of us will get stuck down the back, which won't be particularly pleasant given that the last ten rows on the NRT route are designated as smoking.

After we land in Japan, we'll pile onto the crew bus and by the time we check into the hotel, it'll be lunchtime. After a thirteen-hour flight, and a nine-hour time change, all I'd usually want to do is sleep, but instead of crawling into bed, I'll sit on the edge it and make a phone call.

During that call, plans will be made, and when I hang up, I'll no doubt be smiling, from knowing that a couple of hours later, David will knock on my door.

26th ~ At home

I thought I was dreaming when I felt my arm being gently shaken.

"Karen, wake up."

I peeled my eyes open, to find Lorna standing over me.

"Shit, are we late? My alarm didn't go off!"

"No, doll, it's still early. Your dad's on the phone."

"What?"

"Your dad. He's on the phone."

"What does he want?" I said, tossing the blanket aside.

"He didn't say."

I swung my legs off the couch and when my foot hit the floor, it landed on my clock. I heard, and felt, the glass shattering. "Shit," I hissed, reacting to the pain. "This better be important."

I hopped my way to the hall and picked up the receiver.

"Hello?"

"Karen, it's dad," he said in an unfamiliar tone.

"Is everything ok?" He didn't answer. "Dad? Why are you phoning so early?" My heart was already racing. "Is mum ok?"

"Aye, mum's eh, aye she's ok."

Lorna came into the hall and placed a towel on the floor that I lowered my bloody foot onto.

"Dad you're not making any sense, what's going on?"

After a long, heavy sigh, he uttered, "It's yer nana."

"Is she ok?"

"No, hen, I'm so sorry. Nana's dead."

27th ~ Nana's, Glasgow, Scotland

Five hours on the train felt like days, and mum barely uttered a word, while, around us, people laughed and joked in a way that made me want to scream and tell them to shut up.

A grey curtain of rain followed the taxi, and when we pulled up outside nana's tenement building, mum broke down in tears. In the rearview mirror, the cabbie raised his hand and mouthed, "Nae rush."

This evening was a bit of a blur, with relatives coming and going and mum's siblings choosing this, of all times, to argue about the same unresolved issues they've been arguing about for as long as I can remember.

I don't think it's hit me that nana is gone. I keep glancing at the empty chair by the window, where she drew her last breath.

28th ~ Nana's, Glasgow, Scotland

The letter I sent from Chicago arrived this morning. No sooner did I pick it up off the mat when I turned in the direction of the living room, so I could give it to nana.

When the hearse arrived, I wondered how they'd get the coffin up two flights of stairs, quickly chiding myself for such an absurd thought. I think immense sorrow distorts and jumbles everything to the point where you don't know if you're coming or going.

With nana situated in her bedroom, friends and relatives started arriving, to pay their respects. The night flew by and when only mum and one of her sisters remained, I knew it was time.

I've never liked nana's bedroom, it's always felt damp and eerie, but tonight, with candles circling the coffin, it felt peaceful.

When I touched nana's forehead, I was surprised at how cold it felt. With my hand over the rosary beads laced through nana's fingers, I told her over and over how much I love her, but it wasn't until I told her how much I'll miss her that the tears came.

29th ~ Nana's, Glasgow, Scotland

Watching the train shunting into the Central, I released a huge sigh of relief.

"Welcome to the circus," I said, stepping up my gait to keep up with dad's lengthy strides.

"I take it the animals are well watered?"

"Swimmin' in it!" I said in a thick Glaswegian accent that made him laugh.

Mum was asleep on the couch and dad picked up the candlewick blanket that had fallen on the floor. Gently, he placed it over mum and when he bent to kiss her cheek, she wrapped her hand around his.

Outside nana's bedroom, dad asked if I was ok.

"Uh-huh, are you?"

"Aye," he said with a deep sigh, slowly turning the door handle. "This part's never easy."

Circling the coffin, the flickering candles danced shadows across the patterned wallpaper nana often said she'd like to change. Above the bed she rarely slept in, a picture of the Pope hung at a slight angle.

"Oh, Kate," dad uttered his voice full of emotion as he eased closer to nana. For a while, neither of us spoke, but when dad did, it was with respect and adoration for his mother-in-law of twenty plus years.

During the prayer vigil at the chapel tonight, dad held mum close as she wept into his jacket. It was a beautiful, albeit sad moment to witness of my parents, who, because of the cruel nature of mum's illness, have recently seemed disconnected.

Crammed into nana's living room, with three bars on the electric fire casting a glow, dad managed to lighten the mood by sharing heartfelt stories about nana, particularly when he first met her.

"I couldnae get over the size of her," he said. "I'd rarely seen such a wee wumin."

I felt myself smiling when I recalled nana saying, "Good things come in small packages."

30th ~ On the train

We buried nana today. I don't feel the need to write about it because I know it'll never leave me. Seeing the excruciating agony on mum's face while the rain pelted our cheeks is forever etched on my memory.

I've been listening to Kate Bush's, "This Woman's Work." I've never paid much attention to the lyrics but at this moment in time they make sense, especially given that nana is..was.. a mother of four.

And now home…After the events of the past few days, I hated coming home to a dark, empty house. Tini is with Janice and Terry and if it wasn't so late (almost half eleven) I'd go and get him.

On the mat, sat a tower of post, but stuck halfway through the letterbox was an envelope. Recognising the scribble of my name, I tore it open.

K- So sorry about your Nana.
Ring me when you get home.
I don't care what time it is, just ring me, ok?
I wasted no time picking up the phone. Ben is on his way over.

DECEMBER

1st ~ At home

A few minutes after I unlocked the door last night, Ben lightly tapped on it, before coming in. There wasn't enough room in the phone chair for the two of us, so I slid onto his lap. With my head rising and falling with the rhythm of his chest, we sat in silence, while he slowly brushed his fingers through my hair.

When I got up and held out my hand, Ben looked surprised, but took it willingly. Without speaking, I led him upstairs in the dark, to my bedroom. With the glow from the streetlamp peeking through the thin curtains, we kissed like it was the first time. Slowly undressing one another, we whispered our desires, while our bodies wound together, as if from memory. Throughout the night, my body showed him I still love him. I think I always will.

2nd ~ At home

For the second day in a row, I woke up with Ben. The word blissful barely covers it. The entire day, it felt like the clock had been turned back to a time when we were madly in love and so happy together. There were no hurtful words, no me getting upset over something he'd said, no him getting frustrated with me because of a misunderstanding. No nonsense, just two people enjoying each other in every way possible, six years after their love first blossomed.

While we were stretched out on the living room floor, I let out a laugh.

"What's so funny?"

"The music."

"I thought you liked Sam Cooke?"

"I do, but I doubt it's what most people in their twenties listen to, especially when we have the eighties."

"*Our* decade," Ben said.

"It's weird to think that in less than a month we'll be into the nineties."

"Spooky," Ben laughed.

Lying on our backs, we serenaded the ceiling. "At first, I thought it was infatuation, but oooo it's lasted so long. Now I find myself wanting to marry you and take you home."

With his hand resting on my thigh Ben said, "Where do you think you'll be, ten years from now?"

With you?

"What kinda question is that?"

"One I'm interested in the answer to."

"I'm not sure," I uttered. "Where I end up will depend on so many things."

"Ok, then where would you like to end up?"

"France?"

He laughed. "You've always been drawn to all things French."

"C'est vrai."

He rolled toward me and propped himself up on his elbow. "Je t'aime."

"You do not!" I blurted.

"Shouldn't I be the judge of that?"

"I s'pose."

"I do, you know."

"Hmm," I muttered.

"Why hmmmm?" I fixated on his lips as he drew out the sound.

"I refuse to say her name, especially now, but have you forgotten about *whatsherface*?"

Rolling onto his back, he sighed. "Mandy's a different kettle of fish."

I looked at him, quizzically.

"To you."

"You're just saying that, so I'll drag you upstairs to my lair," I grinned. "Again."

"As much as I love that, and I do, in every sense of the word, it's not the reason I just told you I love you."

"Oh, is that what you said in French? Sorry, your accent was so atrocious I had a hard time understanding you." I tried keeping a straight face, but I failed. Miserably.

"Tu es tres méchante," Ben breathed, with a tantalising slap to my thigh.

"Not as naughty as you. Do you love her?"

"In some ways, yeah, I do."

"*But?*"

"But I don't see us ending up together."

"Why not?"

"I think I'm better with…someone like you."

"Yeah right and just for your information, *monsieur*, I'm still not taking you upstairs."

His face took on a look of seriousness. "Come to think of it, the two of you are polar opposites."

"I'm relieved to hear that!"

Whenever Ben questions something, he scrunches up his nose. This time was no exception.

"I've seen her taste in clothes," I sneered. "Or lack thereof."

"Uh-oh," he said, getting up. "Might be time to change the subject."

"Probably," I said, reaching for his outstretched hand.

"Get up here and dance with me," he grinned, pulling me up to meet him.

3rd ~ At home

320

After an incredibly satisfying time with Ben, I was sad when he left but I was due to pick up mum and dad from the train station so there was no time to dwell on how I was feeling.

When I spotted dad, he smiled and gave a little nod but no wave. I couldn't see mum but the memory of her waving wildly whenever she meets me off the train made me smile.

"Where's mum?"

"She wanted to stay in Glasgow a wee while longer. Hopefully she'll be home in a few days."

Pausing for a second, to choose my words carefully, I said, "I just worry about mum falling into-"

"Don't," dad said. "I'll phone every day and make sure she's ok."

I set the alarm for seven this morning and was up before dad (most unusual) but knowing I was picking up my new car made getting up a breeze. For the first few minutes of driving, I felt nervous but soon got the hang of it. Came straight home and did all the chores I didn't do while Ben was here.

"D'ye fancy going for a wee run?" Dad asked tonight. "Get used to driving the new motor."

"Where should we go?"

"Is Wolverton too far?"

"Not at all but why there?"

"I thought we could get some Chinese take-away at the wee place you and mum like."

Feeling thoroughly stuffed, dad switched on the news.

"This is sum year," he said in response to the declaration by Thatcher, Bush and Gorbachev that the cold war has ended. With such big news, nothing else was being reported, so dad shut it off. He was in one of his talkative moods, not that he's quiet but mum's usually the one to use up all the air in the room. He talked mostly about nana and how she initially didn't accept him because he wasn't Catholic.

"Might have had something to do with the fact you knocked her daughter up before she had a ring on her finger," I said, my boldness spilling out before I could catch it.

"Best surprise ever, hen," he smiled.

4th ~ LHR - MCT
Hotel Inter-Continental, Muscat, Oman

Lovely pax on our eight-hour flight (zero crew rest!) with one very sweet elderly lady who reminded me of nana. Towards the end of the flight, she made her way into the galley and sang my praises to the Purser. I was a little embarrassed but when she hugged me, she said she'd been back in the UK to bury her sister. It took everything I had not to cry, and it served as a reminder that you never know what someone is going through.

Ben rang this morning, looking to find out when I'll be back.

"In a week," I said, which is a lie because I'll be home in a few days. Granted, we just had the most fantastic time together but that doesn't mean I'm reverting to my old, foolish ways. I have no intention of doing that ever again. Not with him. Not with anyone.

We arrived in Muscat before seven pm, and most the crew were meeting up in the hotel bar but I'm not in the mood for socialising.

After we left Scotland and moved to England, I went from seeing nana all the time, to every couple of months. We spent every Christmas together and I went to Scotland as much as I could, plus we were always on the phone, and always wrote. What feels difficult is the end of all of that. Knowing I'll never talk to her again almost feels worse than not seeing her but how does that make sense.

It's half two and I've been cocooned in this plush bed for hours. As usual, I've used every scrap of hotel stationery, most of which is now strewn across the bed. Such a satisfying sight that reminds me of my favourite Erica Jong poem, "I Sleep With."

I sleep with double pillows since you're gone.
Is one of them for you-or is it you?
My bed is heaped with books of poetry.
I fall asleep on yellow legal pads.
Oh the orgies in stationery stores!
The love of printer's ink and think new pads!
A poet has to fall in love to write.
Her bed is heaped with papers, or with men.

I keep your pillow pressed down with my books.
They leave an indentation like your head.
If I can't have you here, I'll take cold type-
& words: the warmest things there are – but you.

Ah, how I love that. Some of the stuff I wrote was about Ben, including a letter I already tore into shreds. I don't think I'm ready to stay away from him, not just yet, but I'll never get anywhere if I keep running back to him.

5th ~ Hotel Inter-Continental, Muscat, Oman

Wonderfully relaxing day on the beach with Catherine from my crew, who, at six one makes stowing luggage in the overhead bins look easy! She's also super slender (ugh!) and recently got engaged. When I commented on how sparkly the Princess cut diamond was, she slipped the ring off her finger.

"Here, try it on."

"I can't do that."

"Go ahead," she said. "See if you like it."

"I already know I like it!" I laughed.

"Then try it on."

"Sorry, no, that would be weird."

"*You're* weird," she chuckled. "It's just a ring."

"But it's your engagement ring."

"I'm sure it won't be my last."

I was a little taken aback so I didn't respond.

"Jacob is cabin crew," she announced, rolling her deep-set eyes. "I expect at some point I'll want to trade up."

I couldn't tell if she was joking so I shrugged, "Of course," if only to see how she'd react.

"I'm glad you understand," she nodded. "Most girls wouldn't."

"How do you think it'll work with both of you flying?"

"We'll do married rosters," she said, nonchalantly.

"So, you'll be together on *every* trip?"

"Yes! Do you think you'd have a problem with that?"

With Ben in mind, I concluded that even in our heyday, I'd have found it difficult to live and work with him. All the time.

"Earth to Karen, where'd you go?" The sight of three or more waving karats got my attention.

"Sorry, I was just thinking about someone."

"Who? Tell me!"

"There's nothing to tell. It's an old relationship that needs to be put to bed."

I'd planned on staying in tonight, but Catherine reminded me I did that last night, so we ate at the Car Park, then popped into the hotel disco, where Catherine spotted a familiar face. While he was making his way over, I asked who he is.

"I don't remember his name, but he was dynamite in bed," she purred. "We had a tryst in…Bermuda? Or maybe it was the Bahamas?"

One drink into their flirt fest, I left them to it, with Catherine towering over her bed buddy.

6th ~ MCT - RUH - LHR

Presently relaxing in seat 1A, which, with the exception of a spot on the flight deck, must surely be the best seat in the house. Surprisingly, there are no pax in the First Class cabin, hence the upgraded crew rest area, which, after a two hour delay leaving Riyadh, is much appreciated.

Anxious to know how mum is and if she's back, I rang home first thing, but there was no answer. I rang Catherine but no reply there either.

About an hour later, there was a knock at the door. When I peered through the peephole, I was delighted to see that Catherine had been reduced to a tiny, round blob.

"Morning," I said, opening the door.

Strutting (no joke!) past me, she said, "Can we order room service?"

"Hi Karen," I said cockily. "How are you? Did you sleep well? Yes, I did actually, thanks for asking, Catherine."

"Saw…ree," she yawned, her arms reaching so high, they came close to grazing the ceiling. "I'm absolutely ravenous."

"Lover boy didn't feed you?"

"We were otherwise occupied."

"Catherine! Didn't you just get engaged?"

"Engaged, yes. Married, no. Can we at least order some tuck before you start lecturing me?"

Without asking what she wanted, I ordered an obscene amount of food.

"You're an angel," Catherine breathed, stretching out on the bed to reveal a perfectly toned tum (ugh!).

"Unlike you."

"I can't seem to help myself."

"Don't you love your fiancé?"

"Of course."

"Then why did you sleep with…what's his name?"

"I knew what was in store and couldn't resist."

Fresh from reading *The Oxford Companion to the Mind*, I suggested she might have impulse control issues, in reply to which she screamed, "I cannot, and I mean *cannot* have this conversation, this third degree right now."

Okie dokie!

"Fair enough. By the way, what is his name?"

Turning the charm back on, she said, "Don't laugh. It's Witton."

"Unusual, but not terrible."

"It means far, by the wood."

"Catherine, last night you couldn't remember his name, and now you know the meaning of it? At what point did he share that little tidbit with you?"

"Somewhere between the floor and the shower," she said, with a satisfied grin.

7th ~ Ben's, MK

Ben and I are at opposite ends of the couch, sharing a blanket, under which our socks are pressed together, but I'm getting ahead of myself.

Mum is home and, all things considered, I think she's doing ok. She said there's comfort in knowing nana didn't suffer. It's too upsetting to think about, I need to write about something else.

By this afternoon, I was falling off my feet, so I got comfy on the couch with Tini (love that) and next thing I knew, the phone woke me up.

"Ugh," I groaned, repositioning Tini, whose disapproving snort matched how I felt.

"Hey you, what are you doing home?"

"I got home this morning," I said, without thinking.

"I thought you weren't due back-"

"Oh yeah, the ehm, there was an unscheduled change to the trip. Why are you ringing?"

"Do I need a reason?"

"Sorry, that came out all wrong. The phone woke me up and I'm a bit groggy from being up all night."

"Too groggy to meet for a drink later?"

Through the frosted glass front door, I spotted dad's silhouette.

"Sorry, I have to go," I whispered. "I'll pick you up at six."

Telling dad the truth of my whereabouts might not have been so bad but if mum knew I was seeing Ben, she'd have had a fit and the last thing I want to do is add to her stress. However, those thoughts all disappeared when Ben opened the door.

"Are you coming in or are we going out?"

"Out. Somewhere far from here," I said, meeting him halfway for a kiss on the lips.

"You smell good enough to eat," he moaned.

"As do you," I said, noting the return of Drakkar Noir.

8th ~ At home

While dad and I were having dinner, the phone rang.

"Want me to get that?"

Dad shook his head. "If it's important they'll phone back."

When it rang again, he got up, and through the glass wall, I watched the colour drain from his face. After a few words, he hung up and came back into the kitchen.

"My da's in the hospital." His voice was tremulous. "He had a heart attack."

"Oh no, poor granda."

"Kathy's there, the others are on their way."

"Oh, dad, I'm so sorry," I said, close to tears.

"The doctors are no saying much aside fae the obvious that granda's eighty-three and this is his fourth heart attack. I'd jump on the train the night but mum's no in any fit state to be left alone."

Getting up, I said, "I'll ring crewing and see if I can get time off."

Looking past me, he let out a heavy sigh. "I wisnae expecting this, I think I need a wee hauf."

After I poured dad a whisky, I mentioned staying home again.

"Naw, I don't want ye to do that," he said, adding a splash of water to the generous tot. "Just give me a wee minute to think, before I go up and tell mum."

9th ~ At home

Granda remains in hospital, in stable condition. Dad decided to stay here with mum, and with no shortage of siblings to keep an eye on granda, I think he made the right choice.

David rang. He'd just received my letter explaining why I never made it to Japan. When he offered his condolences, I felt like he was just going through the motions, and it annoyed me.

"Where are you headed next?"

"New York. Tomorrow," I said, flatly.

"I wish I'd known. I could've met you there. New York is halfway between here and London."

"I'm aware of that," I said, immediately regretting my sharp tone. There didn't seem much left to say so I made an excuse that I had to go but after I hung up, I felt bad about how impertinent I'd been, so I thought I'd call and apologise, but when I picked up the phone, it was Ben's number that I dialled.

I love that Ben knew nana and in our favourite Indian restaurant in Northampton, we talked about her at length. Listening to Ben's recollections of the many times he met nana and the funny things she said was so comforting.

David is new in my life, so it's unfair to expect the same from him, but tonight, I needed to be with someone who knew nana, not someone who never met her, offering hollow condolences through the phone.

10th ~ LHR - JFK
Lexington Hotel, New York

Jerry Hall was in Club, along with her matronly nanny who clearly dotes on the little ones, James and Lizzy, both of whom were sweet and very well-behaved. Clearly no strangers to flying, they popped in and out of the galley like the seasoned travellers I imagine they are.

Ms. Hall consistently tossed her signature mane from side to side (fortunately she was on the aisle and the seat next to her was vacant!). When I mentioned how much I loved her accent, she drawled, "Honey, yours is so much better," in that buttery Southern way. She ate nothing, not a morsel, which may explain her striking, slender figure.

Out on the town tonight with Lydia, who dated a guy from here for almost two years.

"What was the best thing about your long-distance relationship?"

She gave a suggestive smirk.

"Other than that?"

"The excitement of exploring each other's world. He loved England as much as I love it here, so sharing that was satisfying."

"And the worst?"

"Getting home from a trip and not having the person you want to talk to the most waiting for you."

Food for thought.

On Lydia's recommendation, we took a cab to Raoul's in Greenwich Village. Feeling utterly stuffed, we walked until the biting wind got too much. Our mammoth chat continued in the hotel bar, and before I knew it, it was eleven (four am UK time.)

"Do you want another drink?" Lydia asked, her eyes half closed.

"No thanks, I'm calling it a night."

"Me too," she nodded. "I think it's time I went to my room and made a phone call."

"Let me guess, your ex?"

"He's only ten minutes away, so it could be dangerous and yes, I might regret ringing but-"

"You only live once!"

"If you do it right," she winked.

I thought about ringing David but I'm feeling weepy, so it's probably best I don't. Plus, it's frigid, so I need to get my arms under the covers.

11th ~ Christopher's, New York

Woke up feeling like I was suffering from hypothermia, so I rang reception and a kindly girl about my age managed to move me to another room. By the time I hit the sack, it was almost four am, local!

Spent the day with Lydia before she flew home on a combi, with another crew. It was her first time at the Empire State, which was surprising given she'd spent so much time here. She led me to the most amazing bookshop called The Strand, where I bought gifts for Florence, Ben, Millie, and yours truly.

As planned, I met Frankie, in the lobby, when she arrived with her crew. "Naff bunch of drips," she whispered during a tight squeeze.

"Just us, then," I said. "Oh, and can we use your room? I moved last night but I don't think the heat's working in that one either."

Frankie rang Robert and when he said he couldn't join us, she made her pouty face and cooed about how disappointed she was. According to Christopher, Robert has a serious girlfriend and when she found out about Frankie, she hit the roof. She told Robert if he, "stepped out," on her again, she'd "dump his sorry ass!" Seems the girl in question comes from a prominent New York family and Robert has no intention of ruining his chances of a life of luxury.

With Frankie in a buttery, fitted leather jacket and me in dowdy black trousers and a ruffled white blouse, we caught a cab to The Iguana, where Christopher met us after work. I had a margarita waiting for him which he just about downed in one, but I swear he was smiling whilst guzzling.

If Christopher lived in the UK, I imagine we'd spend a lot of time together. I don't fancy him and I'm sure the feeling is mutual. Frankie says otherwise, but what does a girl who goes sleeveless in December know.

Frankie got chatted up by approximately five hundred guys and took full advantage of ample free drinks, during which time I caught up with Christopher. I never hold back with him, and he always has good advice. I told him about nana, and unlike when I talked to David (granted, by phone) his concern came across as sincere, which doesn't mean David wasn't. When Christopher leaned in to give me a hug, I spotted Frankie, behind him.

"Look," I pointed, motioning for him to turn and look.

"Holy shit! That's Gene Anthony Ray."

Leroy from *Fame*. Dancing on the bar. With Frankie.

Frankie and Gene (the new Fred & Ginger!) danced like they'd been rehearsing for months, and I watched in wonder as they made full use of the bar, stepping nimbly between glasses and bags, with synchronised moves that drew raucous cheers from the enthusiastic crowd. When the song ended, Gene held Frankie's hand and encouraged her to take a bow, which kept the applause going.

In the heightened atmosphere, the drinks disappeared faster than usual and hours later, I mentioned to Christopher it was time we got going.

Getting Frankie from the bar to the street and into the cab was no small feat. With Frankie sandwiched between us in the back seat of the cab, Christopher said, "You wanna come to my place?" After one look at Frankie, I nodded, yes.

Sliding down Christopher's couch, Frankie asked for, "A wittle dwinkie."

"Sure," Christopher said, pouring coke into a tall glass. "You want some coke with this Jack Daniel's, Frankie?"

"Yes please beautiful, polite American boy," she said, slipping into the position she passed out in.

Wedged between the wall and the table in Christopher's miniscule kitchen, he said, "I guess you're spending the night?"

"Mr. B," I teased. "That's rather forward."

Shaking his head, laughing, he said, "I'll grab you something to wear." When he brushed against the back of the chair, he gave my shoulder a light squeeze. I felt something stir in me, but I attributed it to the wine.

"Get you," I joked, when I saw the monogrammed pyjama cuffs.

"They were a gift… from my grandmother."

"Aw, in that case, thank you. They look brand new."

"I was saving them for you," he said, leaning in to plant a kiss on my cheek. For a split second I thought about moving my head so his kiss would land on my lips but again, I blamed it on the wine and didn't want to spoil what we have, so a peck on the cheek it was.

The pyjama bottoms were much too long so I rolled them up to my knees. Christopher took one look at me and burst out laughing so much so, that Frankie stirred and mumbled something unintelligible.

"What's that, Frankie?" I said, my hand covering my mouth to stifle my giggle.

She uttered a few words before, as clear as day, she said, "Where's Leroy?"

12th ~ Christopher's, New York

After Christopher left for work, I sat by the window, reading, *The Bonfire of the Vanities* (Sherman McCoy reminded me of Robert) while Frankie continued her beauty sleep.

When we finally left the apartment, it was total déjà vu chatting to Michael the doorman, who hailed us a cab, because I wasn't about to walk-

   a.   In the bitter cold.

   b.   Wearing last night's clothes!

At the hotel, Frankie sprang to life and said we were going skating with a guy she met last night. I assumed she meant Gene and was looking forward to asking him about being on *Fame*, but no, it was someone else. I have no idea who he was (not even his name), but we skated together beautifully in Central Park!

I rang home and happy to hear granda is recovering and expected to go home in a day or so, which is great news. Mum sounded ok. The fact she was up and answered the phone is a good sign.

Frankie was only on a night stop, so I grabbed my stuff from her room. She was so disappointed not to be staying but she definitely made the most of her twenty-four hours!

In my room, the message light was flashing. Flight cancelled! I rang Christopher, mainly to thank him for last night but it came up that I'd be here for another night, so we arranged to meet.

At eight pm on the dot (what is it with me and time freaks?) he showed up with a bottle of champagne (forgiven for being on time!).

"No need for ice," he shivered, as he rang room service for flutes.

If only to escape the baltic room, we drank the bottle in record time.

"My local?" Christopher said when we stepped outside. He gets a kick out of using that expression. As usual, dinner at Coconut Grove was delicious and over dessert he asked if I wanted to come here. Responding to my inquisitive head tilt, he quickly added, "To hang out."

After a quick tussle with the bill, Christopher waited while I paid, which from his awkward stance, it pained him to do, but he's always more than generous.

"You're welcome to stay," he offered as we window shopped our way down Fifth Avenue. "Unless you'd rather return to the igloo."

"I'll stay, but on one condition."

His dark eyebrows raised.

"You'll let me wear your monogrammed pj's again."

Wearing said pj's, I joined Christopher on the couch and over a bottle of Merlot, he opened up about his incredibly accomplished, but *complicated beyond belief,* family. Regarding work, he shared some of his innovative ideas for the world of television, all of which I have no doubt he'll see through. Speaking of tv, we caught the news about Leona Helmsley, who I only know from seeing her face splattered all over the place here. She was sentenced to four years in prison and was fined $7.2 million for tax evasion.

It's now after three. I'm in Christopher's bed and he's out on the couch in the living room. He just made me laugh when he yelled, "Where's Leroy?"

13th – JFK – LHR

I'm a whiz with Christopher's coffee maker (after having watched him use it so many times) so while he was getting ready for work, I made coffee, and while he drank it, he mentioned a trip to London is on the cards and asked if I'd show him around. *But of course*! When he said I was welcome to stay at his apartment, I thought how great it'd be to pen something from that location, but I thought it'd be odd being there without him.

Stepping out from under the green awning, fat snowflakes kisscd our faces and when I stuck out my tongue to catch them, Christopher smiled in that appealing way of his. Walking arm in arm, we chatted about how no two snowflakes are the same, then out of the blue, he said, "You should move here!"

"What?"

"You love the city. You should move here."

"It is my favourite place in the world," I said dreamily.

"Why don't you think about it? I'd help you get set up."

I shot him a look.

"*If* you wanted any help, I'd be there to assist." In an exaggerated accent, he added, "I got people."

I hadn't planned on walking all the way to his office, but before I knew it, we were outside the building.

"You want a cab?"

I said I'd rather walk in the snow, so with people side stepping around us, we hugged in the middle of the busy street.

"Don't be a stranger," he said, disappearing into the crowd.

Back in my room, the message light was flashing. I expected it to be news of another delay, but it was David. He said he was sorry he'd missed me, and he'll ring this weekend. Telling him I spent two nights in a guy's apartment probably wasn't what he wanted to hear, so I didn't call him back.

14th ~ At home

Mum looks slightly better and seems a little more like herself but when I look at her, all I can think about is how painful it must be to lose your mother. Writing the words is enough to make me cry.

15th ~ At home

Now that the end of the year is fast approaching, I'm looking ahead to 1990. As much as I love my parents, I'm craving my own space and privacy, but where that might be is still up in the air.

Moving to New York could work. The commute wouldn't be easy, but I could probably find a place to stay during the times I only have minimal days off between trips. I still love the idea of a home in the French countryside, but New York has captured my heart. Plus, I already have a friend there!

16th ~ At home

Super busy Saturday delivering gifts and packing for my trip. Sad I won't be spending Christmas with mum and dad but as crew, it's pretty much a given you'll be away from home when you most want to be present.

When I went to pick mum up from church, she introduced me to some of her lovely friends. They seemed incredibly supportive of her, and it makes me happy knowing she has additional support, especially now.

Tonight, we opened presents, and ate mince pies (the sole reason for the song, "It's the most wonderful time of the year.") I tried not to think about Ben spending it with you know who and avoided eye contact with mum, who looked close to tears for most of the evening.

Dad, clearly in tune with mum's emotions, played only the cheerful Christmas tunes.

17th ~ LHR - SIN

Frankie is upstairs in the crew bunks, but I need a bit of down time before donning (non-monogramed!) pyjamas and strapping into a bunk. Most of the crew received word about the three-hour delay, but I'd already left (couldn't miss this trip) so it's been a long day.

Annabel's Christmas card featured a sketch of her family's country house. She penned such heartfelt sentiments about our friendship that her words brought a tear to my eye.

Sweet card from Graeme, with two mice under the mistletoe.

The best thing about this year was our trip to Bermuda.

Do you need my number?

G x

Jon rang this morning. "This time last year you were in Florida, and this year you'll be on the other side of the world."

"*Working!*"

"Sorry, McGarr, you do *not* have my sympathy. Ring me when you get back?"

"Of course!"

"Happy Christmas. See you in nineteen ninety."

After I hung up, I felt an overwhelming desire to see Ben, and half an hour later he was in my car.

"Where should we go?" I chirped.

"Not too far," he said. "I'm picking Mandy up soon."

Questioning my sanity and feeling utterly crushed, I drove to Willen Lake, but it was too cold to walk so we sat in the car. Gone was the Drakkar Noir, replaced by something I didn't recognise, probably because it's cheap and nasty and came from you know who (meow!). Ben continually made a point of looking at his watch, and without asking, he switched on the radio, after which we barely talked. By the time I dropped him off, I felt thoroughly depressed and cried all the way home.

When dad eyed me suspiciously, I made an excuse about the cold weather affecting me.

"Ye just missed David, on the phone. He said he set the alarm tae try and catch ye before ye leave."

"Did he leave a message?

"Jist that he was hoping ye'd have time tae phone him back."

"I'll try him after I finish packing," I said, even though my case was already packed.

Just as I was getting the last of my things together, mum came downstairs. Her eyes were puffy and when she hugged me tight and said she'll miss me, I swallowed hard so I could say, "Love you, mum."

Dad put my suitcase in the boot and asked if I had everything.

"I have my ID and passport, that's really all I need."

"Have a nice trip, hen, and if ye can phone at Christmas…" his voice trailed off and his shoulders dropped the way they do when he's feeling emotional.

"I'll try dad but with the time change and everything it might be difficult."

"Aye, I know, hen. Jist enjoy yerself. Merry Christmas."

18th ~ The Westin Stamford, Singapore

Frankie and I have adjoining rooms, both of which are now adorned with tinsel and plastic reindeer, none of which came out of my suitcase.

Frankie's friend, Gam, who lives here, came to her room. He'd barely uttered a few words, when she filled three glasses with vodka, and urged him to, "Drink up!" When his eyes widened in questions, she said, "We're tired, you have to go."

Without so much as a sip, Gam got up, nodded goodbye and left.

"What was that all about?" I asked, bewildered.

"You'll see."

Out came the glitter, at which point I was happy to retreat to my room. Frankie found a radio station playing Christmas music she blasted, shimmying in and out of my room in various stages of what she calls, "Getting dolled up."

When I saw the queue for taxi's, all I wanted to do was go back upstairs and crawl into bed, but Frankie insisted we, "Perk up and press on."

"Where are we actually going?"

"To Benny's," she said, goosebumps appearing on her naked arms.

Benny wasn't home but the housekeeper let us in. Well, when I say, let us in, I mean she opened the door, after which Frankie barged inside, taking me with her because her arm was linked through mine. In the expansive living room, with floor to ceiling windows, Frankie made a beeline for the phone, then proceeded to shout, *a lot*, presumably, to Benny. While Frankie was helping herself to a drink from the bar cart, a man I assumed was Benny, appeared.

"Who are you?" she demanded.

"My name is Paddy. I take you to Mr. Benny."

"Oh goodie," she squealed, downing whatever it was she was drinking.

Off we went in the back seat of a gleaming car, complete with privacy screen. The narrow road wound down towards the hub of the city and when we pulled up outside the Hilton, Frankie pointed to two men, framing the entrance to the hotel.

"That's him," Frankie said, liberally spraying the aptly named Poison.

"Which one?" I asked, mid-choke.

"The tall one. The other one is his bodyguard."

I asked why Benny has a bodyguard, but Frankie was already out of the car.

Benny isn't what I'd call attractive but he's striking. Well over six feet, with inky, slicked back hair, he was dressed in a cream linen suit, with a black t-shirt, against which swung a heavy figaro link gold chain. He was bathed in a cologne I didn't recognise (my hostie nose is failing me!) and I imagine he spends an absurd amount of time in the gym, with his closest friends; mirrors.

From the way Benny reacted to the sight of Frankie slinking past him, he was obviously ready, willing and most definitely able to devour her. I immediately felt out of it and during dinner I tried to think of an excuse to escape, but I didn't want to leave Frankie alone with him, so I focused on the food (ah, the struggle!) which fortunately, was delicious.

After dinner, Paddy dropped the three of us off at the Top Ten club, which is pretty naff, but most of our crew were there, including Sandy, who I worked in Economy with (this is her second trip!) and Matt, who clearly has his eye on Sandy.

Next stop was at Ceaser's, where Frankie and Benny worked their way through the cocktail menu.

"Nightcap, nightcap," Frankie whined, after what felt like several exhausting hours feigning interest in their idle chatter.

"No!" I barked. "We're going back to the hotel."

In the fifteen minutes it took Paddy to drive us, Frankie went from bad to worse and by the time we pulled up, she was hanging like a ragdoll. Paddy made no attempt to help me get her out of the car but fortunately a bellhop appeared, by which time Frankie could barely stand. She's small but the bellhop was even smaller. Thrusting her limp limbs in my direction, he dashed off, and returned, with a wheelchair.

19th ~ The Westin Stamford, Singapore

I was so concerned about Frankie that I left the adjoining door open and throughout the night I popped in and out to check on her. Each time, I found her in a different position, enough to reassure me she was doing ok.

Just as I was about to doze off this morning, Frankie came bounding into my room.

"Morning, gorgeous! You awake?" Her pitch was so high, I covered my ears.

"I am now!"

"Why is there a wheelchair in my room?"

After I filled Frankie in on the reason for her new mode of transport and the events of the latter part of the evening, she covered her mouth and giggled. I tried desperately to maintain my scornful expression but watching her doubled over made me do the same.

"Ok, enough of that, we have to get ready."

"For what?" I asked.

"Gam is coming to pick us up."

"No way!"

"Waaayyyy hey," she said in a mock drawl.

"No," I said shaking my head. "You. Don't. Understand. I'm not going out!"

"You have to, Gam has a full day planned for us."

"I can't. If I don't sleep, I'll die."

"Party pooper," she said, blowing a raspberry.

"And proud of it," I said, gleefully sliding under the covers.

The solitude was heavenly, until the heavy bass coming from Frankie's room woke me.

"Frankie? You there?"

"Come in, gorgeous, I'm in the bathroom. Don't worry, I'm decent!"

Leaning against the door frame, I said, "Why are you all dressed up?"

"D'uh! We're meeting the crew in twenty minutes."

"Shit! I slept all day?"

"Yes, and that's why you're sooooo beautiful," she sang.

Waiting in the lobby, Gam looked like a deer caught in the headlights, as one by one, our crew appeared, which I have to admit is quite a sight when we show up en masse.

On the Captain's recommendation, we made our way to Fatty's restaurant. Frankie's dress sleeves (finally!) were covered in pale pink feathers and every time Alan (Captain) turned to talk to Frankie, he pretended to sneeze. Sandy, Matt and I were walking behind and couldn't stop laughing but Frankie seemed oblivious. The more animated she became, the more her feathers flapped.

At the Top Ten, Benny and his bodyguard (oh, please!) were seated in the VIP area, and when Benny spotted Frankie, he swaggered over to her. Bending close to her ear, he motioned to Gam. The music was blasting so I couldn't hear what was being said, but it was obvious Benny was having none of Gam's presence.

With feathers flying, Frankie shooed Gam away and Sandy and I watched him make his way towards the exit. Benny gestured to our crew to follow him to the VIP area and inside the obnoxious ropes, we lounged in illuminated armchairs. Thanks to Benny, it was bubbles galore, putting us all in good spirits, even the Captain. I joined Sandy and Matt on the dance floor, and in a way that guarantees I'll have no voice tomorrow, I belted out the chorus to, "I Hate Myself for Loving You."

No prizes for guessing who was on my mind.

20th ~ SIN - AUH

Hoarse, but with a clear head, I met Sandy and Matt for breakfast, after which we meandered through several markets, but it was so humid I soon felt drained, as did Sandy, so we came back to the hotel just in time for afternoon tea. We rang Frankie from the lobby but there was no reply. In the Compass Rose on the top floor, we enjoyed the amazing views and laughed at Matt's lesson in, *Pinky etiquette.* Judging from how close he and Sandy sat, I detected a blossoming romance.

Jovial chat abounded on the crew bus, where, surprisingly, Frankie was quiet. I teased her about not seeing the light of day, but she leaned her head against the window and shut her eyes.

Take-off was delayed by two hours but pax were already onboard, so we were subjected to complaint after complaint, until we served dinner (always feels odd doing the meal service without a view of the clouds). The woman in 38H made sure everyone around her heard her declare she's, "Never flying with British Airways ever again!" Given the amount of times she's pressed the call bell, it's a medical miracle her finger hasn't fallen off.

Matt's little brother is obsessed with *Teenage Mutant Ninja Turtles*, and on the crew bus, Matt doled out masks of the various characters. The next time 38H dares to rings the call bell, I'm greeting her in a Donatello mask.

21st ~ AUH - KUL

The crew rest area on the Boeing 747-400 is heavenly, as is pretty much everything on this thoughtfully designed beauty. Located at the rear of the aircraft, the designated crew rest area is accessed from one of two doors we have keys to. Upstairs are the bunks, where we rest/sleep during these lengthy sectors.

My favourite passenger tonight is a gorgeous ginger. He's travelling with his parents and twin toddler sisters, and after tending to the little ones nonstop, the parents seemed overwhelmed, so I offered to take Max for a wander. You don't realise how huge the aircraft is until you walk its entirety, including the upper deck, where Captain Alan made a big fuss of Max.

Shortly after arriving in Abu Dhabi at four am, we hit the dance floor in Safari. The Viking's eyes almost popped out of his head when he spotted Frankie sashaying (practice makes perfect!) in his direction. Dancing to, "Back to Life," they cut some serious moves and it was nice to see Frankie enjoying herself, without a bodyguard looming over her.

22nd ~ Kuala Lumpur, Malaysia

Frankie spent a fortune on a collection of duty-free cologne, and asked if I'd go with her, to drop them off at her friend, Elijah's. After minimum rest in AUH before flying here, I felt absolutely knackered but figured a quick taxi ride there and back wouldn't kill me.

The high-rise building was smack bang in the middle of KL, and the surrounding area was chocka, so the taxi moved at a snail's pace. Due to the thick fumes, we had to keep the windows shut, and without AC (hello darkness my old friend!) it didn't take long before I felt like I was going to pass out.

In the apartment building lobby, I slumped in an oversized, plush chair, quickly straightening up with the sound of instructor Sandi's voice in my head. *No sleeping in uniform*! Willing my eyes to stay open, I waited and waited for Frankie to return.

"Not here," Frankie shrugged, exiting the lift. "His secretary said he went to a meeting, but she doesn't know where it is, and isn't sure when he'll be back."

"Can you ring and leave a message?"

She looked at me as though I'd suggested something sinister. "We'll go to his flat."

"*Now?*"

Another taxi, this time with AC, sadly a short ride.

"I'll wait here for you," I said, scanning the sleek lobby, for a chair without hard edges to collapse in.

"Noooo, come with me."

"I can't. I haven't got the energy."

"Old lady," she pouted, forcing me up.

Resting my weight against the cool, metal door, Frankie jabbed the doorbell at least a dozen times but there was no reply.

"We'll wait."

"Don't be silly," I said. "We'll come back later."

"He might come home soon."

"And he might not!" I snipped, ignoring her pout. "Sorry," I said, making for the lift. "I'm not prepared to wait."

"Where are you going?"

"Hopefully to bed!"

We're using my room on this leg of the trip because it's on a higher floor and it's near the lift (easier for me to drag Frankie back to the room?). After Frankie had chosen the bed she wanted, she started pulling Christmas decorations out of her suitcase.

"Do you mind if we hold off until we get to Bangkok?"

"But it's kwismas."

"Fine," I said. "Chuck some balls over here."

With the room looking like a…*winter wonderland* (that's not what I was going to say, but it's Christmas, goodwill to all and all that rot), Frankie said we should decorate the party room, in preparation for the crew party tonight.

"I'm sure the hotel staff have already seen to it."

"Can we just pop up and take a look?"

"Sure," I groaned, gazing longingly at the bed I doubted I'd ever get to sleep in.

It's just gone five and we're meeting the crew at seven, so I set the alarm for half six. Frankie is already snoring, and I'm more than ready to shut my eyes and drift off to a tinsel free land. If only for a little while.

23rd ~ Kuala Lumpur, Malaysia

I woke up at half six. This morning! Oops, guess we missed the crew party, but obviously needed the rest.

We ordered an assortment of breakfast items from room service and set everything up on the small balcony. Our conversation ran the gamut from love and marriage, to children, hopes, fears, death. And sex (couldn't bring myself to put the last two together!). When Frankie talked about the death of her father (many years ago) some of the emotions she described struck a chord with me about nana's death.

After a day spent traipsing across the city to various markets (might have to buy another suitcase) Frankie cajoled me into going to The Grotto, to see Santa. Matt and Sandy were there, and we had our picture taken with the man who promised to bring us a bunch of goodies.

Over dinner, we made merry, and I felt thankful for such a fantastic crew, especially now. Finished Saturday night off at the Tin Mine and we even managed to get Captain Alan on the dance floor. Sandy requested what has become our trip anthem and once again, with our hands in the air, singing our hearts out, we gave Joan Jett a run for her money.

24th ~ Kuala Lumpur, Malaysia

The first thing I saw when I strained to open my eyes, were specks of tinsel. And the first words I heard were, "It's time to get into the Christmas spirit!"

"Didn't we have enough of that last night?"

"Never!" Frankie squealed, leaping onto my bed. "Let's go to the pool."

Through a lengthy yawn, I said, "Let me wake up first."

"You can do that on a sun lounger. I'll pop my headphones on and promise not to bother you while you read."

I felt totally out of place amongst the bikini clad beauties and hid under an umbrella, until Frankie insisted that we move to the other side of the pool, "for maximum tannage," where we got chatting to some KLM crew we arranged to meet tonight at The Ship.

Back in the room (Frankie was still topping up her tan) my thoughts drifted to nana and how much I miss her. I thought back to the Christmases we spent together and how it will never be the same without her. Dwelling on the past, Ben entered the equation, and I tortured myself by wondering how he (and she) will celebrate tomorrow. Those combined thoughts sent me into a downward spiral, and I sobbed my heart out in a way I haven't for a very long time.

Catching sight (what a sight!) of myself in the mirror, I got up to answer the phone. Expecting it to be Frankie, with a warning she was on her way upstairs, I answered, "Yaaasssss?"

"Karen?"

"Oh, shit, hi," I quickly cleared my throat. "David!"

Act cool, act cool and why am I fluffing up in my hair, it's not like he can see me!

"Are you ok? You sound like you have a cold."

"No, I'm ehm-"

"Surprised?"

"You can say that again! How on earth did you find me? I mean the hotel, and everything."

"I have my ways."

"I like 'em."

"I wanted to say hi and happy holidays from LA."

"Well, hello, and happy Christmas from Malaysia. What time is it there?"

"Twenty after nine."

"At night?"

"Yeah, twenty-one twenty, on the twenty-third."

"Stop confusing me!"

After an easy, uplifting chat, I turned on the radio and blasted Christmas tunes. Then I ordered flutes and an ice bucket from room service, into which I slid a bottle of Dom Perignon I knew Frankie would be overjoyed to see. I yanked a handful of tinsel off the wall, threw it around my neck and suddenly, it began to feel like Christmas.

25th ~ Kuala Lumpur, Malaysia

Christmas day began with Frankie bouncing on my bed trying to wake me, but unbeknownst to her I'd already rang home from the lobby. With the time difference, it was still Christmas Eve at home. Mum said it was a different kind of Christmas but that she and dad were planning on making the most of it. When I mentioned David's call, mum perked up and had a slew of questions, two of which I answered before reminding her I was ringing from the other side of the world.

On the crew bus, Captain Alan led us in, "Good King Wenceslas," and we needed no encouragement to keep going. Knowing all we had to do was operate the shuttle to and from Manila (90 mins each way) made the day ahead seem like a breeze, until a solitary, stinking, inconsiderate passenger was a no show! Unfortunately, his luggage was in the hold, and it took the baggage handlers ages to locate it. The sight of hundreds of pieces of luggage being dragged out of the hold was a sight to behold!

After Scrooge's luggage was eventually located, there was a problem with the flaps. Pax were offloaded, and we remained onboard, while the engineers tended to the problem. Milling around in First Class, we took turns having our picture taken by the gueridon, trying to keep some semblance of Christmas cheer going.

After it was deemed the flaps were operable, the pax boarded again, and just as we began to taxi, we went out of hours! Much to the pax dismay (is there an award for understatement of the year?) an announcement was made to the tune of, *None of us sorry sods will be seeing the Philippines today*!

To add insult to injury, Captain Alan broke the news that he'd received a telex from London. Down route, that's rarely positive, and lo and behold, we're spending a few extra days here in Kuala Lumpur. With dampened spirits (I had better prepare an acceptance speech for the understatement award, which I am most definitely getting!) there was no singing on the crew bus.

In an effort to boost morale, Captain Alan invited everyone to his room. I told Frankie I'm not in the mood, but in no uncertain terms, she reminded me it's Christmas, so off we go. Again!

26th ~ KUL - BKK
Hotel Dusit Thani, Bangkok, Thailand

We woke up to good news (in KUL) that we're staying on the original trip.

Ninety-minute flight to this most interesting of places. Tomorrow will be a full day, so I'm looking forward to exploring, but for now, Frankie is asleep, and I plan on doing the same.

27th ~ Hotel Dusit Thani, Bangkok, Thailand

Now that the end of the trip is in sight, I suggested separate rooms to Frankie. Looking dejected, she said, she'd "much rather not." So, for the next few days we'll be in my room, which is slightly bigger.

On our way out this morning, we bumped into Raymond, from our crew. Raymond strikes me as the type that'll remain with BA until he's forced to retire, and I have a sneaking suspicion he lives with his mother. He has a florid complexion and if he were to hold his head just a tad higher, it'd help eliminate some of his chins. When he asked if he could join us, we couldn't really say no, so he accompanied us to The Grand Palace (the official residence of the Kings of Siam, since 1782). In the cool surroundings, I felt a sense of calm wash over me, but it was short lived.

In a tuk tuk, heading for the Chao Phraya River, the driver scared the living daylights out of us, screaming abuse as he sped past other tuk tuk's, generally acting like he was off his rocker. Every turn forced the three of us to become much more familiar than I'd have liked.

At the floating market, Frankie seemed hell bent on buying one of everything, and the more lethargic I got, the more exuberant she became. When I spotted Carl's brother, Connor, the first thing that came to mind was the morning after Carl's birthday party, when Kimberly crawled into the back seat of Connor's TR7, because his suitcase was up front!

When we hugged hello, I watched Connor's eyes dart to Frankie and when I introduced them, it was obvious he was more than keen to get to know her better. The feeling appeared mutual, and while they were *communicating*, Raymond started banging on about his favourite restaurant in Hong Kong. "We're in Bangkok you nitwit!" I was tempted to yell. Ah, humidity, you sure know how to put me to the test.

Back at the hotel, the minute my head hit on the pillow (I was desperate to take a nap before going out tonight) Frankie went into overdrive. "Tell me everything you know about Connor!"

"I don't really know him that well."

"But you're friends with his brother."

"Yeah, but that doesn't mean-"

"Do you think he likes me?"

"Had I given him a spoon, there'd be nothing left of you."

Frankie chuckled in the way only she can, and I no longer felt tired.

Poured into an orange dress, complete with swaying baubles, Frankie looked dynamite and when she paired the dress with silver sandals, the new pink top that I'd been looking forward to wearing, left me feeling like I'd be better off climbing into the wardrobe and staying there. In the company of Frankie's bejewelled outfits, it might have proved a welcome escape.

Outside the bars lining Pat Pong, scantily clad girls urged us to, "have a peek." We'd arranged to meet most the crew in the Queen's Place, a terrible name for an establishment where most of the employees are starkers, and the entertainment is a live sex show.

Feeling slightly stunned, not so much from the sex show as from the ping pong balls being shot from nether regions (!) we left and made our way to the Rome Club.

28th ~ Hotel Dusit Thani, Bangkok, Thailand

When I got back to, our room in the early hours of this morning, it soon became apparent why Frankie left the Rome Club early. Tangled up in the throes of passion, Frankie and Connor's cries of pleasure covered my awkward, "Sorry!" Unsure whether they'd seen or heard me, I retreated to the corridor.

Claiming to be Frankie, I told the guy at reception I'd misplaced my key, and with nothing other than what I was wearing, I fell asleep on top of the bed.

Woke up with a desperate thirst, ordered room service, and when I rang *my* room, Connor answered.

"I'll be up in ten minutes to grab some clothes," I said, hoping he'd take the hint and skedaddle, but not only was Connor still very much in the room, he and Frankie invited me to stay for breakfast!

"I've been dislodged," I pouted, outside Sandy's door.

"Connor?"

"How did you guess?" I laughed.

"I'm meeting Matt, we're going to the market at the President hotel. Come with us."

After a fun afternoon, I rang my room from the lobby. Connor answered.

"Is Frankie there?" I said, curtly.

"She's sleeping."

Tired? Really? Can't imagine why!

"I'll be up in a few to get more of my worldly belongings."

Failing to catch my drift, he replied, "Alright babe, see you then."

Babe?

While I retrieved the last of my things, Frankie slept on, and Connor cracked jokes I paid no heed to. "Will we see you later?" he smiled (the nerve!) holding the door as I used my foot to push my Samsonite into the corridor.

"I don't think so," I tutted. "I have plans."

Maybe I'll buy some ping pong balls and end my British Airways career in spectacular fashion.

29th ~ BKK – LHR

As soon as I finish this, I'm going up to the bunks, and hopefully I'll sleep because after three hours of crew rest, there'll still be eight hours of the flight remaining. Not only is the flight chocka but we have several people travelling on staff travel, so even the jumpseats are occupied.

I stayed in Frankie's room all day, while she and Connor continued to get acquainted in mine. I ordered chocolate mousse not once but twice (with some other yummies) and watched *Heartburn*, with Meryl Streep and Jack Nicholson. I remember the heated, *lengthy* discussion Ben and I had, about the differences between men and women, after seeing it in London.

Thinking ahead to next year…it'll be interesting to see what 1990 holds in the Love Department (Going up!). Ah, men, guys, boys…what to call them? Jon is mature (ex and now a friend) and come to think of it, Christopher in New York (who I'm very fond of but don't fancy) has his act together. David (who I really do fancy) flies all over representing a company so I'd put the three of them in the man category.

Ben is excluded from the man category! That sounds mean and my intention is to move into the new decade with a positive outlook so perhaps it's time to leave behind any negative thoughts about him. Along with the leg warmers and shoulder pads.

As amazing as this trip has been, all I want is to wake up in my own bed, without having to figure out where the loo is.

30th ~ At home

Just got off the phone with David.
"How was your trip?"
"Great, but I'm glad to be home."
"No place like it," he joked. "I bet your folks are happy to see you."

"My mum literally followed me all over the house. The entire day! Any fantasies of sleeping went right out the window."

"I guess she missed you, huh?"

"This was her first Christmas without my nana, so it's been-"

"I know, sweetie, I'm sorry."

Ah, I really needed that.

"Anyway, how are you?"

"Doing good, heading home this afternoon. I've been here with my folks over the holiday. It's been, wait, hold on..what's that mom?"

In the background, I heard a woman's voice but couldn't make out what she was saying. Mum came into the hall and asked who I was talking to.

"It's David, he's ringing from San-"

"Karen, you there?"

Waving mum away, I asked David if everything was ok.

"My mom wanted to know who I'm talking to, but she disguised it by asking if I wanted food for the ride home."

"Sounds like someone I know! Did you answer any of your mum's questions?"

"You didn't hear?"

"No, all I heard was mumbling."

"I told her I'm talking to a Scottish girl in England, who just flew in from Bangkok."

"That's quite the introduction! And are you getting some nosh for the drive home?"

"I don't know. She looked kinda confused. If I ask for nosh, it might knock her over the edge. What're you doing for New Year's?"

"No plans yet, how about you?"

"Same, but I gotta tell ya, Los Angeles puts on quite a show."

"As does London."

"Aw, man, that'd be awesome. Maybe next year, huh?"

I have everything crossed.

31st ~ At home

"It's the last night of the eighties," dad said, as we tucked into the spread that I put together for mum and dad's 22nd wedding anniversary. "Ye should do something memorable, Karen."

"Dad," I laughed. "I've been doing that all year!"

Quick chat to Pamsy (come down!) Jon (come over!) and Millie (heading to Hong Kong, no invite!). Being close to the phone made me want to ring Ben, but just as I was about to give into the urge, Sebastian rang. "I know it's short notice but is there any way you'd consider being my date tonight?"

"For what?"

Like I have other plans!

"A party. A very posh one."

"Ooohh, you have my attention."

"It's in Notting Hill."

That was all I needed to hear.

"I'll pick you up at eight, but I should warn you, there might be a shortage of straight men."

"Why are you telling me that?"

"Just letting you know that the chances of snogging someone at the stroke of midnight will be slim to none."

I've tried on all the usual suspects; black stuff, bright stuff, more black stuff, a blue dress I hate, a white skirt I love, and plan to wear, if I can find a top to go with it.

"Will ye no be freezing in that wee skirt?"

"The party's inside, mum. Besides, I feel comfortable in it."

"Ye looked smashing in that blue dress ye jist tried on."

"Maybe so, but I can't sit in it. Or breathe."

"Ye won't be sitting, ye'll be dancing."

"Not in the car on the way there, I won't."

"Och, details," she laughed.

With less than five hours to go before 1990 shows up, I should probably get ready, but first, tea. And maybe a few biscuits.

Printed in Great Britain
by Amazon

78167943R00202